DATE DUE

NOV 14 1995	
AUG 26 1999	
SEP 14 1998	
OCT 17 2000	

DEMCO, INC. 38-2931

Science and Racket Sports

OTHER TITLES FROM E & FN SPON

Science and Golf II
Edited by A. Cochran and M. Farrally

Science and Golf
Edited by A. Cochran

Science and Football II
Edited by T. Reilly, J. Clarys and A. Stibbe

Intermittent High Intensity Exercise
Edited by D.A.D. Macleod, R.J. Maughan, C. Williams, C.R. Madeley, J.C.M. Sharp, R.W. Mutton and J. Graham

Sport and Physical Activity
Edited by T. Williams, L. Almond and A. Sparkes

Biomechanics and Medicine in Swimming
Edited by D. Maclaren, T. Reilly and A. Lees

Avanced Materials in Sports Equipment
K. Easterling

Physiology of Sports
Edited by T. Reilly, N. Secher, P. Snell and C. Williams

Kinanthropometry IV
Edited by W. Duqvet and J.A.P. Day

Foods, Nutrition and Sports Performance
Edited by C. Williams and J.R. Devlin

Journal of Sports Sciences

Science and Racket Sports

Edited by

T. Reilly

Centre for Sport and Exercise Sciences,
Liverpool John Moores University, UK

M. Hughes

The Centre for Notational Analysis,
Cardiff Institute, Cardiff, UK

and

A. Lees

Centre for Sport and Exercise Sciences,
Liverpool John Moores University, UK

E & FN SPON

An Imprint of Chapman & Hall

London · Glasgow · Weinheim · New York · Tokyo · Melbourne · Madras

Published by E & FN Spon, an imprint of Chapman & Hall, 2–6 Boundary Row, London SE1 8HN, UK

Chapman & Hall, 2–6 Boundary Row, London SE1 8HN, UK

Blackie Academic & Professional, Wester Cleddens Road, Bishopbriggs, Glasgow G64 2NZ, UK

Chapman & Hall GmbH, Pappelallee 3, 69469 Weinheim, Germany

Chapman & Hall USA, One Penn Plaza, 41st Floor, New York, NY 10119, USA

Chapman & Hall Japan, ITP-Japan, Kyoma Building, 3F, 2-2-1 Hirakawacho, Chiyoda-ku, Tokyo 102, Japan

Chapman & Hall Australia, Thomas Nelson Australia, 102 Dodds Street, South Melbourne, Victoria 3205, Australia

Chapman & Hall India, R. Seshadri, 32 Second Main Road, CIT East, Madras 600 035, India

First edition 1995

Printed in Great Britain at the University Press, Cambridge

ISBN 0 419 18500 3

A catalogue record for this book is available from the British Library

Publisher's Note
This book has been produced from camera ready copy provided by the individual contributors.

♾ Printed on permanent acid-free paper, manufactured in accordance with ANSI/NISO Z39.48-1992 and ANSI/NISO Z39.48-1984 (Permanence of Paper).

First World Congress on Science and Racket Sports
Held at Runcorn, Merseyside
9–13th July 1993

Organised from Liverpool John Moores University
and held at Runcorn, Merseyside

Organisers
Mike Hughes and Thomas Reilly

Organising Committee
Alex Arbuckle
Jonathan Chinn
Jake Downey
Lorna Duckworth
Mike Hughes
Thomas Reilly (Chair)

Scientific Committee
J.P. Clarys
M. Hughes
A. Lees
T. Reilly (Chair)

Organising Secretariat
Michelle Cryer
Deborah Hudson

Contents

PART TWO FITNESS IN RACKET SPORTS

PART THREE BIOMECHANICS OF RACKET SPORTS

PART SEVEN MATCH ANALYSIS

Preface

The first World Congress on Science and Racket Sports was held at Runcorn (Merseyside), England, from July 9 - 13th 1993. The event was organised at Liverpool John Moores University. It was established as an extension of the academic programmes of the World Commission of Sports Biomechanics which is affiliated to both the International Society of Biomechanics and the International Council of Sports Sciences and Physical Education. These programmes have existed for many years in swimming, football and more recently golf. The philosophy on which this Congress was based was to effect a bridge between the science of racket sports and their practice. The broad aim was to bring together scientists whose research work is concerned with racket sports and practitioners in those sports who are interested in obtaining current information about their scientific aspects. Consequently the audience included not only sports scientists but also coaches, sports participants, physiotherapists, physicians and professionals from the racket sports industries. The scientific programme consisted of keynote lectures, open communications, poster presentations and workshops. These were complemented by practical demonstrations and an exhibition of equipment and services dedicated to the rackets sports. The Congress had the support of the major rackets sports in the host country, the Squash Racket Association, The Lawn Tennis Association, the Badminton Association of England and the England Racquetball Association. For this support the Organising Committee was particularly grateful.

Introduction

This volume contains papers from the First World Congress of Science and Racket Sports held in Runcorn from July 9 to 13th, 1993. The programme consisted of 6 keynote addresses, 6 workshop sessions, 28 oral communications and 16 poster presentations. Manuscripts written up following the Congress were subject to peer review and editorial judgement prior to acceptance for the Proceedings. Four of the keynote lectures (by Bruce Elliott, Mike Hughes, Graham Jones and Per Renstrom) are published here.

The volume is organised into parts based on scientific disciplines. Material falling into physiological topics have been split into those that report investigations of demands of racket sports, and those detailing fitness profiles or fitness testing of players. Similarly papers concerned with biomechanics and mechanics have been distinguished into those primarily concerned with force or stroke analysis and those focused on rackets or equipment in the racket sports. The Sports Medicine section includes papers that might have been placed elsewhere in the book but for their highlighting of injury or injury risk. Whole sections are devoted to psychology and to match analysis in the racket sports.

The Proceedings provide an indication of the impact that scientific research has had on the respective sports. The volume cannot, unfortunately, recreate the atmosphere of the Congress itself and the highly successful interaction between theorists and practitioners. To our regret it was not possible to reproduce contributions to the workshops on racket design, the racket sport child, injury prevention in racket sports and others. A notable feature of the Congress was the highly impressive demonstrations of coaching elite players by Jonah Barrington (squash) and Jake Downey (badminton).

The papers published are a testimony of the quality of research currently undertaken in applications to racket sports. They indicate also the transferability of some findings across the various racket sports disciplines. It is hoped that the book will stimulate new projects and provide a solid base for the next time the Congress is convened, in U.S.A. in 1997.

Thomas Reilly, Chair,
Mike Hughes,
Adrian Lees.

Part One
Physiology of Racket Sports

1 A metabolic characterisation of single tennis

M.A. Christmass, S.E. Richmond*, N.T. Cable and P.E. Hartmann
*Department of Human Movement and *Department of Biochemistry, University of Western Australia, Perth, Australia*

1 Introduction

Increased professionalism in tennis has stimulated scientific research into the principles of the game. While this research has resulted in considerable refinement of biomechanical principles associated with stroke production, the metabolic demands of singles tennis are still poorly defined. Fox (1979) estimated that approximately 70% of energy production in a singles tennis player was derived from anaerobic metabolism, whereas Seliger et al. (1973) suggested that aerobic sources provide 88% of the total energy demand. This contradiction may relate to the use of indirect methods (heart rate; work : recovery ratio) to establish the intensity of exercise and thereby predict the metabolic demands of singles tennis. In a more direct approach, changes in plasma concentrations of lactate, glucose and serum electrolytes were measured by Copley (1984) and changes in plasma concentrations of lactate, glucose, cortisol and testosterone were measured by Bergeron et al. (1991) during singles tennis. Both reports indicated little effect of play on either blood glucose or blood lactate. However, a major limitation to these studies was the requirement of relatively large blood samples (5 ml) for the metabolite assays and therefore, disruption to standard match-play conditions.

The development of highly sensitive luminometric methods (Arthur et al., 1989) has permitted the assay of metabolites in capillary blood samples (<100 μl) by finger prick. Furthermore, finger prick blood samples can be collected from tennis players at each change of end without disturbing standard match-play conditions. Thus, we investigated changes in the concentration of glycolytic and lipolytic metabolites in blood during standard competitive singles tennis. These changes are discussed in relation to the intensity of exercise and appropriate training methods.

2 Methods

2.1 Subjects

Eight healthy male State level tennis players volunteered for this study. The procedures were approved by the Human Rights Committee of The University of Western Australia. Subjects' physical characteristics (mean ± SE) were: age 23.3 ± 1.2 years, height 1.81 ± 0.02 m, mass 79.1 ± 2.8 kg.

Science and Racket Sports Edited by T. Reilly, M. Hughes and A. Lees.
Published in 1994 by E & FN Spon ISBN 0 419 18500 3

2.2 Preliminary assessments

During a first laboratory session subjects' height, body mass, adiposity and proportional weight rating (Ward et al., 1989) as well as maximal aerobic power ($VO_{2\,max}$) were measured. For assessment of $VO_{2\,max}$ subjects ran on a motor driven treadmill commencing at a speed of 8 km/h and zero grade. The speed was increased by 2 km/h after two minutes and then by 1 km/h every two minutes until 14 km/h; thereafter, the speed remained constant and the grade was increased by 2% every two minutes until volitional exhaustion. A ventilometer (P.K. Morgan, Kent) system was used to determine inspired gas volumes and expired gas was drawn through a mixing chamber to determine fractions of O_2 (S3A/1 analyser, Ametek, USA) and CO_2 (CD3A analyser, Ametek, USA). A personal computer was used to calculate ventilatory gas exchange variables (VO_2, VCO_2, V_E) each minute. Heart rate (HR) was also recorded each minute using a HR monitor (Polar Electro Sportstester, Kempele, Finland).

During a second laboratory session anaerobic work capacity, peak alactic power and 10 s alactic work capacity were measured as described by Telford et al. (1987).

2.3 Experimental procedures

Singles tennis was performed on an outdoor Plexipave™ tennis court where mean climatic conditions during the matches were: air temperature 20 ± 1°C, court temperature 28 ± 1°C, humidity 76 ± 6% and wind speed 1.4 ± 0.3 m/s. In the 24 hours prior to the match, subjects were requested to refrain from strenuous exercise and the consumption of caffeine and alcohol. They had their last meal prior to midnight on the day before the match and 6 subjects consumed an energy supplement (30g Sustagen Gold™ in 300 ml milk yielding 1313 kJ) 3 hours prior to the match whereas the remaining 2 subjects consumed their energy supplement 5 hours prior to the match. All subjects played against an opponent of similar standard based on singles rankings within the local State League competition. Bipolar pre-cordial ECG leads and a transmitter (Siemens TC 36/T, Erlangen, Germany) were attached to the subjects to monitor HR by radio telemetry. A receiver (Siemens TC 36/T, Erlangen, Germany) and a video camera were linked to a stereo video recorder so that playback through a video monitor and a storage oscilliscope (Tektronix™#2230, Oregan, USA) was synchronized to observe the relationship between HR and specific match characteristics.

Each match consisted of 90 minutes of uninterrupted competitive singles tennis. Capillary blood samples were obtained by finger prick (Unilet, Owen Mumford, Woodstock, England) of the non-dominant hand prior to the warm-up and at each change of end. The blood was collected into heparinized haematocrit tubes, which were sealed, centrifuged to separate the plasma, and stored at -20 °C. International Tennis Federation rules were employed to govern the time characteristics for the matches, four new tennis balls were used for each match, and subjects retrieved their own balls. Subjects were permitted to consume only water throughout the match.

2.4 Exercise intensity

A regression of HR on VO_2 (from $VO_{2\,max}$ test) was used to estimate VO_2 during singles tennis. Oxygen consumption represented as a percentage of $VO_{2\,max}$ ($\%VO_{2\,max}$) was used as an estimate of relative exercise intensity. Time motion analysis using video playback of each match, enabled the number of steps taken (including split steps) during each rally to be counted. The number of steps taken per second (steps/s) provided an alternative estimate of exercise intensity (estimated play intensity).

2.5 Biochemical analysis

Samples were thawed, the plasma removed from the haematocrit tube and deproteinised as described by Arthur et al. (1989). Glucose was measured spectophotometrically (Bergmeyer & Bernt, 1974), whereas a spectrophotometric assay for lactate (Noll, 1984) was modified for assay by luminescence detection (Arthur et al., 1989), glycerol (Kather & Weiland, 1983) and ß-hydroxybutarate (Kiensh-Engel & Siess, 1984) were measured by sensitive bioluminescent methods. The detection limits for the metabolite assays were 39.7µM, 281.3µM, 9.2µM and 2.8µM for glucose, lactate, glycerol and ß-hydroxybutarate, respectively.

2.6 Statistical analysis

Regression analysis and one factor analysis of variance with repeated measures on time were performed using ANOVA® and superANOVA® (Abacus Concepts, Inc., Berkley, Ca, 1989). All results presented are means ± SE unless stated otherwise.

3 Results

3.1 Fitness profiles

The mean fitness profile for the subjects was: $VO_{2\ max}$, 54.25 ± 1.90 ml/kg/min; maximum heart rate, 180 ± 3 beats/min; peak alactic power index, 4; alactic work capacity index, 3; anaerobic work capacity index, 4; adiposity 5 ± 1 and proportional weight rating 7 ± 1.

3.2 Match characteristics

The mean match characteristics were: rally time, 10.2 ± 0.3 s; recovery time, 16.8 ± 0.2 s; work to recovery ratio, 1 : 1.7; number of shots per rally, 4.6 ± 0.1: number of rallies per game, 6.9 ± 0.4; proportion of time in play, 23.3 ± 1.4 %.

3.3 Exercise intensity

After an initial rise from the pre-match level to the second change of end, there was no further significant variation in mean HR expressed as a proportion of maximum HR (PMHR). Mean PMHR during play (rallying) was 86.2 ± 1.0 % and was not significantly different from the 82.9 ± 1.2 % observed during recovery (excluding change of ends). Whereas, relative exercise intensity (72.58 ± 2.01 $\%VO_{2\ max}$) and estimated play intensity (1.13 ± 0.03 $steps.s^{-1}$) did not change significantly during the match (Fig 1), both measures of intensity varied significantly between subjects.

3.4 Lactate

The pre-match concentration of plasma lactate (PLa) was 2.13 ± 0.32 mM. Plasma lactate increased significantly at the fourth change of end (5.05 ± 1.04 mM), reached a peak (5.86 ± 1.33 mM) at the sixth change of end and remained elevated until the end of the match (Fig 2). Analysis of covariance revealed significant variation in PLa between subjects and this variation was correlated ($r = 0.71$, $n = 72$, $P < 0.001$) with estimated play intensity (Fig 3).

3.5 Glucose

The pre-match concentration of plasma glucose (PGlc) was 4.36 ± 0.11 mM. Plasma glucose increased at the third change of end (4.86 ± 0.18 mM; P=0.001), reached a peak (5.32 ± 0.40 mM) at the sixth change of end , and remained elevated until the end

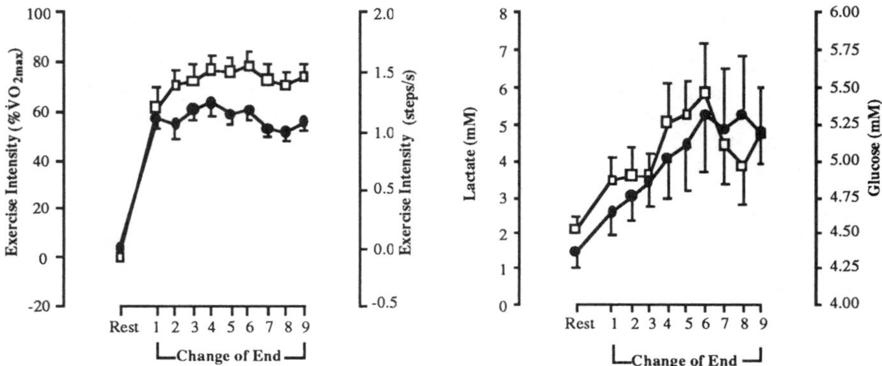

Figure 1. Exercise intensity (□%$\dot{V}O_{2max}$; ●Steps/s)

Figure 2. Concentration of glycolytic metabolites (□ Lactate; ● Glucose)

of the match (Fig 2). Partial correlation analysis with estimated play intensity held constant, revealed that variations in PGlc were correlated with changes in PLa ($r = 0.60$).

3.6 Glycerol

The pre-match concentration of plasma glycerol (PG) was 84 ± 12 μM. Plasma glycerol increased at the first change of end (139 ± 25 μM; $P < 0.001$) and reached a peak (209 ± 21 μM) at the completion of the match (Fig 4). During the match the increases in PG were not correlated with the measures of intensity. However, there was significant variation between subjects and the PG was correlated with the duration of the match (r, 0.57 to 0.98 range) in all but one subject.

3.7 ß-Hydroxybutarate

The pre-match concentration of plasma ß-hydroxybutarate (PB) was 86 ± 24 μM. At the seventh change of end PB had increased to 128 ± 39 μM ($P < 0.01$) and reached a peak (156 ± 54 μM) at the completion of the match (Fig 4).

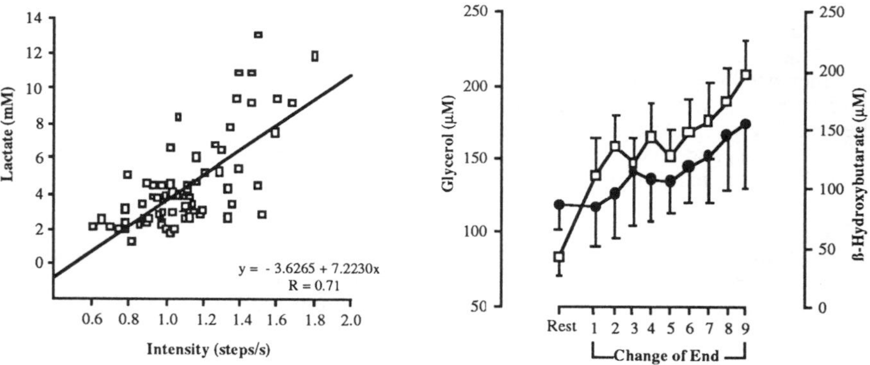

Figure 3. Regression of lactate vs intensity

Figure 4. Concentration of lipolytic metabolites (□Glycerol; ●ß-Hydroxybutarate)

4 Discussion

Subjects in the present study competed at State level, were of similar aerobic fitness to the Collegiate players measured by Bergeron et al. (1991), and above average anaerobic fitness determined by Tri-level age-related standards (Telford et al., 1987). The match characteristics support the findings of Elliott et al. (1985) and Docherty (1982) for high performance players. The work : recovery ratio of 1 : 1.7 (± 0.2) was comparable to 1 : 1.8 for matches played on a similar court surface (Elliott et al., 1985).

Estimates of the metabolic profile of singles tennis have been based upon work : recovery ratios (Fox, 1979). However, the contribution of metabolic systems to energy demand is dependent on the intensity of exercise (Newsholme, 1986). Since, work : recovery ratios do not indicate the intensity of exercise, they are of little value in assessing metabolic responses to singles tennis. Exercise intensity during singles tennis has also been predicted on the basis of HR during play and the results from incremental $VO_{2\,max}$ tests (Elliott et al., 1985; Bergeron et al., 1991). In our study HR did not vary either between rallying and recovery or with duration of the match, which supports the findings of Bergeron et al. (1991) and Docherty (1982), although Elliott et al. (1985) reported a slight increase in HR during recovery between rallies. From evidence of HR elevation between rallies, and the work : recovery ratio during singles tennis, Elliott et al. (1985) speculated that tennis may require minimal assistance from anaerobic glycolysis. In support of this suggestion Bergeron et al. (1991) and Copley (1984) found no significant increase in mean PLa during singles tennis. However, in our study, despite similar HR responses to those reported by Bergeron et al. (1991) and Elliott et al. (1985), a significant increase in PLa relative to pre-match levels was observed. There was considerable variation in this response between subjects (Fig 2) which was not explained by differences in match characteristics because variation in PLa was observed between opponents. In addition, analysis of covariance revealed that the variation in PLa was not related to changes in $\%VO_{2\,max}$. In a further attempt to identify the source of the individual variation in PLa, analysis of covariance with a time and motion assessment of exercise intensity was determined. This estimate of on-court exercise intensity explained 50% of the variation in PLa (Fig 3). Thus a measure of on-court exercise intensity (estimated play intensity) provided a better assessment of the anaerobic glycolyic profile of singles tennis than a relative measure of exercise intensity ($\%VO_{2\,max}$). Therefore, development of more precise measures of on-court exercise intensity may be of value in predicting anaerobic profiles. Since our findings (Fig 2), as well as those of Bergeron et al. (1991) demonstrate large variability in PLa between players in response to singles tennis, generalisations regarding the anaerobic glycolytic profile of singles tennis may be inaccurate. It is more likely that playing style, court surface and the specific stresses of individual matches will determine the lactate profile of singles tennis. Therefore, players should include a proportion of anaerobic glycolytic training within their fitness programmes in order to adequately prepare for singles tennis.

The increase in PGlc demonstrated in the present study contrasts with the findings of Bergeron et al. (1991) and Copley (1984). Variations in PGlc between subjects followed changes in PLa (Fig 2) and therefore can be indirectly attributed to changes in estimated play intensity. During recovery in intermittent exercise, as muscle respiratory rate declines, lactate becomes the preferred substrate for hepatic gluconeogenesis and a large proportion of the reformed glucose is released into the circulation (Brooks, 1986). In addition, high intensity activity results in catecholamine-mediated stimulation of hepatic glycogenolysis (Wahren et al., 1971).

These factors may explain the increase in PGlc which appears to correspond with an elevated PLa response.

The increase in PG during singles tennis (Fig 4) suggests an increased rate of lipolysis from fat stores (Hetenyi et al., 1983) as play progressed, and therefore a shift in the metabolic production of energy towards an enhanced reliance on lipolysis. This result provides clear evidence of the importance of oxidative metabolism for energy production in singles tennis as play progresses. In addition, during prolonged submaximal exercise an increase in the rate of lipolysis inhibits the oxidation of carbohydrate through the glucose - fatty acid cycle, thus sparing muscle glycogen and prolonging time to exhaustion (Randle et al., 1978). Endurance training results in an increased reliance on fat oxidation during submaximal exercise and hence provides an important metabolic adaptation to preserve muscle glycogen (Holloszy, 1990). Therefore, it is important for tennis players to include a significant proportion of endurance training within their preparation, in order to improve oxidative metabolism and spare muscle glycogen during competition.

A moderate increase in PB was observed in all players during the match (Fig 4). This increase in PB is consistent with increased lipolysis and an increase in the hepatic metabolism of fatty acids (Bjorkman, 1986). Furthermore, ketone bodies represent an important fuel to spare glucose under fasted conditions. In our study two players were subjected to a 5 hour "fast" between consumption of the pre-match meal and commencement of the match. These subjects had an elevated PB response. Further study must be directed towards an understanding of the effects of variations in pre-match nutrient intake on performance in singles tennis.

In conclusion, we have demonstrated a large variability between subjects with regard the anaerobic glycolytic profile of singles tennis and the need for further research to establish a measure of on-court exercise intensity that may more accurately predict this profile. In addition, there was an increased reliance on lipid metabolism with duration of play. Although singles tennis may be predominantly submaximal, the possibility for anaerobic glycolytic activity cannot be ignored. Therefore, a proportion of this form of training should be included with the alactic power and aerobic conditioning that form the basis of fitness training for elite tennis performance.

5 Acknowledgements

The authors thank the National Sports Research Program of the Australian Sports Commission for supporting this study, Mr J. Acked, Mr E. Harrison and Mr T. Manford for technical assistance, and Mr S. Dalby for statistical support.

6 References

Arthur, P.G. Kent, J.C. and Hartmann, P.E. (1989) Microanalysis of the metabolic intermediates of lactose synthesis in human milk and plasma using bioluminescent methods. **Anal. Biochem.,** 176, 449-456.

Bergeron, M.F. Maresh, C.M. Kraemer, W.J. Abraham, A. Conroy, B. and Gabaree, C. (1991) Tennis: A physiological profile during match play. **Int. J. Sports Med.,** 12, 474-479.

Bergmeyer, H.U. and Bernt, E. (1974) D-Glucose: Determination with glucose oxidase and peroxidase, in **Methods in Enzymatic Analysis,** 3 (ed H.U.Bergmeyer), Verlag Chemie, Weinheim & Academic Press, New York, pp. 1233-1236.

Bjorkman, O.L.A. (1986) Fuel utilization during exercise, in **Biochemical Aspects of Physical Exercise** (eds G. Benzi, L. Packer and N. Siliprandi), Elselvier, Amsterdam, pp. 245-259.

Brooks, G.A. (1986) The lactate shuttle during exercise and recovery. **Med. Sci. Sports. Exerc.**, 18, 360-368.

Copley, B.B. (1984) Effects of competitive singles tennis playing on serum electrolyte, blood glucose and blood lactate concentrations. **South Afr. J. Sci.,** 80, 145.

Docherty, D. (1982) A comparison of heart rate responses in racquet games. **Brit. J. Sports. Med.**, 16(2), 96-100.

Elliott, B. Dawson, B. and Pyke, F. (1985) The energetics of singles tennis. **J. Human Movt. Stud.**, 11, 11-20.

Fox, E.L. (1979) **Sports Physiology.** W.B Saunders Co: Philadelphia.

Hetenyi, G. Jr. Perez, G. and Vranic, M. (1983) Turnover and precursor-product relationships of non-lipid metabolites. **Physiol. Rev.**, 63, 606-667.

Holloszy, J.D. (1990) Utilization of fatty acids during exercise, in **Biochemistry of Exercise,** VII, (eds A.W. Taylor, P.D. Gollnick, H.J. Green, C.D. Ianuzzo, E.G. Noble, G. Metivier and J.R. Sutton), Champaign, Illinois, pp. 245-259.

Kather, H. and Weiland, E. (1983) Glycerol, in **Methods in Enzymatic Analysis,** 7, (ed H.U. Bergmeyer), Verlag Chemie, Weinheim & Academic Press: New York, pp. 510-581.

Kiensh-Engel, R.I. and Siess, E.A. (1984) D-(-)-3-Hydroxybutyrate and acetoacetate, in **Methods in Enzymatic Analysis**, 8, (ed H.U. Bergmeyer), Verlag Chemie, Weinheim & Academic Press, New York, pp. 60-69 .

Newsholme, E.A. (1986) Application of principles of metabolic control to the problem of metabolic limitations in sprinting, middle-distance, and marathon running. **Int. J. Sports Med.,** 7(Suppl.), 66-70.

Noll, F. (1984) L-(+)-Lactate, in **Methods in Enzymatic Analysis**, 8, (ed H.U. Bergmeyer), Verlag Chemie, Weinheim & Academic Press, New York, pp. 582-588.

Randle, P.J. Sugden, P.H. Kerby, A.L. Radcliffe, P.M. and Hutson, N.J. (1978) Regulation of pyruvate oxidation and the conservation of glucose. **Biochem. Soc. Symp,** 43, 47-67.

Seliger, V. Ejam, M. Pauer, M. and Safarek, V. (1973) Energy metabolism in tennis. **Int. Z. Angew Physiol.,** 31, 333-340.

Telford, R.D. Minikin, B.R. Hooper, L.A. Hahn, A.G. and Tumilty, D.McA. (1987) The tri-level fitness profile. **Excel**, 4(1), 11-13.

Wahren, J. Felig, P. Ahlborg, G. and Jorfeldt, L. (1971) Glucose metabolism during leg exercise in man. **J. Clin. Invest.,** 50, 2715-2725.

Ward, R. Ross, W.D. Leyland, A.J. and Selbie, S. (1989) **The Advanced O-Scale Physique Assessment System Instructional Manual.** Kinemetrix Inc, Burnaby, British Columbia.

2 Investigation of exercise intensity in male singles lawn tennis

T. Reilly and J. Palmer
Centre for Sport and Exercise Sciences, School of Human Sciences, Liverpool John Moores University, Liverpool, UK

1 Introduction

Lawn tennis is played both for recreational and competitive purposes. Activity during matches is intermittent, varying from bursts of vigorous efforts during rallies to relative inactivity periods between points. Standard rest breaks at permitted within each set and also between sets when players change ends. A description of the trends in exercise to rest ratios and of physiological responses to tennis play would help characterise the exercise intensity associated with the game.

This study concentrated on singles tennis play among male club competitors. these players attempt to maintain their standard of play in the winter by practising in indoor facilities. The research was undertaken during the off-season in order to determine work-rates and physiological responses of male singles players to matches indoors.

2 Methods

Subjects were eight top club-standard male players. Their mean age (±SD) was 23.4 ± 3.1 years, height 182 ± 7 cm and body mass 75.1 ± 6.7 kg. Their $\dot{V}O_2$ max and maximal heart rate were determined during an incremental treadmill run to exhaustion. The oxygen uptake ($\dot{V}O_2$) was measured on-line (Sensorimedics, Salford) and heart rate was monitored by means of short-range radio telemetry (Sport-Tester).

Four competitive singles matches were played on an indoor, wooden court surface. The best of three sets indicated victory in each match and subjects were encouraged to treat the matches as realistic competition. The matches were recorded on video film using a Sony Handycam recorder with on-screen timer. Heart rate was monitored using the Sport-Tester device. The clocks on the heart rate monitors and on the video camera were synchronised, accurate to 1 s. The players were matched on ability, $\dot{V}O_2$ max and age. Fluid for ingestion was provided on an ad libitum basis as permitted by the Rules and Regulations of the Lawn Tennis Association.

Finger-prick blood samples were taken before, during and after tennis matches for analysis of blood lactate. During matches the samples were taken only at every

Science and Racket Sports Edited by T. Reilly, M. Hughes and A. Lees.
Published in 1994 by E & FN Spon ISBN 0 419 18500 3

other change of end. The number of blood samples obtained for each subject during match-play was seven (range 5-9). Blood samples were stored at 0-2°C and analysed using an Analox LM3 Lactate Analyser (Analox Instruments, London).

The data from the video recordings were analysed for calculation of exercise to recovery ratios. The heart rates during play were analysed for investigating differences between rally and recovery periods and between server and receiver. These analyses utilised Student's t-test on the VAX Minitab system. A P value of 0.05 or less was taken to indicate statistical significance. The mean heart rates (HR) during play were related to the $\dot{V}O_2$-HR regression lines during the incremental treadmill runs in order to calculate the relative exercise intensity during tennis singles match-play.

3 Results

The mean $\dot{V}O_2$ max determined during the incremental treadmill run was 53.2 (± 7.3) ml/kg/min. The maximal heart rates were 191 (± 11) beats/min.

The total number of games per match was 23 ± 7. The ball was in play for 27.9 (± 3.9)% of the time. Each rally lasted 5.3 (± 1.0) s and 91% of rallies were less than 10 s in duration. The ratio of exercise to recovery time between points was 1 : 2.5 when only the recovery time between points was taken into account; this ratio was increased to 1 : 3.1 when the recovery time in changing ends was also included. The time to take blood samples was not included in the calculations.

The mean heart rates during play (146 ± 19 beats/min) did not differ significantly from values during the recovery periods (147 ± 19 beats/min). The heart rates were higher when serving compared to receiving, both for the exercise periods (149 ± 19 vs 144 ± 19 beats/min) and the recovery (151 ± 18 vs 144 ± 19 beats/min) periods ($P<0.05$).

The mean blood lactate pre-exercise of 1.0 (± 0.1) mM was elevated during match-play to 2.0 (± 0.4) mM. The mean value post-exercise (3 min) was 1.0 (± 0.6) mM and the average peak value attained during play for the eight subjects was 3.0 (± 0.7) mM.

4 Discussion

The mean duration of the four matches was 42.7 min. Two were two-set matches lasting 13.8 and 24.1 min, whilst the other took three sets and lasted 58.3 and 62.8 min. The exercise to recovery ratio was 1 : 2.5 or 1 : 3.1, depending on whether the time taken in changing ends was taken into consideration. The exercise to rest ratio between points gives the more accurate description of game demands in singles tennis, the value of 1 : 2.5 being similar to that reported by Chandler (1990) for the 1988 U.S. Open Men's singles final. The present figures are on the whole consistent with earlier reports which have shown the ball to be in play for 17% (Docherty, 1982), 23.6% (Misner et al., 1980) and 26.5% (Elliott et al., 1985) of the total time.

Morgans et al. (1987), employing 60 min of conditioned games of singles tennis in an indoor court, reported that the ball was in play for 30.5% of the total game. It should be mentioned that none of these studies replicated the format of real match-play, the best of three sets.

The mean duration of a rally was 5.3 (± 1.0) s: this varied from 4.3 and 4.8 s for the two-set matches to 5.2 and 6.7 s for the matches that went to three sets. The average duration of rallies was 4.3 (± 0.6) s, 4.2 (± 0.9) s and 4.0 (± 0.4) s for players of low, medium and high skill levels in the study of Docherty (1982). In contrast, the mean duration of rallies noted by Elliott et al. (1985) was 10 s. These games were played on a hard surface, a factor likely to increase the opportunities for extending rally lengths. The quality of the wooden surface, along with the likelihood that recovery periods are shortened when play takes place in indoor courts with walled restraints compared to the more open outdoor courts, would serve to increase rally length and decrease the time between points (Reilly, 1990). Nevertheless, the rally length is likely to be most affected by the tactics of server and receiver and the emphasis placed on serving and volleying to win points or on using a baseline strategy.

The mean heart rate during match-play of 147 beats/min compares with the 150 (± 10) beats/min reported by Rittel and Waterloh (1975) and 143 (range 132-151) beats/min reported by Seliger et al. (1973) over a 10 min model game. In the present study the subjects were operating at 76.4% of their maximal heart rates. This was similar to the 78% reported by Elliott et al. (1985) for male college players over 60 min. It was higher than the 60% of the age-adjusted maximal heart rate reported by Misner et al. (1980) for recreational players aged 25-52 years, and the values reported by Docherty (1982). In the latter's study, the variation in exercise heart rate due to skill level was not significant and the relatively low exercise intensities are likely to be due to the high percent (81%) of total time that the ball was out of play.

The fluctuations in exercise heart rate in this study were not very great, no difference being noted between the exercise and recovery periods. This confirms the observation of Friedman et al. (1984) that the heart rate over 50 min of play reached a steady state despite the stop and start nature of the game. Elliott et al. (1985) observed mean heart rates of 153 beats/min in between rallies compared with 150 beats/min during rallies and suggested that these recovery periods are used for restoration of energy systems by means of oxygen transport. These authors noted higher heart rates for the server compared to the receiver, the difference being about 10 beats/min while the ball was in play and 8 beats/min between rallies. This trend replicated in the present study and underlines the more dominant role the server takes in dictating the play.

The work-rate and physiological response profiles may be utilised in characterising the energetics of tennis play. When the mean heart rates during play were related to the $\dot{V}O_2$-HR regression line, subjects were estimated to be operating at 76.4 of maximal heart rates and about 53% $\dot{V}O_2$ max. This corresponds to an energy expenditure of 43.6 kJ/min, and agrees with directly measured values during simulated games of 43.5 kJ/min (Bartunkova et al., 1979) and 45.6 kJ/min

(Yamaoka, 1965).

The moderate levels of blood lactate also denote a moderate aerobic loading. The average value was below the 3.0 (± 1.0) mM observed by Kindermann and Keul (1977). Peak values did exceed 3.0 mM during play in only three subjects in the current study, denoting that the blood lactate measurement is influenced primarily by the nature of activity prior to samples being drawn. Such values were rarely attained and this suggests that anaerobic glycolysis does not play a major role in metabolism during tennis play. It seems that a major contribution is made by the phosphagens during activity in conjunction with aerobic metabolism in the short intermissions.

5 References

Bartunkova, S., Sufarik, V., Melicharova, E., Bartunek, A., Seliger, V., Uk, F. and Bures, J. (1979) Energeticky vydaj u badminton. **Teor Praxe del Vych**, 27, 369-372.

Chandler, J. (1990) **United States Professional Tennis Registry Manual on Sport Science (Volume X): Conditioning Players and Monitoring Performance.** United States Professional Tennis Registry, Hilton Head Island, SC.

Docherty, D. (1982) A comparison of heart rate responses in racquet games. **Brit. J. Sports Med.**, 16, 96-100.

Elliott, B., Dawson, B. and Pyke, F. (1985) The energetics of singles tennis. **J. Human Mov't Stud.**, 11, 11-20.

Friedman, D.B., Ramo, B.W. and Gray, G.J. (1984) Tennis and cardiovascular fitness in middle-aged men. **Physician Sportsmed.**, 12, 87-92.

Kindermann, W. and Keul, J. (1977) Lactate acidoses with different forms of sports activities. **Canad. J. Appl. Sport Sci.**, 2, 177-182.

Misner, T.E., Boileau, R.A., Courvoisier, D., Slaughter, M.H. and Bloomfield, D.K. (1980) Cardiovascular stress associated with the recreational tennis play of middle aged males. **Amer. Corr. Ther. J.**, 34, 4-8.

Morgans, L.F., Jordan, D.L., Baegens, D.A. and Franciosa, J.A. (1987) Heart rate responses during singles and doubles competition. **Physician Sportsmed.**, 15, 67-74.

Reilly, T. (1990) The racquet sports, in **Physiology of Sports** (eds. T. Reilly, N. Secher, P. Snell and C. Williams), E. and F.N. Spon, London, pp.337-369.

Rittel, H.F. and Waterloh, E. (1975) Radiotelemetric bei Tennis, Badminton und Tischjennisspieler. **Sportarzt Sportmedizin**, 15, 144-150.

Yamaoka, S. (1965) Studies in the energy metabolism in athletic sports. **Res. J. Phys. Educ.**, 9, 28-40.

3 Seasonal variability in physiological strain: matching performance to demand

R.D. Hansen
Department of Life Sciences, University of Sydney, Australia

1 Introduction

Squash is a physiologically demanding sport (Northcote et al., 1986). Exercise heart rates of 162 beats/min have been reported (Blanksby et al., 1980) during "A" grade matches of 40 minutes duration in mild conditions (air temperature < 22°C, relative humidity < 60%). In 90-minute matches, elite players can exhibit sweat losses of 2 l and increases in rectal temperature of 1.6°C (Noakes et al., 1982). Oxygen uptakes from 2 to 4 l/min have been estimated for the sport (Durnin and Passmore, 1967).

Metabolic heat production in squash must therefore be high. As the sport is popular throughout the world and played in all seasons, it is reasonable to assume that court conditions in the warmer seasons impose considerable *environmental* heat stress on players, additional to the metabolic heat produced, compounding their physiological strain. Seasonal changes in court conditions and physiological demands therefore warrant investigation. The aims of this study were to describe the seasonal variations in environmental heat stress imposed on players in a non-airconditioned Sydney complex, to investigate the influence of these variations on physiological strain, and to determine the implications of this for match preparation and performance.

2 Methods

2.1 Subjects and site

Thirteen male competition squash players gave their informed consent for this study. Seven were subsequently excluded due to infrequent availability or low aerobic capacity. Characteristics of the six subjects who remained in the study are given in Table 1. Each subject played competition squash at the grade indicated, and practised squash regularly, throughout the 20 month study.

A brick, tin-roofed squash court complex in western Sydney was the site for the study. The

Science and Racket Sports Edited by T. Reilly, M. Hughes and A. Lees.
Published in 1994 by E & FN Spon ISBN 0 419 18500 3

region enjoys warm summers and mild winters with a majority of rainfall in summer and autumn. Ceiling fans provided airflow to five concrete-backed courts; windows, louvres and fans provided airflow to three glass-backed courts.

Table 1. Characteristics of the six subjects

Subject #	**Age (yrs)**	**Height (cm)**	**Body Mass (kg)**	**$\dot{V}O_{2\,max}$ (ml/kg/min)**	**Comp. grade**
1	42	185	84.8	46.9	C 5
2	30	192	92.1	45.3	E 6
3	41	173	65.4	43.3	C 5
4	41	181	94.7	38.2	F 6
5	34	171	62.1	49.0	E 6
6	33	177	60.9	39.5	C 5
Mean±SD	37±5	180±8	76.7±15.6	43.7±4.2	

$\dot{V}O_{2\,max}$ = maximal oxygen uptake, estimated from a three stage submaximal step test.

2.2 Protocol

Subjects' physiological responses were recorded during 16 matches of approximately 55 minutes duration with an opponent of similar skill. Each subject was monitored at least once in warm (late spring/summer/early autumn), and once in cool (winter/early spring) conditions. Prior to play, nude and clothed body weight were noted. During breaks in play, exercise heart rate (HR) was palpated at the carotid artery by timing 15 successive beats. Rating of perceived exertion (RPE; Borg, 1970) and perceived warmth (Wm; Bedford, 1936) were also noted during these breaks. Post-exercise rectal temperature (Trec) was taken within two minutes of cessation of play via thermistor probe and digital thermometer. Clothed and nude weight were again recorded. Fluid input and output were measured between pre- and post-exercise weighings.

2.3 Environmental data

Court dry bulb (DB) and wet bulb (WB) temperature for each match were measured by sling psychrometer. Air speed in m/s was estimated via kata thermometer and nomogram (British Standard BS3276). Forty seven additional court DB, WB and air speed observations were made on an *ad hoc* basis.

Outdoor DB & WB data, taken every three hours, were obtained from a Bureau of Meteorology station located 2 km from the squash courts. This permitted a total of 63 comparisons of court and outdoor temperatures.

2.4 Data analysis

The Discomfort Index (DI; Sohar et al., 1978) was calculated as the arithmetic mean of each

set of DB and WB data from the formula: DI = (DB + WB) / 2.
Total sweat loss was calculated as the difference in nude weight before and after exercise, corrected for any fluid input or output. Sweat loss was then expressed as % change in body weight per hour (SL%). Evaporative sweat loss was calculated as the corresponding difference in clothed weight, then expressed as a % of total sweat loss (ESL%). Pearson's correlational analysis, regression analysis, Fisher's test and student's t-tests were used to determine significant relationships between variables at the P<0.05 level.

Table 2. Seasonal trends in court conditions

Season	**DB (^{o}C)**	**WB (^{o}C)**	**Air speed (m/s)**
Winter (n=13)	16.1±0.5	12.7±0.4	0.26±0.04
Spring (n=22)	21.0±0.6*	17.2±0.6*	0.18±0.03
Summer (n=19)	27.6±0.4*A	22.0±0.7*A	0.21±0.04
Autumn (n=9)	26.5±1.2*A	20.5±0.9*A	0.12±0.04**

All mean values ± SE; n = number of observations; * P<0.001 versus Winter; ** P<0.025 versus Winter; A P<0.005 versus Spring.

3 Results

3.1 Environmental conditions

Considerable seasonal fluctuations in court conditions occurred, as shown in Table 2, where the 63 observations are grouped by season and averaged. Hot conditions often persisted late into the evening. No significant differences between concrete- and glass-backed courts were noted. Air speed was <0.25 m/s on 44 occasions.
Court DB & WB correlated significantly with outdoor DB & WB readings (Figure 1). When outdoor DB exceeded 28°C, court DB was often several degrees lower. Court WB was, on average, 2.5^{o}C higher than outdoor WB. When DB & WB were combined to give DI values, the relationship between court and outdoor conditions was: Court DI = 0.772 Outdoor DI + 5.64 (r = 0.91, P<0.001).
Thus variability in outdoor DI accounted for 83% of variability in court DI values.

3.2 Physiological and subjective responses of players

Except for RPE, players' responses in the 16 matches correlated significantly with court DI (Figure 2). Variability in court DI could account for 46%, 31%, 85% and 38%, respectively, of T_{rec}, HR, SL% and W_m variability. The regression lines in Fig. 2 show that when court DI increased from 15°C (early winter conditions) to 25°C (summer), T_{rec} increased, on

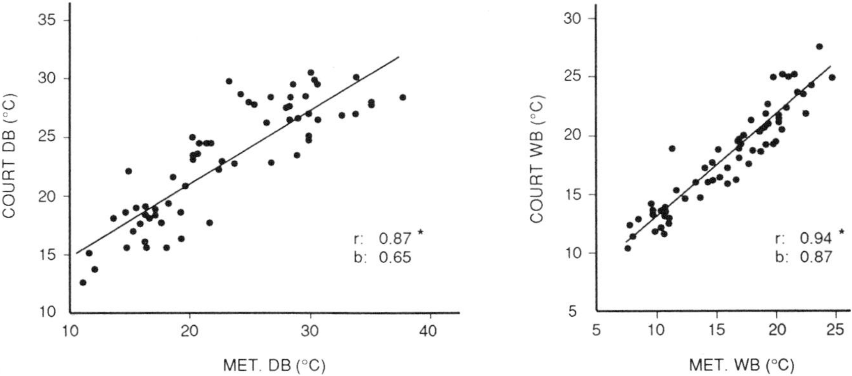

Figure 1. Court versus meteorological temperatures, 63 observations.
Met., outdoor observations at Richmond Meteorological Station;
r, correlation coefficient; b, regression coefficient. * P<0.001.

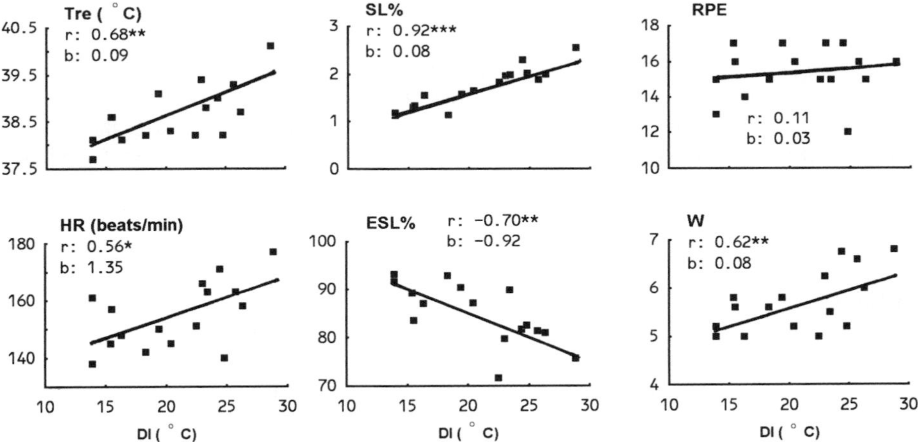

Figure 2. Physiological and subjective responses of players versus court Discomfort Index. RPE, average RPE for match, 12=light work, 18=very hard work; W, average warmth level for game, 5=just warm, 7=much too warm.
* P<0.05; ** P<0.01; *** P<0.0001.

average, from 38.2 to 39°C, HR from 146 to 160 beats/min, and SL% from 1.2 to 2% of body weight/hour. The ESL% decreased from 90 to 81% for these DI values.
When conditions of play were categorised into three DI ranges, there were significant differences between mean values of T_{rec}, SL%, ESL% and W at the hotter versus the cooler conditions (Table 3).

Table 3. Responses of players categorised by three DI ranges

DI range (°C)	T_{rec} (°C)	HR (beats/min)	SL%	ESL%	RPE	W
> 24	39.1±0.3	162±6	2.15±0.12	80±1	15±1	6.3±0.3
19-23.9	38.8±0.2	155±4	1.8±0.08*	84±4	16±0.4	5.6±0.2
< 19	38.2±0.1*	149±4	1.27±0.07#	89.7±2#	15±0.6	5.3±0.2*

Responses are all mean values ±SE; * P<0.025 and # P<0.001 versus the value in the DI > 24 range.

The average (±SE) fluid intake during the 16 matches was 67 ± 33 ml. The hottest match occurred on a midsummer's evening, from 20:30 to 21:45 hours. Court DB was 30°C, WB 27.6°C, DI 28.8°C. The player (#5) had a T_{rec} of 40.1°C. Immediately after the match his HR was 188 beats/min, RPE 18 and W_m maximal. Nude weight loss was 1.97 kg, SL% was 2.55% of body weight/h and ESL% was 76%. He experienced post-exercise nausea and exhaustion.

4 Discussion

4.1 Influence of local weather patterns

The environmental data indicate that heat stress on non-airconditioned courts is heavily influenced by local weather. As daily temperatures are predicted with considerable accuracy nowadays (Bureau of Meteorology, 1991), the relationship between outdoor and indoor temperatures (Figure 1 and equation 2) suggests that forecasts can be used to predict court conditions with reasonable accuracy.

4.2 Degree of heat stress and physiological strain

Summer and early autumn court conditions were characterised by moderately high court DB and WB values, often in combination with poor air movement. High DB values indicate a lessened capacity for convective cooling as air temperature app- roaches skin temperature. Similarly, WB values provide an indication of the resist- ance of the court environments to evaporation of sweat. Air speeds <0.2 m/s imply that both convective and evaporative heat losses are limited (Brotherhood, 1987).

The Discomfort Index integrates the effects on convective and evaporative heat exchange represented by DB & WB. Traditionally, DI values of 24.1 to 28.0°C are associated with "moderate" heat loads and indicate that frequent rest breaks and attention to hydration should accompany vigorous activity. Discomfort Index values >28°C represent "severe" heat loads, indicating that it can be dangerous to engage in vigorous activity (Sohar et al., 1978).

For these six players, the hotter conditions were associated with significant increases in thermoregulatory strain. Increased environmental heat stress makes it difficult for metabolic heat from working muscles to be dissipated from the body. The hypothalamic heat loss centre responds by diverting more blood to the skin and increasing sweat output (Rowell, 1983). However, as the ESL% data clearly show, proportionally less sweat could be evaporated in the hotter conditions (Figure 2 & Table 3). Hence heat loss was prejudiced: this was reflected in higher T_{rec} and W values, even though sweat losses were noticeably elevated.

4.3 The danger of dehydration

This study shows that even in relatively cool conditions the intensity of squash stimulates sweat production above 1% of body weight/h in non-elite players. Noakes et al. (1982) have reported similar sweat losses in elite players. The present study shows, however, that sweat losses in squash can display considerable seasonal variability. Losses above 2% of body weight/h occurred in summer matches.

These sweat loss data highlight the risk of dehydration in prolonged, intense squash matches and round-robin events, particularly in warm conditions. Dehydration- induced performance losses could occur, especially if the player were dehydrated prior to competition (Sawka et al., 1984). The short breaks between games mitigate against fluid replacement during match play.

Subject #5 reported drinking only 1 l in the 4 h prior to play in the hottest match. He drank nothing during the match. His post-match physiological and subjective data are consistent with mild heat exhaustion. It is worthy of note that this match occurred quite late in the evening. Players who work outdoors or in non-airconditioned areas during a hot day have several hours in a potentially dehydrating environment prior to evening match play. This could significantly affect performance. Careful attention to pre-exercise water intake, such that normal body weight is maintained, together with the ingestion of 300 to 400 ml of water during breaks, will minimise these perform- ance decrements (Lamb and Brodowicz, 1986).

4.4 Predicting the physiological demands of a match

The correlation between players responses and court DI values suggests that an envir- onmental heat stress index can predict the general physiological demand of a match. The DI is well-suited to this purpose, as DB & WB data are readily obtained from meteorological records and forecasts, and it is a simple index to calculate. It should enable training to match more accurately expected physiological strain, particularly if competition in a warmer climate is involved. The average increases in T_{rec}, HR and SL% per 1°C increases in DI (that is, the regression coefficients) reported here can serve as a guide for predicting strain and planning training intensity.

Acknowledgement: The expert assistance of Boyd Murray and Virginia Ross and the cooperation of the subjects is gratefully acknowledged.

5 References

Bedford, T. (1936) **The Warmth Factor in Comfort at Work**. H.M.S.O., London.

Blanksby, B.A., Elliot, B.C., Davis, K.H. and Mercer, M.D. (1980) Blood pressure and rectal temperature responses of middle-aged sedentary, middle-aged active and "A" grade competitive male squash players. **Brit. J. Sports Med.**, 14, 133-138.

Borg, G. (1970) Perceived exertion as an indicator of somatic stress. **Scand.J. Rehab. Med.**, 2, 92-98.

Brotherhood, J.R. (1987) The practical assessment of heat stress, in **Heat Stress: Physical Exertion and Environment** (eds J.R. Hales and D.A. Richards), Elsevier Science, Amsterdam, pp.451-468.

Bureau of Meteorology, New South Wales Regional Office (1991). **Annual Report 1990-1991**, p.43.

Durnin, J.V.G.A. and R. Passmore. (1967) **Energy, Work and Leisure.** Heinemann Ltd., London.

Lamb, D.R. and Brodowicz, G.R. (1986) Optimal use of fluids of varying formulations to minimise exercise-induced disturbances in homeostasis. **Sports Med.**, 3, 247-274.

Noakes, T.D., Cowling, J., Gevers, W. and De V. Van Niekerk, J. (1982) The metabolic response to squash including the influence of pre-exercise carbohydrate ingestion. **S. Afr. Med. J.**, 62, 721-723.

Northcote, R.J., Flannigen, C. and Ballantyne, D. (1986) Sudden death and vigorous exercise: a study of 60 deaths associated with squash. **Br. Heart J.**, 55, 198-203.

Rowell, L.B. (1983) Cardiovascular adjustments to thermal stress, in **Handbook of Physiology Section 2: The Cardiovascular System.** American Physiological Society, Bethesda.

Sawka, M.N., Francesconi, R.P., Young, A.J. and Pandolf, K.B. (1984) Influence of hydration level and body fluids on exercise in the heat. **J.A.M.A.**, 252, 1165-1169.

Sohar, E., Birenfeld, Ch., Shoenfeld, Y. and Shapiro, Y. (1978) Description and forecast of summer climate in physiologically significant terms. **Int. J. Biometeor.**, 22, 75-81.

4 Fluid replacement needs of young tennis players

K. Kavasis
Division of Physical Education, University of the Witwatersrand, Johannesburg, South Africa

1 Introduction

Although, there is a considerable amount of information about the fluid replacement needs of the adult athlete [American College of Sports Medicine(ACSM), 1985], little is known for the exercising child and especially the young tennis player. Fluid replacement needs during exercise depend primarily on the exercise intensity, body size, environmental heat stress and fluid intake patterns. This study attempted to determine the fluid replacement needs of young tennis players, while accounting for the influence of exercise intensity, freely chosen drinking patterns and environmental conditions during a competitive tennis match.

2 Methods

2.1 On-Court Test

Three groups of young tennis players (based on age and ability), were studied during five data collection sessions (Table 1). The testing procedures used are presented in Figure 1. Outdoor tennis match conditions were simulated for subjects in Group 2 and 3 and subjects in Group 1 participated in an official interprovincial tournament. Players were allowed to ingest only water, ad libitum, during the match.

Table 1. Selected characteristics of the subjects ($\bar{X}\pm SD$)

	Group 1 (N=8)	Group 2 (N=8)	Group 3 (N=8)	Total Group (N=24)
Age (yrs)	12.8±0.4	12.8+0.6	14.8+0.5^{+}	13.4±1.3
Mass (kg)	45.9±6.2	45.9±10.9	53.3±8.9	48.4±9.3
Height (m)	1.60±0.1	1.54±0.1	1.66±0.1^{++}	1.60±0.1
Fat (%)	10.4±3.6	10.7±4.6	9±2.8	10±3.7

$^{+}$ $P<0.05$ G3 vs G1 and G2; $^{++}$ $P<0.05$ G3 vs G2

Science and Racket Sports Edited by T. Reilly, M. Hughes and A. Lees.
Published in 1994 by E & FN Spon ISBN 0 419 18500 3

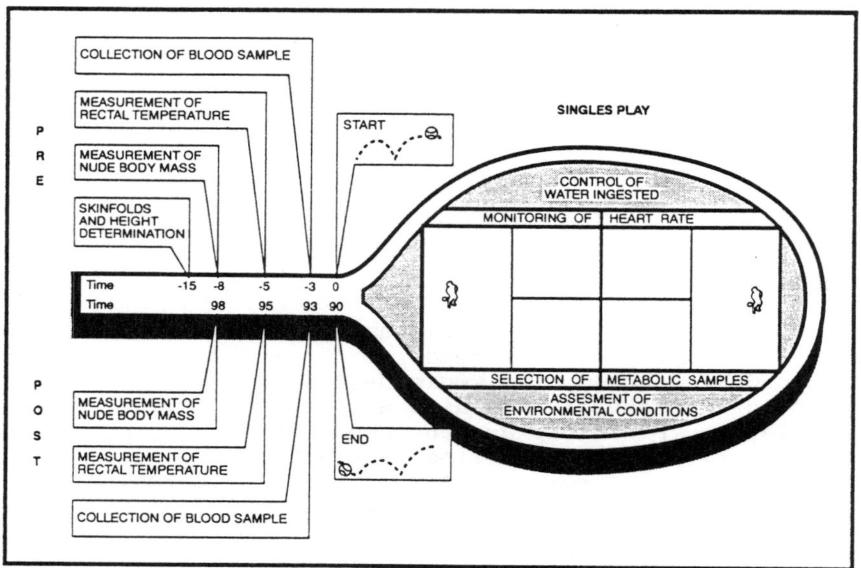

Fig.1. Graphical illustration of testing procedures and sequences. Time denotes minutes relative to the commencement of play. Pre- and post- denotes pre-match and post-match measurements respectively.

The Competitive State Anxiety Inventory-2 (CSAI-2) developed by Martens et al.(1990) was administered to Group 3. The Sport Competition Anxiety Test for children (SCAT-C), (Martens, 1977) was administered to all groups in order to assess the trait anxiety of the subjects.

The environmental heat stress index was obtained using the Wet Bulb Globe Temperature (WBGT) index. Rectal temperature (T_{rec}) was measured using a standard clinical sterilised indwelling rectal thermometer and nude body mass was determined using an electronic scale (Protea Medical, Johannesburg).

Plasma concentrations of electrolyte (Na^+, K^+, Mg^{++}, Cl^-) and total plasma protein (TPP) were measured by the Biuret method. Haemoglobin (Hb) concentration was measured using the S-II counter, haematocrit (Hct) was determined using the Technicon H^* 2 system and plasma volume changes (%) were calculated using the Hct and Hb values (Strauss et al., 1951). Blood glucose concentration was measured using the Beckman Oxygen Electrode method.

Maximum and resting heart rate (HR) were based on the age range of the groups which were obtained from tables published by Siegel(1988). Target HR range (THRR) was set according to the ACSM(1978) exercise intensity criterion for developing and maintaining cardiovascular fitness in adults, which also apply to children (Rowland, 1985).

The portable HR monitor PE 300 (Unilife) was used to record the THRR range by means of radiotelemetry. The PE 3000 (Polar) was used for the continuous measurement (each minute) of HR response and the calculation of the mean HR response of the total group throughout the match from a subset of 13 of the players, was determined.

The Douglas bag technique was used during the tennis matches to measure oxygen consumption ($\dot{V}O_2$). An average of three collections of expired volume, was randomly taken during the match from each player in the neoprene bag (Dynamic Image, Johannesburg). Altogether 80 samples of expired air were collected throughout the measurement sessions. All gas concentrations were analyzed by the Oxycon IV (Mijhardt, Bunnik, Holland) and expressed in STPD units.

2.2 Calculations

A linear regression equation of HR and $\dot{V}O_2$, measured during the test period, was applied to the total group in order to estimate mean $\dot{V}O_2$ (derived from the mean HR data) and corresponding energy expenditure of the subjects.

The net body mass change (after adding liquid intake and subtracting urine voided) was used to determine the amount of total mass loss. This total mass loss included sweat losses, the respiratory tract water losses and the metabolic fuel utilized. Water deficit (WD) was calculated by the use of the formula:

$$WD = [TML - (MFU + MWP)] / 2$$

where TML = total mass loss (kg)
MWP = metabolic water produced (kg)
MFU = metabolic fuel utilized (g)

Energy expenditure and MFU (g) was calculated according to method described by Mc Ardle et al.(1991). The metabolic water produced by mitochondrial oxidation was estimated from the method described by Noakes et al.(1991). Following the recommendations of Olsson and Saltin(1970) water released from glycogen breakdown was not considered as water deficit. In this study it was assumed that 50% of the WD resulted from water released by glycogen breakdown. Percent dehydration was calculated as follows: % dehydration = WD/IBM x 100 [where IBM=initial body mass (kg)].

3 Results

The mean trait anxiety test score(19), revealed that the young tennis players experienced moderate levels of trait anxiety prior to competition. The WBGT index during the five data collection sessions was temperate, ranging from

13-19. In the total group, the time spent within the THRR for cardiovascular development was 24.38 min, 0.48 min were spent over and 64.38 min were spent under the target HRR. One-way analysis of variance revealed that exercise intensity, as reflected by the time spent within each HRR, was not significantly different between the groups ($P>0.05$). The HR-$\dot{V}O_2$ regression line of the total group is shown in Fig.2.

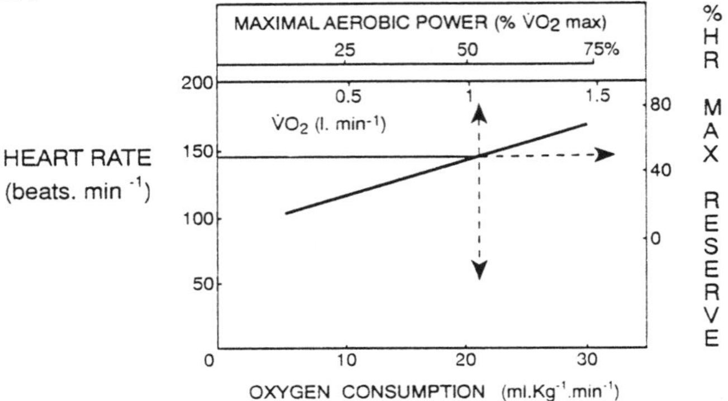

Fig. 2. The HR-$\dot{V}O_2$ relationship of the subjects(N=24). The mean of the continuous HR is used to assess the average $\dot{V}O_2$ demand during the tennis match, as well as the average load expressed as the age adjusted %HRmax reserve and predicted corresponding %$\dot{V}O_2$max.

The estimated mean $\dot{V}O_2$ of 21.38 ml.kg^{-1}.min^{-1} for the total group corresponded to a mean energy expenditure of 1772 kJ during the 90 min playing period. The significant increase in mean T_{rec} of 0.73 Ĉ was unrelated to mean percentage dehydration of 0.80% of the subjects after a 90 min tennis match. Furthermore, post-match T_{rec} did not differ significantly between the groups.

Mean plasma volume changes in group two and three were non-significant but positively related to TPP changes in both groups ($r=0.85$). Non-significant mean electrolyte, TPP and glucose changes were observed in total group. The subjects voluntary ingested a mean amount of 0.427 l of water during the match, whilst the mean mass loss for the whole group was 0.480 kg. However, water deficit was calculated to be 0.390 l.

4 Discussion

As the environmental conditions in this study were temperate and the competitive stress levels of the subjects moderate, it is unlikely that mean HR and/or $\dot{V}O_2$ levels during play would have been greatly influenced by these factors. The mean HR response of the subjects whose continuous HR response was recorded in this study, resulted in the derivation of a mean intensity of effort of 55% of the age adjusted HRmax reserve (Figure 2). This, together with the fact that only 24.3 min were spent within the THRR, over the 90 min period of competitive tennis match, appears to indicate limited possibilities for optimal cardiovascular development in young tennis players through competitive play. Furthermore, the estimated mean $\dot{V}O_2$ max of 50-55% (Figure 2) suggests that playing at a high percentage of $\dot{V}O_2$ max is not a prerequisite for young tennis players. Furthermore, it appears that a high level of metabolic stress is not imposed by this sport in young tennis players.

Blood glucose, thermoregulatory (T_{rec}) and plasma volume change mechanisms seem to function adequately under the environmental conditions of the study, in order to support the intermittent moderate metabolic demand of a 90 min tennis match. Furthermore, the increase in blood glucose response does not support the need for glucose supplementation during 90 min of tennis play in similar conditions. Likewise, the non-significant changes in plasma Na^+ and Cl^- concentration may also suggest that under the conditions of this study, in particular, the exercise intensity and amount of water ingested, supplementation of NaCl is contraindicated.

The American Academy of Pediatrics (AAP, 1983), suggested the enforcement of freely-chosen drinking patterns in children. This should be followed with caution since it is based on a single laboratory study (Bar-Or et al., 1980). In contrast, the subjects in this study who were permitted to adopt freely-chosen drinking patterns, either correctly gauged (Group 1), overestimated (Group 2) or slightly underestimated (Group 3) their fluid replacement needs during tennis play (Fig. 3).

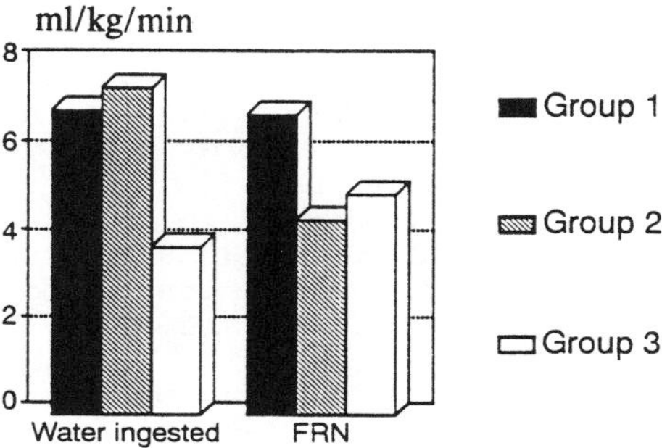

Fig. 3. Calculated fluid replacement needs (FRN) ($ml.kg^{-1}.min^{-1}$) and measured freely-chosen drinking patterns ($ml.kg^{-1}.min^{-1}$) of the three subject groups during a 90 min tennis match (N=24).

The findings of this study do not support the contention of the AAP(1983) that voluntary dehydration is common among exercising children. It is recommended that this statement should be reconsidered and examined in other natural settings of play in children. It is more appropriate that a range of fluid replacement volumes, ought to be determined according to body mass, exercise intensity and the WBGT index on the day of the match-play.

In conclusion, and in order to prevent harmful levels of dehydration and overhydration under warm environmental conditions, at an exercise intensity of tennis match of approximately 55% of HRmax reserve or 50-55% of $\dot{V}O_2max$, consumption of 4.44-6.81 ml kg min or 200-360 ml h of water is recommended in young tennis players possessing a body mass of 45-53 kg.

This study was made possible by a grant from the South African Sugar Association (No. 59). The study was completed in fullfilment of an M.Ed thesis in the Division of Physical Education under the supervision of Edith Futre.

5 References

American Academy of Pediatrics (1983) Climatic heat stress and the exercising child. **Phys.Sportsmed.,** 11, 155-159.

American College of Sports Medicine (1978) Position statement on: The recommended quantity and quality of exercise for developing and maintaining fitness in healthy adults. **Med.Sci.Sports Exerc.,** 10: vii-x.

American College of Sports Medicine. (1985) Position statement on the preventation of thermal injuries during distance running. **Med.Sci.Sports Exerc.,** 16: ix-xiv.

Bar-Or, O., Dotan, R., Inbar, O., et al. (1980) Voluntary hypohydration in 10 to 12 year old boys. **J.Appl.Physiol.** 48, 104-108.

Martens, R. (1977) **Sport Competition Anxiety Test.** Human Kinetics, Champaign, IL.

Martens, R., Burton, D., Vealey, R.S., Bump, L.A., Smith, D.E. (1990) The Competitive State Anxiety Inventory - 2 (CSAI- 2), In D. Burton and R. Vealey (Eds), **Competitive Anxiety,** Human Kinetics, Champaign, IL.

Mc Ardle, W.A., Katch, F.I., Katch V.L. (1991) **Exercise Physiology: Energy, Nutrition and Human Performance,** (3rd Ed.). Lea and Febiger, Philadelphia, London.

Noakes, T.D., K.H Myburgh, J. Du Plessis, Lang, L., Lambert, M., Riet C. Van Der, Schall, R. (1991) Meta bolic rate, not percent dehydration, predicts rectal temperature in marathon runners. **Med.Sci.Sports.Exerc.,** 23, 443-449.

Olsson, K-E., and Saltin, B. (1970) Variations in total body water with muscle glycogen changes in man. **Acta Physiol.Scand.,** 80, 11-18.

Rowland, T.W. (1985) Aerobic response to endurance training in prepubescent children: a critical analysis. **Med.Sci. Sports Exerc.,** 17, 493-497.

Siegel, J. (1988) Children's target heart rate range. **J.Phys.Educ.Rec.Dan.,** 59, 78-79.

Strauss, M.B., Davis, R.K., Rosenbaum, J.D., Rossmeisl E.C. (1951) "Water diuresis" produced during recumbency by the intravenous infusion of isotonic saline solution. **J.Clin.Invest.,** 30, 862-858.

5 Cramps, heat stroke and abnormal biological responses during a strenuous tennis match

A. Therminarias, P. Dansou, M.F. Chirpaz, J. Eterradossi and A. Favre–Juvin
Centre Hospitalier Régional de Grenoble, France

1 Introduction

During a tennis match the exercise intensity may differ considerably according to the ability and the style of partners. Players regularly involved in competition, are often confronted with a strenuous match, generally of high exercise intensity, of long duration and often played in a hot environmental condition. Physiological responses during such matches have been studied in 23 women playing under standardized conditions (diet, ambient temperature, intensity, duration). The values obtained in 19 subjects have been previously published (Therminarias et al., 1991). Among the other women, 3 subjects stopped before the end of the match because of cramps and one because she felt the premonitory symptoms of heat stroke. The aim of the present study was to compare the biological values obtained in these four women to those obtained in the other players who were used as a control goup.

2 Method

All these women were ranked by a national tennis federation at an intermediate level and regularly took part in tournaments. They played the match as an official competition. Each subject chose the opponent that she feared playing the most during official tournaments, preferably a player able to provide long and regular exchanges. For the match, a duration of a minimum of two hours was arbitrarily fixed. All matches were played during the summer.

Before the match each subject was weighed nude and rectal temperature (Trec) was measured. Electrodes were placed to record heart rate (HR) and a blood sample was drawn for blood parameter determination (haemoglobin, plasma electrolytes, lactate, creatinine, uric acid, glucose, adrenaline, noradrenaline, arginine vasopressin (AV) concentrations) and plasma renin activity (PRA).

During the match, HR was measured continuously. The amount of time spent in different phases of activity was evaluated according to 3 levels of intensity: rest, low and high intensity. Each player had at her disposal 500 ml water to drink. Immediately after the match biological measurements were again performed, Trec was measured and the subject was again weighed nude.

Water loss due to transpiration was determined from body weight changes with appropriate correction for water intake. Exercise intensity during the match was estimated from mean HR values obtained on each player during the first 30 min of the match (firstHR), that is after 10 min warming-up and during the last 30 min of play (lastHR). Data are expressed as mean±S.E.M. A Student't-test was used to compare mean values obtained before and after the match.

Science and Racket Sports Edited by T. Reilly, M. Hughes and A. Lees.
Published in 1994 by E & FN Spon ISBN 0 419 18500 3

3 Results and Discussion

3.1 Control group

All players found the matches tiring because of the intensity, long duration, ambient temperature (28.3±0.7°C) and restriction in water intake. Thus the body weight was decreased by 2.7% at the end of the match and lastHR reached 87% of the maximum heart rate (Table 1). When pre-match values were compared to post-match values (Table 2), it was noted that i) plasma electrolyte concentrations did not greatly change except for phosphorus which increased by 36%, ii) plasma lactate concentration increased moderately, iii) PRA, AV, and noradrenaline concentrations were increased while adrenaline did not change.

3.2 Cramps

Three women stopped before the end of the match because of cramps (C1, C2 and C3). In these women, the conditions of match-play and the dehydration were similar to those obtained in the control group. In addition,various abnormal biological values were found.

Table 1. Values are 1) mean ±SEM obtained in 19 players during or after a tennis match (control group);2) values obtained in 3 players who stopped because of cramps (C1,C2,C3); 3) values in one player who stopped because of heat stroke (Heat S).

	Control group	Cramps			Heat S
		C1	C2	C3	
Rectal Tre (°C)					
post-match	38.4 ±0.2	38.1	37.9	36.8	40.4
Heart rate (beats/min)					
firstHR	154 ±2	142	138	145	164
lastHR	158 ±3	167	176	145	182
lastHR/maxHRx100	87 ±2	98	95	72	104
Water loss (g)	1430 ±15	1270	1060	2440	1650

One woman (C1) complained of cramps in the inferior and superior limbs. In this woman, biological values were similar to those of the other players. In addition, the plasma magnesium concentration was measured at the end of the match (Table 2) and a 40% decrease was found compared to the normal rest values (0.80±0.02). A week later plasma and erythrocyte concentrations were measured in this woman at rest and abnormally low values were obtained. Obviously, a deficiency in magnesium pre-existed before the match. Unfortunatly plasma magnesium was not measured in the other players. The change in plasma magnesium concentration during exercise depends on the relative contribution of anaerobic versus aerobic metabolism. Generally, an increase in plasma magnesium concentration is found after short-term exercise while a moderate decrease is observed after prolonged exercise. Thus, plasma magnesium was decreased by 5% at the end of a marathon (Lidgen et al., 1988). Since a low plasma magnesium concentration can lead to neuromuscular dysfunction, tetani or cramps (Brautbar and Carpentier, 1984; Lui et al., 1983), the very low value was probably responsible for the occurrence of cramps.

Table 2. Values are; 1) mean ±SEM obtained on 18 players before and after a tennis match (control group) * $P<0.05$ post-match versus pre-match values; 2) values obtained on 3 players who stopped because of cramps (C1,C2,C3), 3) values on one player who stopped because of heat stroke (Heat S).

	Control group		**Cramps**			**Heat S**
	pre-match	post-match	post-match			post-match
			C1	C2	C3	
Haemoglobin (g/dl)	12.8 ±0.2	13.2 ±0.2*	12.4	15.1	10.8	14.5
Sodium (mM)	140 ±0	142 ±1	141	138	139	145
Potassium (mM)	4.3 ±0.1	4.2 ±0.2	3.5	6.5	3.8	4.8
Chloride (mM)	107 ±1	108 ±1	105	110	105	110
Phosphorus (mM)	1.1 ±0.1	1.5 ±0.1*	1.2	1.4	1.8	2.1
Calcium (mM)	2.25 ±0.01	2.31 ±0.04	2.50	1.61	2.54	2.48
Magnesium (mM)			0.48			
Urea (mM)	5.1 ±0.4	5.6 ±0.4*	6.0	5.3	8.9	6.5
Uric acid (mM)	253 ±11	288 ±7.0*	265	260	292	380
Creatinine (mM)	77 ±5	104. ±7*	102	121	134	170
Glucose (mM)	5.2 ±0.2	5.6 ±0.4*	11.2	8	8.9	6.0
Lactate (mM)	1.27 ±0.12	1.78 ±0.3*	1.9	2.9	3.9	2.9
Nor (pM/ml)	0.79 ±0.17	1.86 ±0.23*	1.19	2.69	2.82	9.20
Adr (pM/ml)	0.41 ±0.05	0.41 ±0.04	0.31	0.56	0.46	0.25
AV (pg/ml)	0.7 ±0.2	5.6 ±1.4*	9.7	3.7	2.9	20.2
PRA (ug/l/min)	71.5 ±12.5	407 ±59*	370	1035	423	1360

Another woman (C2), complained of cramps in the superior limbs and the back. In this woman, the pre-match value of calcium was normal. However, a very low post-match value of plasma calcium was found. This value could explain the occurrence of premonitory symptoms of tetani. This woman was usually on a low calcium diet which might have promoted the decrease in plasma calcium during the match.

A third woman (C3), complained of cramps in the inferior limbs. Several factors could have promoted the occurrence of cramps: i) the pre-match (9 g/dl) and thereby the post-match values of haemoglobin (Table 1) were low, ii) the body weight was decreased by 3.2% at the end of the match, iii) the post-match value of plasma lactate was higher than that observed in the other players suggesting a greater contribution of the glycolytic pathway to the energy expenditure. An anaemia and a low serum ferritin concentration were found a week later. Probably the occurrence of cramps was favoured by the pre-match deficit in iron.

The glycaemia was considerably higher in these three women than in the control group. Obviously a lack of available blood glucose was not a contributing factor. This observation suggests rather that a decrease in blood glucose utilization occurs in the muscles which cannot contract normally.

3.3 Heat stroke

The woman referred to as H4, stopped 5 min before the end of the match complaining of headache, horripilation and shivering. In this woman the skin was hot and dry. The lastHR was higher than the maximum HR previously measured, and rectal temperature reached 40.4 °C (Table 1) .

At the end of the match the values of plasma electrolytes were similar to those obtained in the control group except for a larger increase in phosphorus. Additionally, uric acid and creatinine were greatly increased whilst AV and PRA were higher than those obtained in the other players. Finally plasma noradrenaline concentration reached a very high value.

The greater AV and PRA responses probably serve as a mechanism blunting the decrease in blood pressure and plasma volume. The greater noradrenaline response might be a consequence of hyperthermia. However, since noradrenaline is known to have a calorigenic effect, this secretion could have favoured the abnormal increase in central temperature.

4 Conclusion

The occurrence of cramps and heat stroke during a tennis match is favoured by numerous factors, such as long duration, high intensity, hot ambient temperature and dehydratation. However, different abnormal biological values pre-existed in two subjects who complained of cramps. Moreover match conditions had been similar in all these women. These observations suggest that the physiological state before the match greatly influences the occurence of cramps or heat stroke.

5 References

Brautbar N. and Carpenter C. (1984) Skeletal myopathy and magnesium depletion : cellular mechanisms. **Magnesium**, 3, 57-62

Lidjen P., Hespel P., Fagard, R., Lysens, R., Vanden Eynde, E. and Amery, A. (1988) Erythrocyte, plasma and urinary magnesium in men before and after a marathon. **Eur. J. Appl. Physiol.**, 58, 252-256

Lui K., Borowski G.and LI. Rose (1983) Hypomagnesemia in a tennis player. **Physician Sportsmed.**, 11; 79-82,

Therminarias A., P. Dansou, M.F. Chirpaz-Oddou, C.Gharib. and Quirion, A., (1991) Hormonal and metabolic changes during a strenuous tennis match . Effect of ageing. **Int. J. Sports Med.**,12, 10-16

6 Physiological demands of training in elite badminton players

M.G. Hughes
British Olympic Medical Centre, Harrow, UK

1 Introduction

Upon first impressions, badminton is a highly explosive sport, involving a unique movement technique over a relatively small court area. At various skill levels, Coad and co-workers (1979) and Docherty (1982) have found average rally length to be around five seconds. A rally was typically followed by an average recovery period of five to ten seconds. However, elite players expect rallies to be considerably longer at their level. High class competitive matches can last up to one hour. Given these combined elements of power and endurance, the physiological requirements of badminton may not be obvious and it would be of benefit to those involved in the sport to reach a more complete understanding of these demands.

At the elite level, training for badminton can be categorised into i) off-court conditioning, ii) on-court technical practice, iii) on-court physical practice and iv) game situations. Each type of session has different fitness and technical demands and these may be specific to given parts of the players' training cycle. During the competitive season, players may spend up to two hours per session in practice games and this forms a major part of the training programme. Consequently, it was considered to be of particular interest to establish the demands of this type of exercise.

Supplementary work was carried out where structured training routines were monitored. These routines were either 'multifeed' work or 'shadow play'. These techniques are typically used in the players' training and both involve high intensity on-court work. Shadow play involves normal on court movements but the player works without a shuttlecock. Depending on the exercise intensity, this can be used to improve footwork at varying degrees of physical fatigue. Multi-feed practice involves the player returning shuttles, directed by a coach, from various points of the court. This is generally a high speed, high quality exercise with a strong technical element. These results are also presented in this study.

The major purpose of this study was to assess the physiological demands of the practice games and then to view those findings in the context of, and in comparison to, the results obtained from work in the other on-court training situations.

2 Methods

Thirteen senior national squad members took part in the study. The following measurements were made at squad training camps.

Science and Racket Sports Edited by T. Reilly, M. Hughes and A. Lees.
Published in 1994 by E & FN Spon ISBN 0 419 18500 3

Table 1. Descriptive data for subjects in part 2.1

(n=8)	Mean	S.D.
Age (yrs)	23.0	3.0
Height (cm)	166.5	6.4
Body Mass (kg)	63.6	5.4
Body Fat (%)	23.6	3.3
$\dot{V}O2$ max (ml/kg/min)	51.5	4.5
HR max (beats/min)	193	7

2.2 Monitoring of training routines

Measurements were also made on players performing typical on-court training routines. Players were monitored for BLa during these forms of training. Only five individuals have been tested in this way.

i) Two female players performed a combination of shadow and multifeed work for one minute (30 seconds for each mode of training), followed by a 4.5 minute recovery for ten repetitions. Lactate measurements were made after the fifth and tenth repetition.
ii) Two male players performed a multifeed session working for 20 shuttles. Mean work duration was 57 $\pm$ 10 s (mean $\pm$ S.D.) with a mean recovery duration of 45 $\pm$ 12 s. Fourteen repetitions were performed, with blood samples taken immediately upon completion of the session.
iii) One male player performed a maximal intensity shadow play session with a work : rest ratio of 20 : 40 seconds for 11 repetitions. Post-exercise BLa and also HR were measured for this player.

2.3 'Competition simulation'

In addition to the routines described above, one female player was tested while playing against a male international. This was done in an attempt to simulate the demands of competition on the female player. Both HR and BLa were monitored in this instance and the male player attempted to subject the female to game situations similar to those experienced in competition.

3 Results

3.1 Practice games

The results obtained from the practice games on the eight players tested showed that during play, HR was greater than 80% of the measured maximum HR for over 85 % of the time. Mean game length was 9.7 $\pm$ 2.9 min. Players commented that the quality of play was relatively low compared to competition and this may be related to the short game length. The blood samples obtained after each game showed the mean BLa concentration to be 1.5 ± 0.4 mM.

3.2 Practice routines

i) Measurements made from the two players performing the {1 minute on : 4.5 minute off} routine showed the BLa concentration to be 4.0 mM and 4.8 mM after five repetitions, rising slightly to 4.6 mM and 4.9 mM respectively at the end of the session (10 repetitions). The players reported that the fatigue experienced in this way was more intense than would normally be experienced in competition.

ii) The 20 shuttle multifeed session resulted in post exercise BLa values of 4.2 mM and 4.0 mM in the two players monitored.

iii) The maximal shadow play session, 11 x [20 s on : 40 s off] elicited a post-exercise BLa of 7.2 mM. The HR data are shown in Figure1.

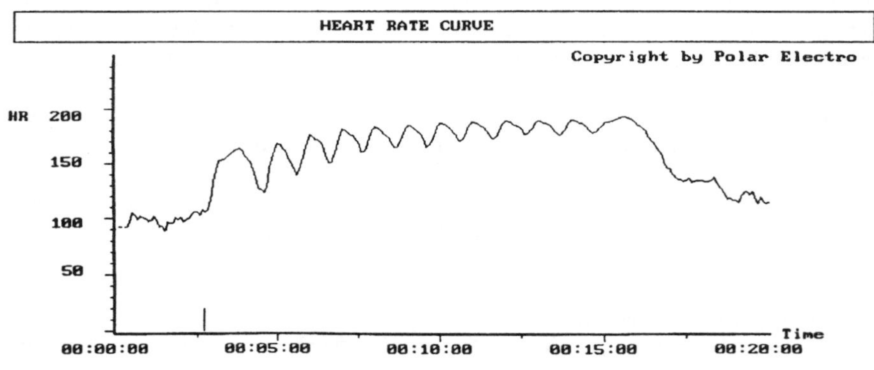

Figure 1. Heart rate trace for maximal shadow play

3.3 'Competition simulation'

The highest BLa concentration from the female player was 3.1 mM during play. After completion of the game, (duration = 13.5 minutes) BLa was 2.4 mM. The player sustained HR above 80% of maximum (HR max = 186 beats/min) for 96% of the playing time (Figure 2).

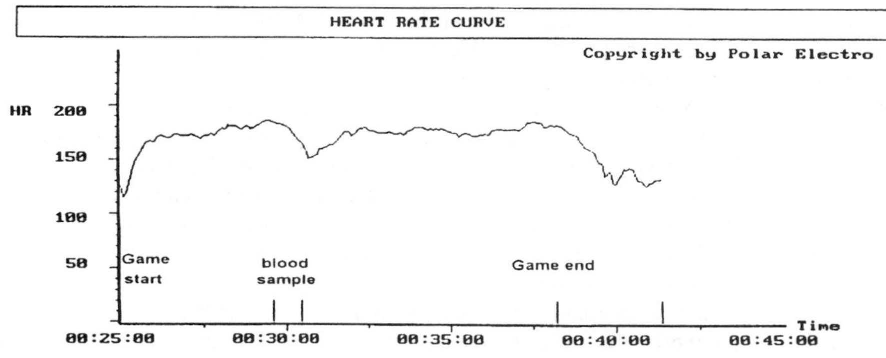

Figure 2. Heart rate trace for 'competition simulation'

4 Discussion

Using the data presented here, it is possible to understand more fully the training demands of badminton performance at the elite level. The results obtained from practice games appear to show that there is a low contribution from the anaerobic system in supplying the necessary energy for activity. The usual work : rest durations are such that the ATP - PC system is not likely to be well replenished in the limited recovery time available (Plisk, 1991). While it is acknowledged that the measured BLa concentration is the net result of production and removal, it does appear that the aerobic contribution to practice performed in this way is very high. The aerobic system is instrumental in delaying the increase in blood lactate as well as in its removal. The high % of maximum HR which was sustained throughout play illustrates a considerable stress on the cardiovascular system. The concomittant low BLa concentration tends to indicate that these players exhibit a high degree of aerobic fitness in this activity. This agrees with the findings of a study carried out on elite Danish players. Mikkelsen (1979) found high levels of the 'aerobic' type I muscle fibre in the quadriceps muscles of the players. Low lactate readings from game- situations were also found and it was concluded that, due to the short intermittent exercise involved, myoglobin has a vital role in providing energy for this sport. Myoglobin can act as a short term supplier of oxygen molecules, particularly at the onset of activity .

It is accepted (Åstrand & Rodahl, 1986) that intermittent exercise can be controlled in such a way that high quality exercise may be performed at what is essentially an 'aerobic intensity'. In other words, manipulation of the work : rest ratio can result in high quality performance without the increase in blood lactate which would occur if the work periods were extended at the same intensity.

There seems little evidence available to indicate that intermittent work of this type is associated with the high HRs measured in this study. Reilly (1990) referred to reports of high

HR measured in badminton and suggested that the postural demands of isometric contraction along with the short recovery periods could lead to a deviation from the normal oxygen uptake - HR relationship. Further work will be needed to confirm this.

Results from BLa analysis of the structured training routines show that badminton training in the elite does stress the anaerobic energy system. This confirms the coaching aim for these sessions in that they induce varying degrees of fatigue in the player. The subjective comments of the players would also tend to confirm that lactate may accumulate, to some extent, in competitive situations. At this stage it has not been possible to investigate post-exercise BLa results from tournaments, but as can be seen from these data, post - game readings may not indicate the intensity of work achieved earlier in a game.

Although these conclusions are based on results from a limited number of subjects, the effect of altering the work : rest ratio and the nature of the exercise can be seen. Multifeed practice with approximately 1 minute on : 1 minute off work : rest ratio produced a BLa of 4.0 - 4.2 mM in two players. However, changing the mode of exercise to shadow play and shortening the work period to 20 and the rest period to 40 seconds appeared to alter the nature of the training effect. This maximal shadow play session elevated BLa to 7.2 mM.

Combining shadow play and multifeed work into a one minute work period elicited a similar post-exercise BLa to that from the one minute multifeed session. However, the recovery period must be considered and the longer rest in this 'combined' session would suggest that the fatigue is less accumulative and that each exercise bout is probably more intense than that for the multifeed - only session. It is likely that the lower technical requirement of shadow play allows the player to operate at a greater exercise intensity than is possible for the multifeed work.

There would seem to be some conflict between the relatively modest VO2 max results measured in international laboratories (Akira, 1988; Mikkelsen, 1979) and the aerobic performance during play. If the action of myoglobin during intermittent work is so instrumental in maintaining low lactate results, then there may be a good case for some modification in the modes of physiological testing for this sport. This point is supported by recent work on soccer players (Bangsbo & Lindquist, 1992). These authors compared intermittent and continuous work with actual play and found that only the intermittent protocol was a suitably sensitive test of endurance fitness in this sport. The importance of myoglobin at the onset of exercise is clear, and it could be that continuous tests of aerobic fitness may neglect this important consideration.

5 Concluding Remarks

It would seem that training games in elite badminton performers is predominantly an aerobic activity. However, specific training routines have been monitored which are sufficiently intense to cause an increase in BLa concentration. This type of training is likely to be especially beneficial for competitions where one might expect a greater reliance on anaerobic glycolysis in order to sustain work over rallies and games longer than those reported here. The role of myoglobin in supplying oxygen to active tissue in this intermittent sport may be very significant. This may be an important consideration when physiological test programmes are devised for players.

Further work is required to describe the physiological demands of competitive play and in investigating the specificity of aerobic adaptation to training in this sport.

Acknowledgements- The author is very grateful to colleagues at the BOMC and to all of the players and coaches who have been so helpful in making this study possible.

6 References

Akira, H. (1988) Physical fitness characteristics of the Yamaha Chinese national women's team players. In : **Physical Working Capacity of Chinese Badminton players**, Yamaha Badminton coaching seminar reference material. pp. 5 - 12.

Åstrand, P.O., and Rodahl, K. (1986) **Textbook of Work Physiology, Physiological Bases of Exercise (3rd edn.)** McGraw-Hill, Singapore.

Bangsbo, J.and Lindquist, F. (1992) Comparison of various exercise tests with endurance performance during soccer in professional players. **Int. J. Sports Med.**, 13, 125 - 132.

Coad, D. Rasmussen, B. and Mikkelsen, F. (1979) Physical demands of recreational badminton. In : **Science in Racquet Sports** (ed. J.Terauds) Academic Publishers, Del Mar, California. pp. 43 - 54.

Docherty, D. (1982) A comparison of heart rate responses in racquet games. **Brit. J. Sports Med.,** 16, 96 - 100.

Mikkelsen, F. (1979) Physical demands and muscle adaptation in elite badminton players. In : **Science in Racquet Sports** (ed. J.Terauds) Academic Publishers, Del Mar, California. pp. 55 - 67.

Plisk, S.S. (1991) Anaerobic metabolic conditioning : A brief review of theory, strategy and practical application. **J. Appl. Sport. Sci. Res.,** 5 (1), 22 - 34.

Reilly, T. (1990) The racquet sports. In : **Physiology of Sports** (ed. T. Reilly, N. Secher, P. Snell and C. Williams.). E & F.N. Spon, London. pp. 337 - 369.

7 Physiological evaluation of specific training in badminton

R. Dias and A.K. Ghosh
Sports Authority of India, Jawaher Lal Nehru Stadium, New Delhi, India

1 Introduction

Elite badminton players exhibit a high aerobic peak (VO_2max) through a combination of training and endowment (Mikklesen, 1979; Reilly, 1990). Physical training improves the cardiorespiratory fitness and such improvements are reflected by VO_2max (Wenger and Bell, 1986).

Scientists have used cycling, running or other aerobic or interval type training programmes to observe adaptations in cardiorespiratory fitness. In recent years, the "anaerobic threshold" has gained emphasis, especially in continuous events, due to its high correlation with endurance performance (Jacobs, 1986). The importance of "anaerobic threshold" in non-continuous intermittent games has also been discussed (Bunc et al., 1987). The "anaerobic threshold" is generally determined from blood lactate concentration where it increases steeply after a certain exercise intensity and is known as the "lactate threshold" or by the gas exchange method known as "ventilatory threshold" (T_{vent}) estimated from the deviation point of VE-VO_2 from linearity (Beaver et al., 1985). It has been claimed (Wasserman et al., 1973) that T_{vent} coincides with the blood lactate threshold and that the relationship is causal. While improvement in lactate threshold through physical training is evident (Jacobs, 1986), contradictory observations on improvement in T_{vent} are available (Gaesser and Poole, 1986). Every sport activity has its own specific training to build up fitness levels of the players for that sport. Similarly in badminton, there are sports-specific specialized training drills to improve the fitness required for the game. In a short pre-competition training camp, the sports specific training programme dominates the other physical conditioning programmes.

The main objectives of this study were (i) to investigate the effects of a short (3 weeks) training schedule, dominated by sports specific training, on physiological variables $\dot{V}O_2max$ and T_{vent} of a group of female badminton players in the age range 13-14 years; (ii) to quantify the intensity of the sports-specific training by studying the heart rate and blood lactate response and (iii) to observe the short-term adaptations of these cardiorespiratory parameters in pubescent female badminton players.

Science and Racket Sports Edited by T. Reilly, M. Hughes and A. Lees.
Published in 1994 by E & FN Spon ISBN 0 419 18500 3

2 Materials and Methods

The study was conducted on five selected female badminton players (age: 13-14 yrs; height: 160-165 cm; mass: 47.0-51.5 kg) which included at least the semi-finalists in the sub-junior and junior national championships in 1988. The study was conducted during a training camp held at Netaji Subhas National Institute of Sports, Patiala. The $\dot{V}O_2max$ and T_{vent} of each player were measured at the commencement of the training camp and immediately after the cessation of the camp. The $\dot{V}O_2max$ was evaluated by analysing the expired air continuously on an automatic analyser (Erich Jaeger, FRG) during a graded running protocol on a treadmill. The initial speed of the treadmill was 6 km/h (1.66 m/s) and was increased at the rate of 2 km/h (0.55 m/s) after every 2 min to exhaustion. The T_{vent} was determined from gas exchange data using the VE-VO2 relationship (Beaver et al., 1985)

The three week training schedule contained basic speed work (2 sessions per week), basic endurance (1 session per week), specific training on the court (6 sessions per week). There were three sessions each day (morning, forenoon and evening). The morning session was devoted to basic speed work, endurance work and specific training on the court (3 days in the morning session were devoted to the singles game). The forenoon session (3 days) on three days comprised teaching skill, technique and tactics. Each of the above activities was preceded by a basic warm-up of stretching exercises. The endurance run contained a 2.4 km slow run, the duration of which was 12-13 min. Basic speed work consisted of a 60 m all-out sprint repeated ten times with 1 min rest in between and three sets were performed by each player. In between each set, a 5 min rest was given. The evening game contained competitive practice with technical corrections.

Specific training on the court was a simulated activity of the game where a player had to run to strike the shuttle at different corners of the court starting from the middle and, after striking, come back quickly to mid-court (the starting zone). Each player had to perform three sets of 10 repetitions where the ratio of work to rest was 1:1 (1 min short burst of activity was followed by 1 min of rest). In between the sets a 5 min rest was allowed. Specific training on the court was divided into two parts, training with and without the shuttlecock (shadow practice), on alternative days. The intensity of the training schedule was evaluated by measuring the heart rate and blood lactate concentration, during training sessions. The heart rate was measured in all the training sessions with short-range radio telemetry (Sport Tester PE 3000 Computerized System, Polar Electro, Finland). The blood lactate was measured only during specific training on the court since the training programme was dominated by the specific training schedule and our main objective was to evaluate the intensity of such sports-specific training. Blood samples were collected from the finger tip within 2 to 2.5 min after the training activities. These were analysed using a standardised automatic lactate analyser (YSI, USA). Special care was taken to prevent contamination with sweat.

For observing the differences in the physiological variables, before and after training, the paired `t' test was applied.

3 Results

The pre- and post-training $\dot{V}O_2max$ of the players (Table 1) showed a significant difference ($P < 0.05$). The improvement in the relative $\dot{V}O_2max$ was, on average, 6% from the pre-training value. Of the five cases, the $\dot{V}O_2max$ had improved from 2 to 11% in four cases, but remained unchanged in one case. The $\dot{V}O_2$ of each player at T_{vent} before and after training (Table 2) demonstrated a significant difference ($P < 0.05$). The improvement in T_{vent} varied from 7 to 12% over the five cases. For the subject (S3) whose $\dot{V}O_2max$ remained unchanged as a result of training, there was an improvement of 6.5% in T_{vent}.

The mean heart rate response of the players in each training programme and the blood lactate response in specific training programmes are given in Table 3. The heart rate and blood lactate responses during specific training without a shuttlecock (shadow practice) were higher ($P < 0.05$) than during training with a shuttle.

Table 1. Pre- and post-training values of $\dot{V}O_2max$

Subjects	Pre-training $\dot{V}O_2max$		Post-training $\dot{V}O_2max$	
	l/min	ml/kg/min	l/min	ml/kg/min
S1	2.06	43.8	2.10	44.7
S2	2.04	42.5	2.23	46.4
S3	2.68	52.0	2.67	51.8
S4	2.06	43.8	2.29	48.7
S5	1.75	37.2	1.91	40.6
Mean	2.11	43.8	2.24*	46.4*
± SD	0.34	5.3	0.28	4.2

*P < 0.05

Table 2. Pre- and post-training values of $\dot{V}O_2$ at T_{vent}

Subjects	Pre-training $\dot{V}O_2$		Post-training $\dot{V}O_2$	
	l/min	ml/kg/min	l/min	ml/kg/min
S1	1.50	31.9	1.68	35.7
S2	1.24	25.8	1.37	28.5
S3	1.73	33.5	1.84	35.7
S4	1.55	32.9	1.68	35.7
S5	1.40	29.8	1.55	32.9
Mean	1.48	30.8	1.68*	33.7
± SD	0.18	3.1	0.17	2.2

*P < 0.05

4 Discussion

Physical training improves the $\dot{V}O_2max$ which is evident from the literature (Åstrand and Rodahl, 1986). The intensity of physical exercise is the most important factor in developing $\dot{V}O_2max$. A significant improvement is observed at training intensities of 80-95% of the maximum aerobic capacity, when the training session is for a long duration (30-40 min) (Pollock, 1977). The training schedule in this study was dominated by specific training on the court, where the intensities were 78 and 90% of the maximum heart rate, with and without a shuttlecock, respectively. The movements became a little slower during specific training with the shuttle compared to without the shuttle. This is evident from the higher heart rate and blood lactate ($P < 0.05$) responses during training with and without a shuttle (Table 3).

Table 3. Mean heart rate (beats/min) response of badminton players during each training item. Mean blood lactate response during specific training is shown

Training item	S1	S2	S3	S4	S5	Mean
Warm up	124	104	136	129	138	126
	(10)	(13)	(14)	(16)	(16)	(17)
Endurance run	181	161	191	180	203	183
	(12)	(7)	(9)	(21)	(12)	(12)
Speed work	162	169	172	174	204	176
	(1)	(5)	(2)	(2)	(2)	(2)
Specific training						
(a) With shuttle	153	153	160	165	177	161
	(5)	(11)	(4)	(10)	(5)	(7)
Blood lactate	3.2	3.5	3.9	4.1	5.0	3.9
mM	(0.7)	(0.5)	(0.6)	(0.8)	(0.9)	(0.7)
Rest Pause	138	140	149	145	1266	147
	(6)	(7)	(10)	(12)	(16)	(10)
(b) Without shuttle	176	175	193	187	193	185
	(5)	(5)	(10)	(6)	(7)	(7)
Blood lactate	4.6	5.1	6.8	7.0	7.5	6.2*
(mM)	(1.0)	(0.8)	(0.4)	(0.5)	(0.5)	(0.6)
Rest Pause	157	156	174	165	182	167
	(9)	(11)	(14)	(12)	(8)	(10)
Game practice	170	156	174	165	177	168
	(2)	(7)	(13)	(4)	(15)	(8)

Figure in parentheses indicate SD.
*(without shuttle vs with shuttle, $P < 0.05$)

Endurance training comprising continuous exercise can improve the $\dot{V}O_2max$ in young adults (Fringer and Stull, 1974) but intermittent exercise sessions are most effective (Åstrand and Rodahl, 1986). Intermittent training results in the greater increase in $\dot{V}O_2max$ and maximal exercise capacity whereas continuous training improves the muscles' oxidative capacity and delays the accumulation of blood lactate during maximum exercise.

The specific training of badminton is intermittent in nature and the total duration for each subject in this study was 40 min. Three weeks of specific training, the intensity of which was 78-90% of the maximum heart rate improved the $\dot{V}O_2max$ of 13-14 years old female badminton players by 6% (Table 1).

Gaesser and Poole (1986) did not observe any change in T_{vent} of untrained persons as a result of three weeks endurance training of a continuous type at 70-80% of the $\dot{V}O2max$, whereas Poole and Gaesser (1985) found a significant change in T_{vent} as a result of interval or intermittent training. Our study also indicates that intermittent/ interval training can improve T_{vent} to a greater extent than $\dot{V}O_2max$ (Table 2).

The objective assessment or quantification of training intensity in sports can be done by studying the physiological responses, especially the heart rate and blood lactate. The mean blood lactate values during specific training were 3.9 mM and 6.2 mM during training with and without the shuttlecock respectively (Table 3). Blood lactate concentration of 3.9 mM can be considered as at lactate threshold level or at the aerobic to anaerobic transition level (Jacobs, 1986). Even the mean heart rate during this training (161 beats/min) corresponds to the "anaerobic threshold heart rate" of the badminton girls studied by Ghosh et al. (1990). On the other hand, a blood lactate level of 6.2 mM during specific training without the shuttle-cock is considered to be in the aerobic overload region by many scientists (Troup, 1986; Pyne and Telford, 1989). Endurance training/interval training which elicits a blood lactate concentration of 4-6 mM is considered optimal and the improvements in such cases are observed more in the aerobic to anaerobic transition level than in $\dot{V}O_2max$ (Jacobs, 1986). In this study the degree of improvement in T_{vent} of the players was more than that noted in the mean $\dot{V}O_2max$ after three weeks of a specific training programme.

The following may be concluded from the present study:

(i) The intensity of sport-specific training observed in badminton was 78-90% of the maximum heart rate. This elicits a blood lactate response of 3.9-6.2 mM which corresponds to an aerobic overload region.

(ii) The three week training schedule dominated by specific training in badminton can alter the $\dot{V}O_2max$ as well as the T_{vent} of the players. The degree of improvement in T_{vent} level was more than in the $\dot{V}O_2max$.

(iii) At a pre-competition training camp, coaches and sports scientists depend on sports specific training to develop not only the skill level of the players but also the physiological variables. A separate conditioning programme to develop these variables may not be needed.

5 References

Åstrand, P.O. and Rodahl, K. (1986) **Textbook of Work Physiology**. McGraw-Hill Book Co., New York.

Beaver, W.L., Wasserman, K. and Whipp, H.J. (1985) A new method for detecting anaerobic threshold by gas exchange. **J. Appl. Physiol.**, 60, 2020.

Bunc, V., Heller, J., Leso, J., Sprynarova, R. and Zdanowivz, R. (1987) Ventilatory threshold in various groups of highly trained athletes. **Int. J. Sports Med.**, 8, 275.

Fringer, M.N. and Stull, G.A. (1974) Changes in cardio- respiratory parameters during periods of training and detraining in young adult females. **Med. Sci. Sports**, 6, 20.

Gaesser, G.A. and Poole, D.C. (1986) Lactate and ventilatory threshold: disparity and time course of adaptation to training. **J. Appl. Physiol.**, 61, 999.

Ghosh, A.K., Mazumdar, P., Goswami, A., Ahuja, A. and Puri, T.P.S. (1990) Heart rate and blood lactate response in competitive badminton. **Ann. Sports Med.**, 5, 85.

Jacobs, I. (1986) Blood lactate, interpretation for training and sports performances. **Sports Med.**, 3, 10.

Mikklesen, F. (1979) Physical demands and muscle adaptation in elite badminton players, in **Science and Racquet Sports** (ed. J. Terauds), Academic Publishers, Del Mar, CA, pp. 55-67.

Pollock, M.L. (1977) Submaximal and maximal working capacity of elite distance runners, Part 1: Cardio- respiratory aspects. **Ann. New York Acad. Sci.**, 301, 310-322.

Poole, D.C. and Gaesser, G.A. (1985) Response of ventilatory and lactate thresholds in continuous and interval training. **J. Appl. Physiol.**, 58, 1115.

Pyne, D.B. and Telford, R.D. (1989) Classification of swimming training sessions by blood lactate and heart rate responses. **American Swimming Coaches Association Magazine,** Feb. 7.

Reilly, T. (1990) The racquet sports, in **Physiology of Sports** (eds T. Reilly, N. Secher, P. Snell and C. Williams), E. and F.N. Spon, London, pp. 337-369.

Troup, J. (1986) Setting up a season using scientific training. **Swimming Technique,** May-July 9.

Wasserman, K., Whipp, H.J., Koyal, S.N. and Beaver, W.L. (1973) Anaerobic threshold and respiratory gas exchange during exercise. **J. Appl. Physiol.**, 35, 236.

Wenger, H. and Bell, G.J. (1986) The interaction of intensity, frequency and duration of exercise training in altering cardiorespiratory fitness. **Sports Med.**, 3, 346.

8 Physiological effects of squash participation in different age-groups and levels of play

T. Reilly and D.L. Halsall
Centre for Sport and Exercise, School of Human Sciences, Liverpool John Moores University, Liverpool, UK

1 Introduction

Physical exercise represents a major means of realising active health promotion programmes. This applies especially to coronary health, particularly in view of the high incidence of coronary heart disease in industrialised countries (Poole, 1984). Improvement in cardiovascular risk factors has been linked with reduced incidence of heart disease (Haskell, 1991). Such factors include elevated blood pressure, serum lipids, excess adiposity and inactivity.

Physical activity regimens have been implemented within the rubric of health promotion programmes. Surveys in the U.S.A. (Paffenberger et al., 1986; Darga et al., 1989) have provided support for the belief that regular exercise is beneficial in preventing hypertension. Clarkson et al. (1981) reported that subjects participating in aerobic exercise showed beneficial effects on blood lipid profiles whereas those engaged in anaerobic training did not. A longitudinal study by Wood et al. (1983) demonstrated that the amount or volume rather than the intensity of training was influential in raising high density lipoprotein cholesterol levels. Hypertension (both systolic and diastolic pressures) and hyperlipidaemia are both more common in overweight individuals than in those with normal body composition. Whilst attempts to decrease body fat levels generally entail restrictions of caloric intake, a combination of diet and a systematic exercise regimen is likely to provide the best results. Prevention of the onset of obesity in adults is strongly related to physical activity patterns (Pollock et al., 1984).

'Sport for all' programmes have encouraged the participation in sports for purposes of acquiring health benefits (Oja and Telama, 1991). As squash imposes demands on the oxygen transport system compatible with a training stimulus (Beaudin et al., 1978; Mercier et al., 1987; Reilly, 1990a), this sport has been encouraged as a recreational activity. Such participation may present problems in older players, in view of the decline in coronary health status with age in inactive populations. As a result of observing electrocardiographic changes in male subjects (aged 33 $\pm$ 6.5 years) during and after playing squash, Northcote et al. (1983) suggested that older players, with the risk of silent coronary artery disease should not participate in squash because of the increased risk of 'sudden death'.

Science and Racket Sports Edited by T. Reilly, M. Hughes and A. Lees.
Published in 1994 by E & FN Spon ISBN 0 419 18500 3

The aims of this study were:- (i) to investigate the demands of playing squash on a recreational group of squash participants; (ii) to compare results with those obtained on an age-matched and on a younger group of competitive squash players; (iii) to relate these demands to the fitness profiles of the respective groups.

2 Methods

Twenty one male subjects, equally subdivided into three groups completed the study. These were selected after responses were obtained to publicly placed invitations for recreational players aged 35 years and over to volunteer. Respondents completed a questionnaire to provide background information on current health status and anthropometry (age, height, body mass). The members in this group played squash occasionally (approximately twice a month) and were not engaged in any fitness training programme. Subjects among the other groups were recruited from competitive squash players, constituting a young (mean age 22.4 years) and an older (mean age 42.4) group matched to the ages of the recreational group (mean age 45.3 years). Information in the questionnaire about skill level was used in matching subjects when required to play against others within their group.

Measurements were made of body mass using a beam balance scale (Avery) and the sum of four skinfolds was used to estimate percent body fat (Durnin and Womersley, 1974). Resting values whilst seated were obtained for heart rate and blood pressure (syphgmomanometry). A blood sample was obtained from a fingertip for analysis of cholesterol using reflective photometry (Mannheim Boehringer Lipotrend C system). The multi-stage 20 m shuttle run was used to predict maximal oxygen uptake ($\dot{V}O_2$ max).

Each subject was required to play squash against another matched for skill level. A 5 min warm-up preceded each match which was terminated after 20 min. The subject was fitted pre-exercise with a short-range radio telemetry system (Sport-Tester 3000) for measurement of heart rate during play. At the end of the match the subject rated the level of exercise during play for whole body exertion, breathlessness and muscle fatigue according to Borg (1970).

3 Results

A comparison of the anthropometric profiles between the three groups was made using a one-way analysis of variance (ANOVA). This showed a significant result for all the variables examined (Table 1), except that when fat free mass was computed the difference between the groups disappeared. Follow-up tests showed that the groups were significantly separated according to estimated body composition (from skinfolds) and heart rate. The older competitors did not differ significantly from their younger counterparts for either blood pressure variable, or for serum cholesterol levels.

The difference in estimated $\dot{V}O_2$ max was significant, the recreational group

Table 1 Anthropometric and physiological measures of the three groups (n = 21)

	Younger Competitors	Older Competitors	Recreation Group	F Value
Body Mass (kg)	71.0 ± 4.8	78.1 ± 3.8	83.0 ± 4.9	13.31[b]
Fat Free Mass (kg)	60.6 ± 1.4	64.4 ± 2.7	62.0 ± 2.3	2.24
Body Fat (%)	10.5 ± 2.0	17.4 ± 2.9	25.2 ± 2.9	57.41[b]
Systolic BP (mm Hg)	116 ± 5	116 ± 5	124 ± 5	5.42[a]
Diastolic BP (mm Hg)	71 ± 4	74 ± 8	80 ± 5	3.65[b]
Heart Rate(beats/min)	58 ± 3	63 ± 4	74 ± 2	40.34[b]
Serum Cholesterol (mM)	4.9 ± 0.4	4.9 ± 0.6	6.1 ± 0.4	4.69[b]
$\dot{V}O_2max$(ml/kg/min)	58.8 ± 2.9	49.4 ± 2.9	33.3 ± 2.9	64.89[b]

a denotes P<0.05; b denotes P<0.005

being significantly poorer than the other two. Whilst the estimated values for the older competitors was on average 84% of those attained by the younger players, the difference did not reach statistical significance.

The heart rate response to match-play was lower in the older competitors than in the other two groups whose values did not differ between each other. When values were expressed as a percentage of maximal heart rate (measured during the shuttle run test), the older competitors had similar results to their younger counterparts but significantly lower values than the recreation players of similar age (Table 2).

Subjective responses to match-play were significantly higher for the recreation group than for the other two categories. This applied to all three ratings of perceived exertion. Although ratings were higher in the older compared to the younger competitive players, the differences did not reach statistical significance. The ratings were highest for breathing and lowest for muscles, except in the recreation group where the whole-body ratings reached the same levels as the perceived exertion related to breathing.

Table 2. Responses to match play (mean ± SD) for the three categories of players

	Younger Competitors	Older Competitors	Recreation Group	F Value
Heart Rate(beats/min)	163 ± 5	150 ± 6	166 ± 5	18.5[b]
Heart Rate (% max)	82.4 ± 2.7	84.6 ± 4.9	95.1 ± 1.2	31.68[b]
Perceived Exertion:				
Whole body	12.1 ± 1.3	13.4 ± 1.2	16.0 ± 1.1	19.5[b]
Breathing	14.2 ± 1.1	14.4 ± 0.8	16.0 ± 1.4	5.92[a]
Muscles	8.8 ± 0.7	9.6 ± 0.9	12.3 ± 1.4	18.73[b]

a denotes P<0.05; b denotes P<0.005

4 Discussion

The observations during this study of squash play confirm a number of previous reports in the literature relating exercise participation and health. The competitive squash players had anthropometric and fitness profiles suggestive of accrued training effects on body composition and cardiovascular status. The older competitive squash players in general had profiles more closely resembling those of the younger players than the age-matched recreation players. Whilst inferences from the present study must be guarded because of the small sample size, observations support the belief that regular and frequent participation in squash has favourable effects on coronary risk factors. This applies to blood pressure, serum lipids, body composition and aerobic power among the variables that were monitored.

The recreation group had blood lipid levels in the range where counselling with regard to risk factors in development of coronary heart disease is recommended (European Atherosclerosis Society, 1987). The activity programmes of the older competitive squash players seemed to have been effective in preventing this rise. The greater skinfold thicknesses in the recreation group reflected the higher proportion of fat mass computed for these players. The values for estimated $\dot{V}O_2$ max were compatible with aerobically trained games players only in the younger competitive players (Reilly, 1990b). Whilst there is a decline in this function with ageing and with inactivity, this fall was offset to some degree in the older squash players.

Casual participation in squash seems to have little favourable effect on fitness profiles among older players. Of concern is the fact that such participation imposes greater physiological strain on these players compared to their well-trained counterparts who practice more frequently. The older players appear to adjust the exercise intensity better to their capabilities than do the recreation players. The former were exercising at 85% of their maximal heart rates, the latter at 95%.

According to all the indices of perceived exertion, the recreation group exercised subjectively harder than the others. Whilst the ratings were higher for breathing than for whole-body and muscles in the other groups, the older inactive group reached levels for both whole-body exertion and breathing corresponding to a feeling of hard to very hard. It may be that competitive factors, inherent to the game, force an excessively high exercise intensity in this group, whereas skilled players can regulate the exercise intensity to one they find more acceptable. Older, untrained individuals should be cautioned to approach the game with due care.

5 References

Beaudin, P., Zapiec, C. and Montgomery, D. (1978) Heart rate response and lactic acid concentration in squash players. **Res. Quart.**, 49, 406-412.

Borg, G. (1982) Psychophysical bases of perceived exertion. **Med. Sci. Sports Exerc.**, 14, 377-381.

Clarkson, P.M., Huntermeister, R., Fillyaw, M. and Stylos, L. (1981) High density lipoprotein cholesterol in young adult weightlifters, runners and untrained subjects.

Human Biology, 53, 675-682.

Darga, L.L., Lucas, C.P., Spafford, T.R., Schork, M.A., Illis, W.R. and Holden, N. (1989) Endurance training in middle-aged male physicians. **Physician Sportsmed.**, 17, 85-101.

Durnin, J.V.G.A. and Womersley, J. (1974) Body fat assessed from total body density and its estimations from skinfold thickness: measurements on 481 men and women aged 16 to 72 years. **Brit. J. Nutr.**, 32, 169-179.

European Atherosclerosis Society Study Group (1987) Strategies for the prevention of coronary heart disease. **Europ. Heart** J., 8, 77-88.

Haskell, W.L. (1991) Dose-response relationship between physical activity and disease risk factors, in **Sport for All** (eds. P. Oja and R. Telama), Elsevier, Amsterdam, pp.125-133.

Mercier, M., Beillot, J., Gratos, A., Rochcongar, P. and Lessard, Y (1987) Adaptations to workload in squash players: laboratory tests and on-court recordings. **J. Sports Med. Phys. Fit.**, 27, 98-104.

Northcote, R.J., McFarlane, P. and Ballantyne, D. (1983) Ambulatory electrocardiography in squash players. **Brit. Heart J.**, 50, 372-377.

Oja, P. and Telama, R. (eds.) (1991) **Sport for All**. Elsevier, Amsterdam.

Paffenberger, R.S., Hyde, R.T., Wing, A.I. and Hsieh, C.C. (1986) Physical activity, all cause mortality and longevity of college alumni. **N.Eng. J.Med.**, 314, 605-613.

Pollock, M.L., Wilmore, J.H. and Fox, S.M. (1984) **Exercise in Health and Disease: Evaluation and Prescription for Prevention and Rehabilitation**. W.B. Saunders, Philadelphia.

Poole, W. (1984) Exercise, coronary heart disease and risk factors. **Sports Med.**, 1, 341-349.

Ramsbottom, R., Brewer, J. and Williams, C. (1988) A progressive shuttle run test to estimate maximal oxygen uptake. **Brit. J. Sports Med.**, 22, 141-144.

Reilly, T. (1990a) The racquet sports, in **Physiology of Sports** (eds. T. Reilly, N. Secher, P. Snell and C. Williams), E. and F.N. Spon, London, pp.327-369.

Reilly, T. (1990b) Football, in **Physiology of Sports** (eds. T. Reilly, N. Secher, P. Snell and C. Williams), E. and F.N. Spon, London, pp.371-425.

Wood, P.D., Haskell, W.L. and Black, S.N. (1983) Increased exercise level and plasma lipoprotein concentrations: a one-year randomised controlled study in sedentary middle-age men. **Metabolism**, 32, 31-39.

Part Two
Fitness in Racket Sports

9 Development of an on-court aerobic test for elite badminton players

M.G. Hughes and F.M. Fullerton
British Olympic Medical Centre, Harrow, UK

1 Introduction

The development of any new fitness testing protocol should reflect the physiological and technical demands of a sport. In order to enhance the sensitivity of the test, the results should be obtained from a situation which is as similar to competition as is practical. This may be especially important for a sport like badminton where the pattern of movement adopted during play is highly specific and cannot be simulated on any ergometer. The evidence which is available on the physiological demands of badminton play suggest that it is a predominantly intermittent aerobic activity with only a modest contribution from the anaerobic energy system (Mikkelsen, 1979; Hughes, 1993). Consequently, one of the important requirements for an appropriate programme of physiological monitoring is a valid test of endurance fitness whose results can be applied to the on-court situation. The benefits of such a test should be considerable, as it should monitor activity on the court as opposed to using other non-specific activities (e.g. running) which badminton players may undertake in their usual off-court endurance training. In this test, players work on the court, thus incorporating the typical movements for the sport which cannot be monitored in the laboratory.

This study describes a novel aerobic test specifically designed for badminton players to perform at their usual training venue. The test is based on a mode of training frequently used by players whereby their normal movement pattern is executed around the court without use of a shuttlecock. Although in training, this work is quite random in nature, controlling the distance and speed of movement can allow this to be used as a basis for fitness testing. Data are presented here which have been obtained from national squad junior players performing the test at two phases of their training year.

A number of authors have found that $\dot{V}O2$ max, as determined in laboratory conditions, is less sensitive to changes in endurance fitness than the assessment of blood lactate concentrations at sub-maximal intensities (Jacobs, 1986). Based on this observation, heart rate and blood lactate were selected as the physiological parameters to be measured in this test.

Science and Racket Sports Edited by T. Reilly, M. Hughes and A. Lees.
Published in 1994 by E & FN Spon ISBN 0 419 18500 3

2 Methods

2.1 Description of protocol

The test is performed with each player using one half of a badminton court. The player must move around the court touching the floor with the racket at the points (1 to 4), explained below. Players are instructed to use their normal movement pattern and consequently must return to a central base after each movement. The order of movements is always from 1 to 4 until completion of the three minute exercise period. Points '1' and '2' are between the singles and doubles side-lines in the extreme forecourt. A line 0.5 metres from the net post is made and the racket must touch the box marked on the floor just beyond the line. Points '3' and '4' are also between the sidelines, but are situated in the extreme rear court area. The doubles service line acts as the marker for the box to be touched by the racket. The four points represent the greatest distance which a player can cover within the confines of the half - court.

Movement speed is controlled by means of a BBC microcomputer programmed to sound a tone, via an external loudspeaker, at a given frequency. The players must commence each movement when the tone sounds and to have returned to the base, being prepared to move again, when the next tone sounds. The test is discrete and incremental comprising three work stages of three minutes duration. An eight minute recovery period is given between each stage. When setting the movement speed for the respective stages, it is intended for the first stage to represent very low speed movement, with little blood lactate accumulation. The third stage should be sufficiently intense to elicit a considerable blood lactate concentration while still allowing completion of the entire stage. The second stage should be at a speed mid-way between the first and third.

Earlobe blood samples are taken within one minute of completing each stage and analysed on site for blood lactate concentration using Analox portable lactate analysers (Analox Instruments Ltd., UK) calibrated on 5 mM standard solution. Heart rate is monitored throughout the test using telemetry (Polar Sports Tester) with a five second sampling frequency; peak heart rate for each stage is noted for use in the interpretation of results.

2.2 Gathering the experimental data

The subjects whose results are described here were thirteen (5 male, 8 female) members of the England under 18 national squad (aged 17 to 18 years at the time of testing). Assessments took place at the National badminton Centre at two training camps in the 1992 - 93 season. The first test was timed to coincide with the start of the players' Summer conditioning phase ('pre-training'). The Summer is typically the time of year when most off-court aerobic training is accomplished. The second test was performed in the competitive phase of the season ('post-training').

After consultation with the coach, movement speeds were determined based on sex and fitness level. Three groups were formed in this way to allow for within-group variation in these factors. Each movement was commenced at the sound of the tone and the duration between tones ranged from 3.65 seconds (stage 1, slowest group) to 2.5 seconds (stage 3, fastest group). A summary of the movement times is shown in Table 1.

Table 1. Movement times required for each group performing the test.

Movement time (seconds)

	Group A (n=3)	Group B (n=5)	Group C (n=5)
Stage 1	3.65	3.5	3.1
Stage 2	3.3	3.2	2.8
Stage 3	2.95	2.9	2.5

3 Results

Group mean blood lactate concentrations are displayed in Table 2. Note that members of groups A,B and C have been presented together in this table. Lactate results were not obtained for three subjects during stage 1 of their post-training test. However, they did perform the test in every way as described in the text.

Table 2 Results from pre- and post-training tests.

Blood lactate concentration Mean + S.E. (mM)

	Pre-training	Post-training	Difference
Stage 1	2.8+0.2 mM (n=10)	1.5+0.2 mM (n=10)	1.3+0.2 mM***
Stage 2	2.8+0.2 mM (n=13)	1.9+0.2 mM (n=13)	1.1+0.2 mM***
Stage 3	4.3+0.4 mM (n=13)	2.7+0.3 mM (n=13)	1.6+0.3 mM***

*** Denotes statistically significant difference ($P<0.001$), Student's paired 't' test.

4 Discussion

It can be seen that there is a significant reduction in blood lactate concentration when the 'post-test' is compared with the 'pre-test'. It appears that the fitness improvements which would be expected between the two test occasions have been detected. Heart rate data are not presented here because it was impossible to collect this information on the first visit. On later visits and when the test had been performed on senior players, heart rates were recorded and the evidence suggests that changes in the heart rate occur in the same direction as changes in lactate concentration. It is considered favourable to monitor both quantities, but heart rate information merely tends to confirm the lactate results.

There are still a few minor refinements which may be made before the test's development is complete, but there are various advantages to this type of testing, particularly when comparisons can be made to laboratory test procedures. Firstly, the test is similar to the players' normal on-court activity and training routines. This gives the advantage of making the test specific to the sport's demands as well as ensuring that it is easy to perform and to administer. Secondly, the sub-maximal nature of the test is favourable when compared to the exhaustive and motivation-dependent $\dot{V}O2$ max measurements. Maximal tests cannot be performed by members of a group simultaneously, making them less time efficient, and notably in this case, they also use movements which are alien to competitors in the sport. Thirdly, the test can be performed at any training location, thus making it suitable for use at squad and club gatherings.

Some further work is needed in the development and validation of the protocol. This must continue, where possible, to be performed alongside standard laboratory assessments of aerobic fitness. It is important that the results from this test can be compared to more recognised indicators of endurance fitness such as those obtained from treadmill or cycle ergometry.

Acknowledgements - The authors acknowledge the help received from the coaches and players of the 1992-93 England Under-18 National Badminton Squad.

5 References

Hughes. M.G. (1993). Physiological demands of training in elite badminton players. **Communication to the First World Congress of Science and Racket Sports.** Liverpool, U.K. July 1993.

Jacobs, I. (1986). Blood lactate: Implications for training and sports performance. **Sports Med. 3**, 10 - 25.

Mikkelsen, F. (1979) Physical demands and muscle adaptation in elite badminton players. In: **Science in Racquet Sports** (ed. J.Terauds). Academic publishers, Del Mar, California, pp 55 - 67.

10 A phosphate decrement test for adolescent racket sport players

G.F. Treble, K. Wood and A.R. Morton*
University of Western Sydney,
**University of Western Australia*

1 Introduction

An original "phosphate decrement test" was designed by Morton (1986) to measure the average percentage deterioration in performance of a 40 m sprint when the sprint was repeated every 30 s. It was a test that purported to determine the efficiency of the alactic energy system to utilize and resynthesize the phosphagens. In this test, the 40 m sprint was repeated sixteen times.

Many individual and team sports are characterised by short bursts of intense effort followed by a limited opportunity for recovery. This applies particularly to field games and racket sports. The ability to use and quickly restore phosphagen is an important fitness component for players of these games. Indeed, points or contests may often get lost if restoration of phosphagens is delayed.

Most anaerobic tests do not measure this ability to repeatedly restore phosphagens. For example the Wingate Test (Bar-Or et al., 1977) is used purportedly to estimate the alactic anaerobic capacity and the lactacid capacity (Tamayo et al., 1984), i.e. it determines the maximal power observed in a 5 s period (alactacid capacity) and/or the total work performed in 30 s (lactacid capacity). The Margaria-Stair-Run Test which is used to compute alactic anaerobic power (Margaria et al, 1966) can predict with reasonable success a 40 m sprint ability but favours the heavier performer in some instances (Powers and Howley, 1990).

It is important that a test of the phosphagen system reflects the ability to regenerate phosphagens not merely running speed. Unlike the original 'Phosphate Recovery Test' of Dawson et al. (1984), which measures the ability to repeat bursts of intense activity, Morton's "Phosphate Decrement Test" does not penalise the slow runner. That is, someone who may be able to replenish phosphate quickly and efficiently may score poorly on the original test of Dawson et al. because of the inability to run at the high speed of another player. In Morton's decrement calculation every repetition is scored relative to the initial 40 m sprint.

The "Phosphate Decrement Test" is designed in such a way that the athlete must perform a series of 40 m sprints with a short recovery period between each sprint. Previously tested athletes have completed anywhere between 8 and 16 sprints. However, the greater the number

Science and Racket Sports Edited by T. Reilly, M. Hughes and A. Lees.
Published in 1994 by E & FN Spon ISBN 0 419 18500 3

of sprints, the higher the blood lactic acid levels are likely to rise With the higher number of sprints, the test becomes more a test of lactic acid tolerance, rather than the body's ability to replenish and re-use the phosphate energy stores.

The recovery between each sprint is not long enough to allow full replenishment of phosphate, thus causing a decrease in performance throughout the series of sprints. That is, the time it takes to complete the 40 m sprint takes longer each time, so long as the athlete is giving an all-out effort for each sprint. The phosphate restoration is very rapid during rest. It takes about 3-5 minutes for recovery with a half-reaction time of about 30 s (Hahn, 1992), i.e. half of the phosphate store is replenished in 30 s and 75% of it is replenished in one minute.

Morton's original Phosphate Decrement Test was designed for specific game fitness. The athletes must repeat 16 sprints for 40 m every 30 s. While this may be an appropriate distance and length of time for adults, it is not appropriate for adolescents. Indeed, when attempts were made on the adult-type test, there were negative reactions from the athletes. These reactions appeared justified given the physiological demands placed on adolescent performers. Therefore the purpose of this study was to modify the adult version of the phosphate decrement test to make it appropriate for use with adolescent athletes. Specifically the study determined appropriate sprint distances to be repeated every 30 s and the number of repetitions to be attempted.

2 Methods

Male (n = 172) and female subjects (n = 123) ranging in age from 12 to 17 years, participated in this investigation. The tests were performed during physical education classes at Westfields Sports High School by students who were members of sports teams. They were informed orally as to the general nature of the investigation. Most of the subjects had previously experienced a "phosphate decrement test". Three groups were formed, namely 16 and 17 year olds (Group 1), 14 and 15 year olds (Group 2) and 12 and 13 year olds (Group 3).

All athletes were requested to refrain from eating for three hours prior to the session of testing. A thorough warm-up preceded all sprint tests.

Group 1, the 16 and 17 year olds, was the initial group tested in order to establish a base time for adolescents. Each subject ran two 40 m sprints with approximately 5 min rest between each sprint. The times were recorded and the means calculated for the male and the female athletes.

A Lafayette timing clock and infra-red photo electric alarm-type timing gates were placed at the start and end of the 40 m track. All subjects ran on a grass surface. The mean score for males was 5.68 s and the mean score for females was 6.78 s. Once the sprint time was established the distance that could be covered in that time (to the nearest metre) was determined for both sexes in each of the other age groups, i.e. Group 2 (14-15 years) and Group 3 (12-13 years).

To measure the distance covered by Groups 2 and 3, marker cones were placed at 1 m intervals along the track with a tape measure extending from the start to the 40 m mark (see Fig. 1). Three subjects ran at a time with three testers observing the distance covered by each runner. A timekeeper called "ready", then gave a blast of a whistle for the start. At 5.7 s for the boys, the timekeeper, using a stopwatch, called "stop". The testers then called out the distances which were recorded by an assistant. For the girls, the timekeeper called "stop" at 6.8 s, after which their distances were also recorded. In this study, the testers were experienced physical education teachers or coaches and sport science university lecturers.

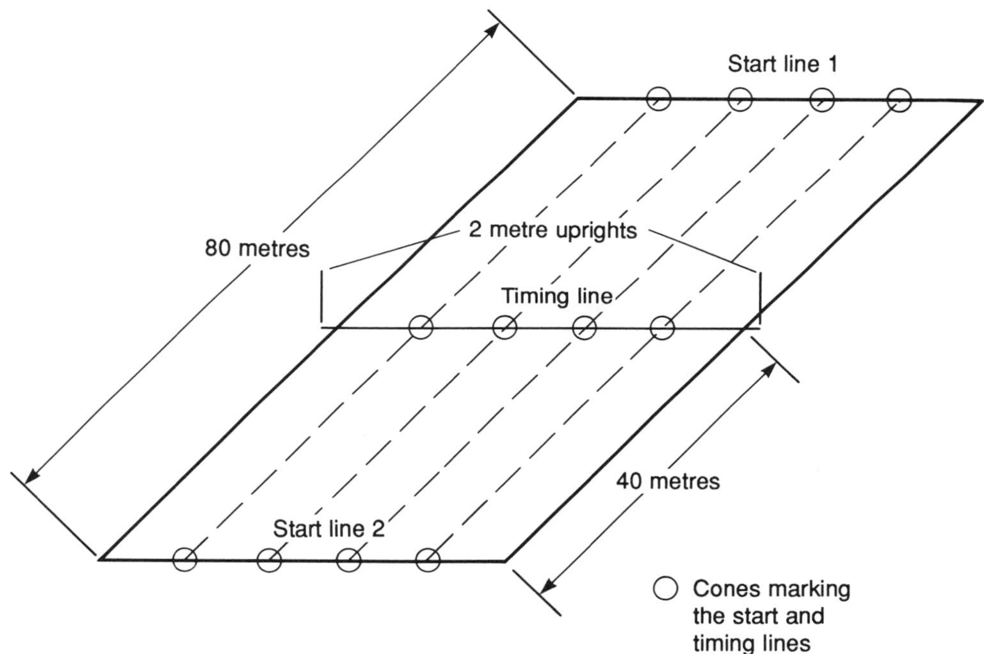

Fig. 1. Track marking for the 'phosphate decrement test'.

3. Results and Discussion

The results initially used as a base sprint time for adolescents are shown in Table. 1. The aim of this study was to determine what distance appeared appropriate for adolescents to complete during Morton's design of a Phosphate Decrement Test. Adults run a series of 40 m sprints with each sprint repeated every 30 s. If adolescents are to perform this same test in order to

Table 1. The base sprint times for adolescents.

Sex	N	40 m sprint times:	Vel(m/s)
Males	33	5.68 s	7.05
Females	25	6.78 s	5.89

determine the efficiency of the alactic energy system to utilize and resynthesize the phosphagens, then a shorter distance than 40 m must be established. This is because adolescents take longer to sprint 40 m and are, therefore, going to reach far higher levels of fatigue in attempting to complete the same number of sprints as that required of the adults.

Table 2. Distances covered, in the established base time, by athletes of age 12 and 13, 14 and 15 years

Group	Mean distance (m) covered in 5.68 s by males		Vel m/s	Mean distance (m) covered in 6.78 s by females		Vel m/s
	Mean	S.D.		Mean	S.D.	
Ages 12&13	33.62	2.91	5.9	36.94	3.03	5.45
Ages 14&15	35.03	2.53	6.16	36.40	3.49	5.37

An examination of the results indicates the 16 and 17 year old boys covered greater distances in 5.68 s than the younger age male groups. For the girls, in 6.78 s, the 16 and 17 year olds covered 40 m while the 14-15 year old girls covered a mean distance of 36.40 m and the 12 and 13 year olds 36.94 m.

When attempting to establish an appropriate distance for the adolescent group to run, it must be taken into consideration that 12 and 13 year old boys and girls are similar in sprinting ability. Since, in this study the girls were sprinting for 6.78 s whereas the boys were only sprinting for 5.68 seconds, it is understandable that the distance covered by the girls was marginally further than that for the boys.

It would appear that adolescents in the younger age groups should not be running 40 m sprints for the Phosphate Decrement Test. Even though this study has established shorter distances for the younger boys and girls, these comparisons have only been made against the 16 and 17 year age group, not adults. If the comparisons were made against adult scores, the established distances for the younger group may have been even shorter.

As a result of this investigation the recommendations for reduced distance of repeat efforts for males and females from age 12 through 15 are as shown in Table 3.

Table 3. Recommended distances for the "phosphate decrement test" for male (M) and female (F) adolescents

AGE	SEX	DURATION (s)	NUMBER OF REPEATS	DISTANCE (M)
12-13	M	30	10	30
12-13	F	30	10	30
14-15	M	30	10	35
14-15	F	30	10	35
16-17	M	30	10	40
16-17	F	30	10	40

The repetitions suggested are in agreement with Dawson and Ackland (1991). Negative psychological reactions have been consistently observed where repetitions are excessive. It is advisable to familiarise racket athletes with repetition type running. Racket athletes should be made aware of the importance of speed on the court and be encouraged to perform maximally in the initial sprint (done some time previously to the Phosphate Decrement Test). The motivation to perform every sprint as fast as possible is important.

4 References

Bar-Or, O., Dotan, R. and Inbar, O. (1977) A 30 second all-out ergometric test: its reliability and validity for anaerobic capacity. **Israel J. Med. Sci.**, 13, 326.

Dawson, B. and Ackland, T. (1991) Repeated effort-testing: the phosphate recovery test revisited. **Sports Coach**, 14(2):12-17.

Dawson, B., Ackland, T. and Roberts, C. (1984) A new fitness test for team and individual sports. **Sports Coach**, 8 (2):42-44.

Hahn, A. (1992) Physiology of training, in **Textbook of Science and Medicine in Sport** (eds.

J. Bloomfield, P.A. Fricker and K.D. Fitch). Blackwell Scientific, Melbourne, pp. 66-86.

Margaria, R., Aghemo, P. and Rovelli, E. (1966) Measurement of muscular power (anaerobic) in man. **J. Appl. Physiol.**, 21, 1661-1664.

Morton, A.R. (1986) **Field test for phosphate decrement in Australian Rugby players.** N.S.W. State Sports Academy.

Powers, S.K. and E. Howley (1990) **Exercise Physiology, Therapy and Application to Fitness and Performance**. W.C. Brown, Dubuque, Iowa.

Tamayo, M., Sucec, A., Phillips, W., Buono, M., Laubach, L. and Frey, M. (1984) The Wingate anaerobic power test, peak blood lactate and maximal oxygen debt for elite male volleyball players; a validation study. **Med. Sci Sports Exerc.**, 16, 126.

11 Influence of physical fitness specific to the game of tennis, morphological and psychological factors on performance level in tennis in different age groups

P. Unierzyski
Academy of Physical Education, Poznan, Poland

1 Introduction

In recent years tennis has developed dramatically in its various aspects. On one hand it has become one of the most popular types of leisure and a mass sport practised by millions of people every day, on the other hand, it is a top sport and source of income. The development of the game and a systematic improvement of performance in tennis make it necessary to start training in early childhood and for a player to achieve top ranking requires serious commitment and sacrifices. Hence, there is a need to carry out a scientific research which would provide the data necessary to organize training and to identify and select gifted children for high competitive tennis.

The game itself, as well as the training and frequent journeys, requires specific predispositions and physical and mental traits on the players' side. Which of these factors are crucial to the present and future level of performance is an issue of the utmost importance for the development of the game and for the solving of practical problems.

The purpose of this work was to construct a battery of tests for selection to the national team, which would be useful for the training planning of particular players. The most important condition, which worked as a limiting factor too, was the necessity to work out a very cheap and easily applicable project to be utilized even in poorly equipped laboratories and sports clubs. Anthropometric and psychological studies as well as research on physical fitness have been carried out in several countries dominating in world tennis. However, there have been few studies tackling the whole complex of factors which influence the level of performance. Against this background, the studies carried out by Schonborn (1984), supported by the German Tennis Association, are recognized as the closest to this ideal. In this work limiting factors have been introduced. This term stands for factors which, if not possessed by players in their optimum, limit their potential for improvement. Among motor abilities the most vital of limiting factors are: coordination-agility and speed-endurance. Specifically tennis skills were also mentioned among the limiting factors. These were footwork and tennis technique. According to the research, mental features belong to the limiting factors, either, for example, self-stimulation (motivation, confidence, strong will); steering features (endurance, self-control, concentration ability); intellectual traits (ability to receive and process information, match cleverness, anticipation). The research progrmme was defined; its aims were as follows:

Science and Racket Sports Edited by T. Reilly, M. Hughes and A. Lees.
Published in 1994 by E & FN Spon ISBN 0 419 18500 3

- Testing to what degree the factors mentioned in the title of the work determine young tennis players' performance.

- Testing how that influence changes depending on the age and the years of players.

Answers to these questions could be vital in planning training and in selection for top tennis. They would help avoid errors stemming from selection based on the results achieved in the very first matches in which the more experienced children and those accelerated in their biological development would succeed.

2 Material and Method

In the years 1988-1992 more than 500 youngsters were tested. The tests were carried out twice a year during the preparation period for the indoor and outdoor season. The results taken for efficiency analysis were those of the anthropometric tests given to a player once a year. Since there was not a methodological need of repeating the psychological tests (the features in question are relatively stable), each player was given this test only once and its result was included with the results of this analysis in the following or previous year.

Overall, the results of 381 (217 boys and 164 girls) players, representing different sports competency, were analysed. The age of the players tested ranged from 11 to 14 years and they were divided into 3 groups according to the performance level they represented at the time of testing:-

A) top ranked players, good international level,
B) national ranked players up to number 30 on present level ranking,
C) other players.

The following studies were carried out:

1. Psychological tests:
   a) drive features of the nervous system,
   - type of nervous system examined by use of the Strelau Inventory (Strelau, 1985),
   - motivation for achievement (Wiederszal-Bazyl Questionnaire, 1978),
   b) intellectual level tested by means of the Raven Matrix Scale.

2. Anthropometric tests:
   - height and weight,
   - percentage body fat,
   - index of maturity (Drozdowski, 1992) which determines the degree of acceleration or retardation of the biological development,
   - playing age - how many years the examined player has been training.

3. The tests of motor abilities:
   - 5 m run measuring starting speed,
   - side run - 9 x 6 m criterion of agility and coordination,
   - medicine ball throw from above the head forward,

standing broad jump.

The methodology developed by Wachowski et al. (1990) was used in this study. Variation analysis was utilized in examining the data, besides the usual characteristics (arithmetic mean, standard deviation); this enabled investigation of how the characteristics varied with different players and their influence on the actual performance level of the individuals.

3 Results

3.1 Psychological tests

The average results of the psychological characteristics are shown in the Table 1. The variations between groups A, B and C are not statistically significant in most cases, but they indicate certain tendencies. Among boys, the better players showed a lesser inhibition - depending on their age. It was noted that the group of better players (A) of boys aged between 11 to 14 and girls aged 13 to 14 showed generally bigger nervous system mobility than players from group B. As for the girls, better players achieved better results in the Raven test on average - the differences between A and B were significant in the age groups from 12 to 13.

3.2 Anthropometric tests

The means and importance of differences between the groups of players at various sports levels, as far as their playing age and anthropometric traits are concerned can be seen in Table 2. It can be noted that the differences between the groups drawn on the basis of the playing age are most significant with players aged 11 and 12. With 13 year old boys and 13-14 year old girls the difference is most clearly drawn between group A and the remaining two, i.e. B and C. It was found that the differences between the groups of boys aged 14, tested according to their playing age, were statistically insignificant. It was found that better players were taller on average. The differences became more visible while comparing groups A and C. No such differences were found while comparing the average height of the girls. The analysis of the fat percentage in the body shows that the players of higher sports level have generally lower percentage of body fat. The mean values of the biological maturity coefficient indicate that boys with greater sports competence are accelerated in their biological development more than their peers from group B and C. The difference is the greatest at the age of 13, after which it shows a tendency to grow smaller. Among the girls the differences in the biological development acceleration are most visible at the age of 12 to the advantage of group A. Then, the situation reverses, 13 and 14 year old girls from group B even gain advantage over the female players from group A.

3.3 Testing motor abilities specific for tennis

Table 3 shows the average results achieved by players of different sports level in the tests characterizing motor abilities. As far as the differences are concerned, the 11 and 12 year old players did not show much difference in terms of their physical fitness in general. The differences between the groups investigated became bigger with age and were most significant at the age of 14 as far as the starting speed, agility and dynamic strength of the legs were concerned.

Table 1. Results of physical traits and significance of differences between investigated groups of tennis players.
* - significant difference at the level 0.05, ** - significant difference at the level of 0.01

	BOYS			COEFFICIENT			GIRLS			COEFFICIENT		
AGE	A	B	C	AC	AC	BC	A	B	C	AB	AC	BC
	Stimulation											
11	61.9	61.0	57.4				61.5	61.0	59.7			
12	64.1	63.3	64.2				60.4	62.1	63.8			
13	68.9	68.4	60.8				63.6	63.5	63.5			
14	69.4	67.8	63.5				60.4	63.6	66.4			
	Inhibition											
11	60.9	63.7	62.9				64.1	66.4	66.6			
12	59.2	66.7	69.9				61.3	65.1	66.3			
13	60.5	67.1	64.9				63.9	61.8	67.4			
14	64.0	71.2	66.0				63.9	61.8	67.4			
	Mobility											
11	62.0	57.0	60.6				57.7	59.1	60.7			
12	65.0	60.8	65.9				57.3	61.4	65.4			
13	67.8	63.6	62.5				64.2	62.5	60.4			
14	68.1	67.6	63.2				66.3	62.8	60.3			
	Motivation											
11	66.6	65.1	61.2				66.7	64.6	63.5			
12	68.6	65.2	63.9				64.8	64.7	63.1			
13	68.1	68.6	65.6				66.2	67.3	66.2			
14	68.1	67.7	63.2				66.4	69.1	65.2			
	Intellectual Level											
11	38.4	43.3	44.2				49.1	45.9	44.6			
12	43.8	43.8	46.3				50.2	42.8	44.7			
13	47.5	45.3	47.8				49.6	44.1	47.9	*		
14	49.3	48.8	46.9				49.5	49.5	47.4	*		

Figure 1 shows how strong the examined characteristics influenced the division into groups A, B and C, that is how they determined the actual performance level and how that influence altered with age. Because of lack of space only the most significant cases are shown here. The diagram shows how the influence of the motor abilities tested (starting speed and agility) intensified with age. At the same time the playing age loses its meaningfulness.

Table 2. The averages and significance of differences between the groups of various sports level, in the sphere of playing age and selected anthropometric traits.
* - significant difference at the level 0.05,** - significant difference at the level 0.01

	BOYS			**COEFFICIENT**			**GIRLS**			**COEFFICIENT**		
	A	B	C	AC	AC	BC	A	B	C	AB	AC	BC
AGE												
	Playing Age (Years) +											
11	5.0	3.9	2.8	**	**	**	4.8	3.6	2.8	**	**	**
12	5.9	4.8	4.4	**	**		5.3	4.1	3.7	**	**	
13	6.5	5.6	5.1	**	**		6.1	5.3	4.8	*	**	
14	6.7	6.4	5.9				7.1	5.9	5.7		**	**
	Height (cm)											
11	150.6	145.6	145.00	**	**		151.2	149.9	146.2			
12	157.5	153.1	151.2				158.1	155.9	153.7			
13	167.9	161.9	161.2				160.2	162.4	158.5			
14	176.3	172.4	164.3		**	**	165.6	165.5	166.1			
	Body fat (%)											
11	15.3	15.3	16.8		*	*	15.3	16.1	16.1			
12	15.3	16.2	26.1		.		15.0	26.2	16.3			
13	14.2	16.3	16.3	**	**		15.1	16.9	16.9			
14	14.2	16.2	16.45	**	**		15.9	19.1	17.1	**		*
	Index of maturity											
11	7.1	0.6	-0.8				6.0	4.7	-2.2		**	*
12	5.4	0.9	-0.3				14.2	2.8	0.3	*	**	
13	11.3	4.3	2.2	*	*		3.5	13.9	4.0			
14	13.2	10.9	0.1		**	**	9.2	14.9	11.0			

4 Discussion

The results of the studies indicate that the investigated factors exert very different influences on the successes of young players and that these influences depend upon their age and duration of the training. Initially the successes of 11 and 12 year old tennis players are determined mostly by their experience (playing age); they contribute as well to more intensive biological development. The present results confirm the findings of Muller (1990).

Table 3. Results of motor abilities specific to the game and significance of differences between the groups of competitors of various sports level.
* - significant difference at the level 0.05, ** - significant difference at the level 0.01

	BOYS			COEFFICIENT			GIRLS			COEFFICIENT		
	A	B	C	AC	AC	BC	A	B	C	AB	AC	BC
AGE												
	5 m (m/s)											
11	4.72	4.76	4.56				4.70	4.61	4.57			
12	4.93	4.79	4.78				4.85	4.75	4.66		**	
13	5.11	5.01	4.83		**	**	4.93	4.76	4.77	**	**	
14	5.45	5.15	4.94	**	**	**	5.10	4.83	4.76			
	9 x 6 m (sec)											
11	19.80	20.68	21.43	*	**		20.51	20.86	21.71		**	*
12	19.52	19.96	20.10				19.94	20.57	21.02	*	**	
13	18.61	19.06	20.37		**	**	18.95	19.82	20.28	**	**	
14	17.94	18.66	19.73	*	**	**	18.44	19.55	20.18	**	**	**
	Standing Broad Jump (cm)											
11	182.1	181.9	172.9		*	*	178.1	178.2	169.2			
12	193.2	191.6	186.0				188.9	183.4	179.7			
13	217.2	211.2	195.3		*	**	206.9	191.3	185.4	**	**	
14	235.0	220.6	203.5	*	**	**	215.0	199.1	190.0	**	**	
	Med Ball Throw (m)											
11	6.01	6.08	6.32		*	**	5.77	5.39	5.01		*	*
12	7.26	6.71	6.64				6.96	5.69	5.31	**	**	
13	8.89	8.17	7.26		*	**	7.52	7.19	6.27		**	*
14	11.23	9.65	8.12	*	**	**	8.51	7.90	6.83		**	*

A tendency for the influence of motor efficiency specific to tennis on actual sports level to increase with age is clearly visible; at the same time the importance of playing age becomes less. Analysis of the factors related to the body constitution indicates that competitors of higher sports level have less body fat level and are taller compared with the other competitors, which confirms the features observed in 'adult' tennis (Groppel, 1987; Unierzyski, 1993). The results of psychological studies seem to be a little less consistent, among others due to less significant differences between groups A, B and C. Differences in the level of mobility of the nervous system seems to confirm (Gracz and Sankowski, 1991) that this trait enables players to succeed in the game due to a quick and adequate reaction as well as frequent changes of position.

Similarly, the better results were achieved by the girls of Group A in the Raven test. The results of this test reflect the predisposition to proper tactical solutions.

5 Conclusions

1. During the first years of sport practice, competitive results are predominantly affected by playing experience, reflected also by the playing age. The influence of this factor becomes smaller with age.

2. The role of motor abilities, particularly agility and starting speed, increases with age and becomes predominant about 14 years .

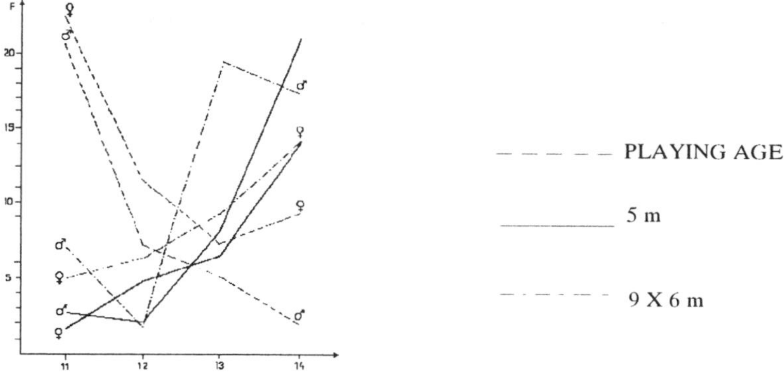

Figure 1. Changes of the force of influence of the starting speed, agility and playing age on the sports level observed with the age of tennis players.

3. Some mental and morphological traits (mobility of the nervous system, intellectual level among the girls as well as height among the boys and low body fat) positively influenced performance. Further in-depth research in this sphere seems to be required.

4. During selection of young competitors for high competitive tennis, the results not only showed the actual level of the sports abilities should be taken into account, but also the potential to optimise development for a future sport career.

6 References

Drozdowski, Z. (1992) Antopologia w wychowaniu fizycznym. **AWF, Poznan**

Gracz J., Sankowski, (1991) Psychologia dzialalnosci sportowej. Skrypt 94, **AWF, Poznan**

Groppel J.L. (1987) Going for the Gold. **World Tennis,** 10.

Hornowski, B. (1970) **Analiza psycholpgiczna skali.** J.C. Ravena, PWN, Warszawa

Muller E. (1990) Sport Motor Ability Test for Talent Selection in Tennis, ETA Coaches Symposium, Norwich.

Schonborn, R. (1984) Leistungslimitirende und Leistungabestimende Faktoren.in **Talentsuche und Talentforderung im Tennis (**eds H. Gabler and B. Zein). Czwalina, Ahrensburg,.

Strelau, J. (1985) **Temperament, osobowosc.** Dzialanie, PWN, Warszawa.

Unierzyski, P. (1993) Tendencje rozwojowe tenisa ziemnego.In Drozdowski, Z. (ed) **Tendencje rozwojowe sportu.** AWF, Poznan

Unierzyski, P., (1994) Wplyw poziomu zdolnosci motorycznych o charakterze dynamicznym (silowo-szybkosciowym), stazu sportowego oraz stopnia rozwoju biologicznego na sukcesy sportowe we wczesnym okresie uprawiania tenisa ziemnego. **Scientific Annuals of the AWF, Poznan** (In press).

Wachowsk, E., Strzelczyk, R. and Osinksi, W. (1990) **Pomiar cech sprawnosci motorycznej osobnikow uprawiajacych sport.** AWF, Poznan

Weiderszal-Bazyl, M. (1978) Kwestionariusz do mierzenia motywu osiagniec. **Przeglad Psychologiczny,** 2.

12 A comparison of kinanthropometric profiles between county and club female tennis players

T. Reilly and K. Benton
Centre for Sport and Exercise Sciences, Liverpool John Moores University, Liverpool, UK

1 Introduction

In sport it is axiomatic that demands of match-play increase with the level of participation and are reflected in fitness profiles of players. This has not always been confirmed in racket sports, as players of low, medium and high skill categories may demonstrate similar heart rate responses to participation in play (Reilly, 1990). Nevertheless competitors at different levels may be distinguished by their training programmes or their fitness profiles. This may apply particularly to female lawn tennis players, for whom there have been few studies reported in the literature. The aim of this study was to provide a kinanthropometric profile of female county lawn tennis players and compare this with club standard players.

2 Methods

Thirty three female subjects volunteered for the study. They included seventeen players (age 30.6 ± 7.0; height 164.5 ± 6.2 cm; body mass 64.4 ± 8.8 kg) from 6 clubs in Staffordshire and sixteen county players (age 24.6 ± 6.5; height 169.7 ± 11.3; body mass 60.9 ± 8.8 kg) from Staffordshire and Lancashire.

Anthropometric measures included body composition established using bio-electric impedance (Bodystat, Isle of Man) and somatotype according to the Heath-Carter method. Hand length, wrist and elbow diameters were measured on both sides to examine evidence for asymmetry. Grip, back and leg strength were determined using a portable dynamometer (Takei Kiki-Kogyo, Tokyo). Standing broad jump and vertical jump were used as muscular performance measures and 40 m sprint time (best of 2 trials) was used as an index of running speed. Forward flexibility was measured from a raised platform with the subject reaching forward and downward, legs kept extended; the best of three trials was recorded using a digital system (Takei Kiki- Kogyo, Tokyo).

Science and Racket Sports Edited by T. Reilly, M. Hughes and A. Lees.
Published in 1994 by E & FN Spon ISBN 0 419 18500 3

3 Results and Discussion

The county players were taller than the sample of female club players, confirming a trend towards greater stature the higher the level of tennis competition (Reilly, 1990). The county players were, in fact, taller than the average of the Western Australian Senior Women's Squad studied by Pyke et al. (1974), but were similar to the professional players examined by Copley (1980). The greater than average stature (and segmental length) affords an advantage in reaching to play a shot and in leverage for serving.

The county players were also more mesomorphic than their club counterparts (4.2 ± 1.6 vs 2.6 ± 1.2) and more ectomorphic (3.0 ± 1.0 vs 2.0 ± 1.0). Both calf and upper arm girth were significantly larger ($P < 0.05$) in the county players. The lower value for ectomorphy in the county players was reflected also in the body composition estimates, whether computed from the sum of skinfold thicknesses or from the impedance measure (Table 1). There was no evidence of assymetries between limbs in either group.

Grip strength was greater in the county players than in the club players ($P < 0.05$), mean difference being 53.7 N for the dominant arm and 35.6 N for the non-dominant side. The differences between dominant and non-dominant sides in grip strength (51 N for county, 34 N for club players) was not significant ($P > 0.05$).

Table 1. Anthropometric and performance data for female club and county tennis players

	Club (n = 17)	County (n = 16)
% Body Fat	28.8 ± 3.5	18.8 ± 3.1*
Back Strength (N)	720 ± 317	1018 ± 355*
Leg Strength (N)	630 ± 227	739 ± 277
40 m Sprint (S)	6.8 ± 1.0	6.1 ± 1.0
Flexibility (cm)	6.8 ± 6.6	11.2 ± 6.3*
Vertical Jump (cm)	31.6 ± 3.7	34.5 ± 2.8*
Broad Jump (cm)	144.8 ± 20.5	161.5 ± 23.2*

*indicates significant differences ($P < 0.05$)

The two groups were distinguishable on the basis of their kinanthropometric and performance profile (Table 1) according to discriminant function analysis (Roy's test, $P < 0.05$). In view of the potential effect of age on the performance profiles of the two groups, the data were re- examined using analysis of covariance. This established that the age difference between the groups accounted for the differences in flexibility, strength and jump performances. However, the significant differences in body composition and somatotype measures remained ($P < 0.05$).

The frequency of competing and participating in tournament play was established by questionnaire to be similar in the two groups. The county players spent significantly more hours in training per week than did the club players ($P < 0.05$). Since the hours spent practicing rather than competing discriminated between the groups, the anthropometric findings may be related more strongly to training than to match-play demands.

4 References

Copley, B.B. (1980) A morphological and physiological study of tennis players with special reference to the effects of training. **S. Afr. J. Res. Sport, P.E. Recr.**, 3, 33-44.

Pyke, S., Elliott, C. and Pyke, E. (1974) Physiological and anatomical characteristics of outstanding female junior tennis players. **Brit. J. Sports Med.**, 8, 80-86.

Reilly, T. (1990) The racquet sports, in **Physiology of Sports** (eds T. Reilly, N. Secher, P. Snell and C. Williams), E. and F.N. Spon, London, pp. 337-369.

13 Physiological profiles of squash players of different standards

S. Mellor, M. Hughes, T. Reilly and K. Robertson
Centre for Sport and Exercise Sciences, School of Human Sciences, Liverpool John Moores University, Liverpool, UK

1 Introduction

Playing squash is largely accomplished with energy supplied by means of aerobic mechanisms. Although the activity during play is non-rhythmic, a high level of strain is maintained on the oxygen transport system. Mean heart rates of squash players observed during match-play have varied from 147 to 161 beats/min or 79 to 88% of the subjects' maximum heart rates (Reilly, 1990). As a consequence of this, it is likely that regular and frequent participation in squash provides a physiological training stimulus to the heart and to the oxygen transport system.

Recreational participants are attracted to squash due to its purported health promotion benefits. These apply particularly to positive effects on physiological factors that might predispose towards coronary heart disease. Concern about the safety of the game for otherwise sedentary individuals followed reports of sudden death during or after playing squash (Northcote et al., 1984). It may be that the game is inappropriate for individuals with coronary heart disease predispositions and that participation in squash as a recreation activity on an unsystematic basis affords no benefit on coronary risk profile status.

The present study was undertaken to compare fitness and blood lipid levels of squash players of different standards. Of interest was the comparison of recreational players with those competing at club and at county levels.

2 Methods

Subjects were recruited for longitudinal and cross-sectional studies on the training effects of participation in squash. Participation in the study was solicited by advertising posters placed in squash clubs and recreation centres and through personal contacts at the clubs. The cross-sectional investigation is reported here.

The sample consisted of three groups:-

i) recreational players (n=14). These were non-competitive in that they did not play in any Leagues but did play for fun at least once a week;

ii) club players (n=10). These were specialists in squash and did not engage in other sports but competed regularly in inter-club matches;

iii) county players (n=13). These were currently playing representative squash for their counties. Their mean age was 27.5, compared with mean age of 35 years in each of the other two groups.

The anthropometric profile included body mass and sum of four skinfolds (Durnin and Womersley, 1974). Performance tests of the alactacid energy system included a stair run (Margaria et al., 1966) and a standing broad jump. Physiological responses to a graded treadmill run test included measurement of oxygen consumption using an on-line system (P.K. Morgan, Rainham) and heart rate using a three-lead electrocardiogram. Each stage lasted 5 min but the subjects were not required to exercise to voluntary exhaustion as the index of aerobic capacity was taken to be the $\dot{V}O_2$ corresponding to a heart rate of 170 beats/min. The $\dot{V}O_2$-170 was calculated by interpolation (or extrapolation) of the regression line relating $\dot{V}O_2$ and heart rate on the incremental treadmill test.

Serum profiles were determined by photometric methods. Both total cholesterol and high density lipoprotein fractions (HDL) were calculated.

Data were analysed by means of ANOVA. Follow-up LSD tests were employed to localise significant differences between groups.

3 Results

The three groups were similar in body mass. The groups were separated on skinfold measures ($P<0.05$), the highest values being observed in the recreation players, the lowest in the county players (Table 1).

This trend was evident also when the anaerobic performance measures were examined. The recreation players performed most poorly on the stair run, the club players were intermediate in performance, whilst the best performances were by the county players. These results were not completely replicated in the standing broad jump. Whilst the county players were significantly better than the other two groups ($P<0.05$), the club players did no better than their recreational counterparts.

The aerobic capacity ($\dot{V}O_2$-170) showed a progressive increase according to standard of play. The significant trend was evident also when values were corrected for body mass values ($P<0.05$).

Lowest values for total cholesterol were observed in the county players (Table 1). The other two groups did not differ significantly from each other although they were well below the risk threshold of 6.5 mmol/ℓ suggested by the British Medical Association and the standards of the European Atheroscleroses Society (1987).

The HDL values were expressed as a proportion of total cholesterol for comparative purposes. In this instance the recreation and club players did not differ significantly from each other, whereas the recreation group had higher values than those of the county players ($P<0.05$). All groups were below the threshold of worry about coronary disease risk suggested by the British Medical Association.

Table 1. Cross-sectional comparisons of squash players at three levels of participation. Values are mean ± S.D.

	County	Club	Recreation
Body mass (kg)	73.7±5.3	71.1±7.2	72.0±7.0
Sum of skinfolds (mm)	31.8±10.1	39.0±10.0	45.0±15.9
Stair run (ms)	421±44	454±33	483±52
$\dot{V}O_2$-170/kg (ml/min)	55.8±8.9	50.8±7.0	43.9±5.6
Total cholesterol (mmol/ℓ)	4.8±0.8	6.0±0.6	72.0±0.7
HDL/Total Cholesterol ratio	0.29±0.08	0.28±0.08	0.25±0.08

4 Discussion

The county players demonstrated an all-round superior fitness level to the other groups. The aerobic capacity test in particular set them apart. This is likely to have been due to the frequency of training and competing and to the intensity of play at that level of skill.

Whilst the aerobic capacity test used does not permit comparisons with data in the literature for other groups of athletes, the present results demonstrated its validity. Its main use specific to the present studies is for monitoring changes in health-related physical fitness over a long-term in subjects not inclined in the first instance to exercise at maximal aerobic power.

The stair run test proved to be a more powerful discriminator between the groups than did the broad jump. This may be because of the contribution of anthropometric measures, notably leg length, to performance in the broad jump. The stair is a more dynamic test and resembles more closely the type of anaerobic efforts employed by squash players in that a rapid acceleration over a short series of strides (rather than one single explosive jump) is called for.

The superiority of the players at county level was manifested also in the sum of skinfolds and in total cholesterol level. Despite having the highest values for these measures, the club players were still below danger levels as indicated by the British Medical Association, and the European Atherosclerosis Society (1987). The HDL-total cholesterol ratio for the recreation players may represent an attitude towards health, of which participation in squash is only one part. In contrast the similar profile of the club players may raise questions about their holistic attitudes towards health and fitness, and the systematic nature of their dietary and training programmes. These questions may be resolved by adoption of more sensitive criteria in recruitment of subjects.

Findings indicate that regular and frequent participation in competitive squash is associated with a positive profile of coronary health. Players at county standard have values indicative of aerobic capacity, fat free mass, anaerobic performance and lipid profiles that separate them from their less proficient counterparts. Clarifying the health benefits of recreational participation requires a longitudinal approach where the discrete effects of squash play can be isolated more effectively.

Acknowledgements: this work benefitted from a grant from the Health Promotion Research Trust which is gratefully acknowledged.

5 References

Durnin, J.V.G.A. and Womersley, J. (1974) Body fat assessed from total body density and its estimation from skinfold thickness: measurements on 481 men and women aged 16 to 72 years. **Brit. J. Nutr.**, 32, 169-179.

European Atherosclerosis Society Study Group (1987) Strategies for the prevention of coronary heart disease. **Europ. Heart J.**, 8, 77-88.

Margaria, R., Aghemo, P. and Rovelli, E. (1966) Measurement of muscular power (anaerobic) in man. **J. Appl. Physiol.**, 21, 1661-1664.

Northcote, R.J., Evans, A.D.B. and Ballantyne, D. (1984) sudden death in squash players. Lancet, 1, 148-150.

Reilly, T. (1990) The racquet sports, in **Physiology of Sports** (eds. T. Reilly, N. Secher, P. Snell and C. Williams) E. and F.N. Spon, London, pp. 337-369.

14 The physiological profile of elite junior squash players

C.A. Mahoney and N.C.C. Sharp*
The Queen's University of Belfast, Belfast, Northern Ireland
**University of Limerick, Limerick, Eire*

1 Introduction

An increasing awareness in the application of sport science in recent years has led to the development of physiological testing in various sports. The results have enabled better training principles to be administered and monitoring to occur more objectively. Sports such as hockey (Reilly & Borrie, 1992), soccer (Green, 1992), rowing (Shephard, 1991) and swimming (Costill et al., 1992) have made successful use of such testing opportunities. However, very little has been done to describe the physiological requirements of elite squash play, though van Rensburg et al. (1982) have completed a comprehensive study of league players and Montpetit (1990) has reviewed applied physiology of squash. This limited research at any level of squash is unusual when it is listed among the top ten sports played in Great Britain from the General Household Survey (1987).

Squash has been described as a sport placing demands on aerobic and anaerobic pathways (Sharp, 1979). With games lasting between 30 minutes and 2 hours, common work to rest ratios of 1:1 and rally lengths between 5 and 20 seconds (Docherty & Howe, 1978; Montgomery et al., 1981), squash is a sport which requires intense training of a wide range of physiological parameters.

The importance of physiological monitoring to professional squash players is perhaps unclear, but insufficient data available for comparative assessment hinder this judgement. Physiological profiling of any sport must not become merely a data acquisition exercise; though the correlation with success may be only marginal, the data can assist in identifying weaknesses, providing optimal training programmes and motivating players to train. This has benefits for young players, full playing professionals and coaches.

The aim of this study was to assess selected physiological variables of elite junior squash players entering a career as professionals. In addition the ongoing development of baseline data of functional capabilities and developing a battery of tests effective in identifying change, were paramount.

Science and Racket Sports Edited by T. Reilly, M. Hughes and A. Lees.
Published in 1994 by E & FN Spon ISBN 0 419 18500 3

2 Method

Five junior international male squash players ranked in National Open competition provided informed written consent to take part in the study. The players had just entered or were about to enter full time professional careers as squash players. All players were in peak physical condition, currently playing professional tournament squash, National League competition and possessing National senior rankings. Subject details are provided in Table 1.

Table 1. Subject details and anthropometric measurements

	Mean ± SD	**Range**
Age (years)	16.8 ± 1.3	15 - 18
Height (cm)	173.0 ± 6.4	165 - 182
Mass (kg)	67.0 ± 10.3	50 - 77
Body Fat (%)	10.9 ± 1.8	8.0 - 12.5

The subjects were asked to refrain from strenuous activity during the preceding day and were given complete verbal instructions and demonstration prior to each test. A warm up was completed by each subject before the test was performed.

All measurements were taken in the laboratory using standard protocols. Body fat was estimated from skinfold measurements taken at bicep, tricep, subscapular sites and suprailiac, using the equation of Durnin and Womersley (1974). From this information fat free mass was estimated, and body surface area calculated using the Dubois formula.

The Abalokov test (TKK jump metre) was used to indicate "explosive leg power". Grip strength was measured using a hand grip dynamometer. Balance and agility was measured on a Layfayette stabilometer using 5 degrees of freedom over a 30 second time trial. A 30 second all out Wingate anaerobic test was used to assess anaerobic power, which was repeated following a five minute recovery.

The aerobic fitness of the players was assessed using an incremental treadmill test (Powerjog M30) in which the subject commenced running at 10 km/h increasing every three minutes by 2 km/h. Expired gas was measured and the expired air was analysed for O2 and CO2 using an automated system (Cardio Kinetics Ltd Oxycon 4). Variables including $\dot{V}E$, $\dot{V}O2$, $\dot{V}CO2$, R and $\dot{V}E/\dot{V}O2$ were determined. The test was terminated when two or more of the following criteria were achieved;

1. a test heart rate within ± 5 beats/minute of theoretical age related maximum;

2. a respiratory exchange ratio greater than 1.15;

3. a plateau in $\dot{V}O2$ indicated by less than 2 ml/kg/min increase with increasing exercise intensity;

4. volitional exhaustion.

Each subject's heart function was monitored throughout the test via a CR7 Cardiorater ECG.

3 Results and discussion

The laboratory test results are summarised in Table 2. Very few studies have considered any physiological variables related to squash other than aerobic fitness. This provides a void of comparative evidence with which to make assessment of these junior elite players.

The results from this study suggest squash is a sport demanding relatively high levels of physiological fitness in a variety of parameters. Most research with squash players has placed particular emphasis on aerobic fitness. The $\dot{V}O2max$ results in this study compare with those of Montgomery et al. (1981) and Mercier et al. (1987), but are generally lower than those of Steininger & Wodick (1987) or van Rensburg et al. (1982). Wilmore (1979) found $\dot{V}O2max$ values of 60-80 ml/kg/min were common in endurance athletes, while athletes specialising in sports with low endurance demands had values of 30-40 ml/kg/min. The values in this study support the notion that aerobic fitness is necessary in squash but high levels are not essential. In fact a level of motor fitness above average, with cardiorespiratory fitness between normal population values and elite marathon runners in addition to a high anaerobic fitness, are possibly the more effective predictors of success necessary to elite junior squash.

Table 2. Laboratory results and physiological measurement

Test Parameter	**Mean ± SD**
Lean Body Mass (kg)	59.7 ± 8.8
Body Surface Area (m^2)	1.8 ± 0.2
Grip Left (N)	436.1 ± 63.7
Right (N)	501.3 ± 98.1
Abalokov Jump (cm)	66.1 ± 11.3
Balance (seconds/30 seconds)	26 ± 2.5
Wingate Test:-	
Peak Power (watts)	899 ± 254
Peak Power (watts/kg)	13.2 ± 0.9
Fatigue Index (watts/s)	-15 ± 6.4
Total Work (kilojoules)	20.1 ± 4.5
Recovery (%)	89.7 ± 6.9
$\dot{V}O2max$ (ml/kg/min)	52.6 ± 3.6

This study has shown a high inverse Spearman rho correlation between sum of skinfolds and $\dot{V}O2max$. ($r = -0.84$, $P<0.05$). This accounts for over 60% of the variance and indicates body fat may be a factor limiting performance. Significant inverse Spearman rho correlations were also found between Abalokov jump and junior ranking (r = -0.92, P<0.001) and Wingate results with junior ranking (r = -0.89, P<0.001).

The level of strength in racket players can often restrict performance. In longer games the onset of fatigue will increase the likelihood of injury and reduce the effectiveness of skill. Grip strength values in excess of 450 N for the dominant hand would seem adequate. Using the stabilometer to estimate balance, values greater than 26 seconds of balance using 5 degrees of freedom would appear most acceptable.

The Wingate anaerobic test results show peak power approaching 1000 watts can be expected from elite junior squash players. This will assist on-court strength and concomitant speed. Taking account of body mass differences, a mean peak power of 13.2 watts/kg is suggested as an appropriate output. During each bout of activity a fatigue index of less than 15 watts/second and preferably 10 watts/second is desirable, since squash is a multiple sprint sport requiring continued bursts of peak power and the ability to repeat such activity is essential. This 30 second period of intense exercise should be possible again within 5 minutes as an indicator of anaerobic recovery potential. In such instances the rest period should elicit a recovery index of at least 90% in power output.

The Abalokov jump test to indicate "explosive leg power" has also supported the notion that a high level of anaerobic potential is necessary in squash. An average score of 66 cm for the squad is well above population norms and approaching values commonly found in basketballers, jumpers and footballers.

During squash play heart rates are often elevated above 80% of maximum (Docherty & Howe, 1978) which will improve cardiorespiratory fitness during play, but also place great demands on the cardiorespiratory system of the individual. With games lasting from 30 minutes to over 2 hours and the ball in play for 69% of the match (Montgomery et al., 1981) players must be highly trained aerobically and anaerobically.

With average rally lengths of 16.9 seconds (Docherty and Howe, 1978), limited time between rallies to recovery and distances between 10 and 30 metres covered during the rally, squash can be described as a multiple sprint sport with underlying aerobic requirements. Training should therefore emulate this to fulfil the requirements of specificity. Elite squash performance is limited by factors including overheating, dyspnoea and muscle fatigue. The game demands extremely quick visual and locomotor reflexes because of ball speed and the propinquity of players. It requires quick anticipation and response to movements of opponents, ball, footwork and stroke production. Games lasting over 30 minutes with intense activity require optimal physical fitness, stamina and an intense determination to win. Success in squash is dependent upon developing skill, fitness and mental abilities to their optimum level. The physiological requirements of the sport are associated with optimising those talents genetically possessed. Elite junior squash performance is closely linked with body fat levels approaching those of elite distance runners, grip strength scores over 493 N (50 kg) for the playing arm (necessary to diminish the likely loss of form due to local muscle fatigue in the arm), Abalokov jump scores in excess of 60 cm (directly linked with anaerobic capability), peak power output above 13 watts/kg with recovery indices of 90% or greater and $\dot{V}O_2max$ values above 52 ml/kg/min.

The lack of comparative data in squash, less than 12 papers in refereed journals, and only one paper on junior squash, makes comparison of data difficult. Steininger and Wodick (1987) who completed assessment of $\dot{V}O2max$ on German junior players, found higher values than the present study, but they gave no indication of the method of assessment, they combined males and females together and age, anthropometry or the completion of other tests were not included in the results. Further work is required to fully establish a comprehensive profile of the physiological requirements of elite junior male squash player.

4 References

Costill, D.L., Maglischo, E.W. & Richardson, A.B. (1992) **Handbook of Sports Medicine and Science: Swimming.** Blackwell Scientific Publications, Oxford.

Docherty, D. & Howe, B. (1978) Heart rate response of squash players relative to their skill level. **Aus. J. Sports Med.,** 10, 90-92.

Durnin, J.V.G.A. & Womersley, J. (1974) Body fat assessed from total body density and its estimation from skinfold thicknesses. **Brit. J. Nutr**., 32, 77-97.

General Household Survey. (1987) Office of Population Censuses and Surveys. London.

Green, S. (1992) Anthropometric and physiological characteristics of South Australian soccer players. **Aus. J. Sci. Med. Sport**, 24, 3-7.

Mercier, M., Beillot, J., Gratas, A., Rochcongar, P. & Lessard, Y. (1987) Adapation to work load in squash players: laboratory tests and on-court recordings. **J. Sports Med. Phys. Fit.,** 27, 98-104.

Montgomery, D.L., Malcolm, V. & McDonnell, E. (1981) A comparison of the intensity of play in squash and running. **Physician. Sportsmed.**, 9, 116-119.

Montpetit, R.R. (1990) Applied physiology of squash. **Sports Med.**, 10, 31-41.

van Rensburg, J.P., van der Linde, A., Ackerman, P.C., Keilblock, A.J. & Strydom, N.B. (1982) Physiological profiles of squash players. **S. Afr. J. Res. Sport Phys. Ed. Recr.**, 5, 25-66.

Reilly, T. & Borrie, A. (1992) Physiology applied to field hockey. **Sports Med.**, 14, 20-26.

Sharp, C. (1979) Fitness for squash; how to build your aerobic power. **Squash Player Int.,** 8, 15-17.

Shephard, R.J. (1991) Testing the rower. **Can. J. Sport Sci.**, 16, 243.

Steininger, K. & Wodick, R.E. (1987) Sports-specific fitness testing in squash. **Brit. J. Sports Med.**, 21, 23-26.

Wilmore, J.H. (1979) The application of sport science. Physiological profiles of male and female athletes. **Can. J. Appl. Sport. Sci.**, 4, 103-115.

15 Determination of pre-season physiological characteristics of elite male squash players

M. K. Todd and C.A. Mahoney
The Queen's University of Belfast, Belfast, Northern Ireland

1 Introduction

Squash entails moderate to high intensity intermittent exercise where players are active 50 to 70% of the playing time (Montpetit, 1990) which taxes the players' cardiac, respiratory, metabolic and musculoligamental capacities (Mercier et al., 1987). Games can last up to three hours (Steininger and Wodick, 1987) and therefore a high level of energy reserves for anaerobic glycolysis and aerobic process in required (Blanksby et al., 1973).

Factors associated with physical fitness in squash include aerobic capacity, anaerobic power, strength, speed, flexibility, balance and co-ordination (van Rensburg et al., 1982). The game demands fast reactions, quick acceleration, fast arm, leg and whole body movements and an ability to change direction quickly (Reilly et al., 1990). Pre-season

training must concentrate on elevating these factors through suitable training methods to facilitate successful performance during the competitive season.

The present study involved the monitoring of 12 Irish elite male squash players aged 15-22 years. The project is part of a continual monitoring of the players and the results presented are the initial pre-season characteristics which may be subject to seasonal variation.

The project is concerned only with the physiological assessment of the players from which comparative research data are being used to provide detailed analysis of the current status of the individuals. A major outcome of the work is the production of individualised training programmes together with an underlying educational objective.

2 Methods

In the laboratory anthropomorphic measurements were taken for height (Holtain stadiometer), body mass (Secca scales) and skinfold thickness (Harpenden skinfold callipers). Body composition was estimated using the equation of Durnin and Womersley (1974), grip strength was measured using a grip dynamometer and abdominal strength was measured by counting the number of sit-ups performed in 60 seconds. Speed and agility were measured using a 30 metre maximum sprint test and

Science and Racket Sports Edited by T. Reilly, M. Hughes and A. Lees.
Published in 1994 by E & FN Spon ISBN 0 419 18500 3

10 x 5 metre shuttle run. Hamstring and lower back flexibility were assessed using a sit-and-reach test and `explosive leg power' was determined using an Abalokov jump test. Anaerobic power was measured using a 10 x 6 second multiple Wingate test with a load resistance of 8% of the subject's body mass, from which fatigue indices showing reductions in power were determined.
Maximal oxygen uptake ($\dot{V}O2max$) was directly measured using an Oxycon Beta (Mijnhard BV) expired gas analyser during a progressive test on a treadmill (Powerjog M30). The test commenced at 12.9 km/h with increments in treadmill gradient of 2.5% every three minutes according to the British Association of Sports Sciences (BASS) guidelines (1988). Lactate concentrations were obtained from a 30 ml sample collected at the end of each work bout and analysed using an Analox GM7 analyser. The test was terminated when the subject reached volitional exhaustion or three of the following occurred (BASS, 1988);

1. a plateau in the oxygen uptake/exercise intensity;

2. a respiratory exchange ration of 1.15 or above;

3. a heart rate of within 10 beats/min of the age related maximum;

4. an exercise blood lactate concentration of 8 mmol/l or more.

3 Results and Discussion

3.1 Aerobic power

Maximum oxygen uptake ($\dot{V}O2max$) is defined as the maximum rate an individual can take up and use oxygen whilst breathing air at sea level and it is effectively a measure of cardiovascular function. It provides an indicator of endurance performance potential and, to a lesser extent in trained subjects, training status (BASS, 1988).
The average $\dot{V}O2max$ value for the Irish squad was 63.3 $\pm$ 3.1 ml/kg/min (Table 1). This is higher than the findings of Mercier et al. (1987), Loots and Thiart (1987), Montpetit et al. (1987), Steininger and Wodick (1987), Docherty and Howe (1987) and van Rensburg et al. (1982). The English senior county players assessed by Winter et al. (1984) had $\dot{V}O2max$ values similar to the Irish players.

3.2 Body composition

The percentage of total body weight occupied by body fat is of great importance to squash players. Whereas a minimum of 3% body fat is essential for survival in males, percentage body fat values of elite athletes seem to be well below the average of 15% for young adult males (Lamb, 1989). Low percentage body fat improves the ability to dissipate metabolic heat which is of primary importance in maintaining thermal balance during competition (Reilly et al., 1990). Excess body fat constitutes extra body mass that adds directly to the energy cost of a game of squash.
The percentage body fat of the Irish players (13.6 $\pm$ 0.6 %) is higher than English county players (Winter et al., 1984), the top 50 British players (Jaski & Bale, 1987),

South African players (van Rensburg et al., 1982) and top class Western Australian players (Pyke et al., 1974), but lower than top class French players (Mercier et al., 1987). Despite the fact that comparisons between body fat assessed in different populations may be unreliable, due to differing conversion equations and the inaccuracy associated with body fat determination, it is still possible that high body fat may be a limiting factor associated with achievement in Irish players.

3.3 Anaerobic capacity

Anaerobic capacity is defined as the ability to persist at the maintenance or repetition of strenuous muscular contractions that rely upon anaerobic mechanisms of energy supply (Lamb, 1989). To measure maximal anaerobic power and capacity a 10 x 6 second maximal sprint Wingate test was performed on a cycle ergometer with a load ratio of 8% of the subject's body mass. This test was designed to assess the maximal power exerted, the mean power output over 6 seconds, and the reproducibility of both measures over ten six-second repetitions. Maximum power (898.7 ± 36.1 watts) was similar to the scores of English county players (Brookes & Winter, 1985). From these data peak power decline (PPD) and mean power decline (MPD) fatigue indicators were calculated. For example;

PPD = 100 * [(highest peak power - lowest peak power)/highest peak power]

Table 1. Physiological characteristics of elite Irish squash players (n=12)

Variable	**Mean ± SE**
Height (cm)	174.5 ± 0.7
Body mass (kg)	72.8 ± 1.6
Body fat (%)	13.6 ± 0.6
30m sprint (s)	4.84 ± 0.4
10 x 5 m sprint (s)	17.6 ± 1.5
Text>Sit-ups (/60 s)	42.8 ± 2.0
Abalokov jump (cm)	56.2 ± 1.3
Grip strength (N)	507.4 ± 16.7
Flexibility (cm)	28.0 ± 1.6
$\dot{V}O_2max$ (ml/kg/min)	63.3 ± 3.1
Wingate Test :-	
Max power decline (%)	18.1 ± 2.3
Mean power decline (%)	22.1 ± 2.5

Acceptable power declines for mean and peak power in this population was estimated at 10%, considering their elite status. The percentage power decline of the Irish players (PPD = 18.1 ± 2.3; MPD = 22.1 ± 2.5) indicates a possible limitation to performance. Since athletes with a greater percentage of fast twitch fibres seem to produce greater anaerobic power during the Wingate Anaerobic Test (Jacobs, 1980), it is possible that the state of anaerobic conditioning of the players is a more dominant variable associated with performance than anthropometric variations. These fatigue values may have implications for the intermittent nature of squash in which recovery time is insufficient to reduce stroke volume, heart rate or oxygen consumption (Saltin, 1976).

3.4 Strength

Isometric and isotonic contractions were measured to provide an indication of strength in two areas important to squash - trunk strength and grip strength. Isometric (static) strength (grip strength) - a good gripping strength is important to the squash player for maintenance of rackety control for possibly five games in a match. The isometric grip strength of the Irish players was 507.4 ± 16.7 N which is comparable with other players tested in our laboratory.

Isotonic (dynamic) strength and endurance was measured using the sit-up test. Abdominal strength is important because of the twisting and turning that is involved in high level squash. The sit-up test results of the Irish players were lower than expected (42.3 ± 2.0). Results of greater than 55 sit-ups per minute are commonly achieved by elite level athletes in this laboratory and are not uncommon in racket sports.

3.4 Speed and agility

Running speed and agility (10 x 5 metre shuttle run) - running speed and agility are very important to the squash player due to the variation in the speed, height and angle of approach to the ball. The ability to cover short distances quickly will be of great advantage to the squash player who covers 12 metres per rally on average. The average score of the Irish players was 17.6 ± 1.5 s.

Maximum speed (30 metre sprint) - leg speed, stride length and stepping cadence all contribute to the overall maximum speed of an athlete. Due to both the nature of the game and the size of the court it is vital for the squash player to reach his maximum speed as quickly as possible. The average time for the 30 metre sprint was 4.84 ± 0.4 s.

Explosive power (Abalokov jump) - explosive power will enable the squash player to move quickly from the "T". The Abalokov jump test showed results for the Irish players of 56.1 ± 1.3 cm, which was greater than the Sergeant jump results of English county players (Brookes and Winter, 1985).

3.6 Flexibility

The sit and reach test was used to measure hamstring and lower back flexibility in the subjects. The flexibility of the Irish players was 28.0 ± 1.6 cm which is better than many other sporting groups. Maintenance of trunk flexibility is important in minimising the chance of chronic lower back pain (Lamb, 1989), in all sports but particularly squash.

4 Conclusions

This study has revealed the training status of the Irish squash players to be comparable with players in other studies. The average $\dot{V}$O2max value for the Irish squad was higher than the findings of Mercier (1987), Loots and Thiart (1983), Montpetit et al. (1987) and Steininger & Wodick (1987), though similar to Winter et al. (1984). The percentage body fat of the Irish players is high compared to other studies (Winter et al., 1984; Jaski & Bale, 1987; van Rensburg et al., 1982; Pyke et al., 1974), but lower than Mercier et al., (1987). Possible factors considered as a limit to performance of the Irish squash players were abdominal strength and endurance, the percentage fat and the decline in power caused by fatigue. A consequence of the study has been the development of individualised training programmes for the Irish squad which are monitored by the National Coach and updated according to further testing and alterations in the players' training behaviours (e.g. injury, tournaments, leagues). In addition the educational value of the programme is being monitored to assess the effectiveness of such projects in bringing about change in training behaviours and fitness parameters commensurate with success in squash.

This project and on-going research are in part funded by the Irish Squash Rackets Association, whose assistance is gratefully acknowledged.

5 References

Blanksby, B.A., Elliott, B.C. and Bloomfield, J. (1973) Telemetered heart rate responses of middle-aged sedentary males, middle-aged active males and "A" grade male squash players. **Med. J. Aust.**, 2, 477-481.

British Association of Sports Sciences. (1988) **Position statement on the physiological assessment of the elite competitor**. White Line Press, Leeds.

Brookes, F.B.C., and Winter, E.M. (1985) A comparison of 3 measures of short duration, maximal performance in trained squash players. **J. Hu. Mov't. Stud.**, 11, 105-112.

Docherty, D. and Howe, B. (1978) Heart rate response of squash players relative to their skill level. **Austra. J. Sports Med.**, 10, 90-92.

Durnin, J.V.G.A. and Womersley, J. (1974) Body fat assessed from total body density and its estimation from skinfold thicknesses. **Brit. J. Nutr.**, 32, 77-97.

Jacobs, I. (1980) The effects of thermal dehydration on performance of the Wingate anaerobic test. **Int. J. Sports Med.**, 1, 21-24.

Jaski, A. and Bale, P. (1987) Physique and body composition of top class squash players. **J. Sports Med. Phys. Fit.**, 27, 23-26.

Lamb, D.R. (1989) **Physiology of Exercise Responses and Adaptations.** MacMillan, Co. N.Y.

Loots, S.L. and Thiart, B.F. (1983) Energy demands of league and social squash players. **S. Afr. J. Res. Sport.Phys. Ed. Rec.**, 6, 13-19.

Mercier, M., Beillot, J., Gratas, A., Rochcongar, P., Lessard, Y., Andre, A.M. and Dassonville, J. (1987) Adaption to work load in squash players; laboratory tests and on court recordings. **J. Sports Med. Phys. Fit.**, 27, 98-104.

Montpetit, R.R., Beauchamp, L. and Leger, L. (1987) Energy requirements of squash and racquetball. **Phys. Sportsmed.**, 15, 106-112.

Montpetit, R.R. (1990) Applied physiology of squash. **Sports Med.**, 10, 31-41.

Pyke, S., Elliott, C. and Pyke, E. (1974) Performance testing of tennis and squash players. **Brit. J. Sports Med.**, 8, 80-86.

Reilly, T., Secher, N., Snell, P. and Williams, C. (1990) **Physiology of Sports.** E & F.N. Spon, London.

Saltin, B. (1976) Cardiovascular and pulmonary adaption to physical activity. **Med. Sport (Basel),** Vol. 9.

Steininger, K. and Wodick, R.E. (1987) Sport-specific fitness testing in squash. **Brit. J. Sports Med.**, 21, 23-26.

van Rensburg, J.P., van der Linde, A., Ackermann, P.C., Kielblock, A.J. and Strydom, N.B. (1982) Physiological profile of squash players. **S. Afr. J. Res. Sport Phys. Ed. Rec.**, 5, 25-56.

Winter, E.M., Fairley, R.T.D. and Kidd, D. (1984) The relationship of VO2max to fat free mass and running performance in competitive squash players. **Proc. Sport Sci. Conf.**, Bedford College, B1, 1-5.

Part Three
Biomechanics of Racket Sports

16 The biomechanics of tennis stroke production

B.C. Elliott
Department of Human Movement, The University of Western Australia, Perth, Australia

1 Introduction

All racket sport skills have a biomechanical base. Successful achievement of any stroke is therefore greatly influenced by the technique with which the player hits the ball. One of the most important objectives of a coach should then be to help pupils develop "good technique".

The decision on what constitutes good technique is based on a number of important factors. These include past experiences, current world trends and individual player characteristics.

1.1 Past experiences as a coach or player

The decision to initially teach a semi-western grip for a forehand drive to beginner tennis players may be based on the fact that experience has shown that small children need this type of grip to keep the racket vertical to the court, at impact, for balls that generally bounce relatively high compared to their stature. Another reason may have been that as a player, the coach found that this grip was the best for hitting topspin. This occurred as it not only permitted a vertical racket-face through a variety of ball heights, but also made the low-to-high racket path, necessary for topspin, easier to perform.

1.2 Current world trends

Data produced by Richard Schonborn (1992), the German National Coach, on international players on the European circuit, provide coaches with technique information from top level players. For example, on the forehand drive the great majority use a looped backswing, do not step into the ball and use an open stance. Also, information that players using a "leg drive" in the service action recorded 100% less double faults than players with no drive, provides coaches with obvious implications for teaching this aspect of service technique.

1.3 The individual flair of the player

Coaches must always consider the natural flair of the player when modifying technique. A dogmatic approach to coaching technique would probably have stifled the natural flair of a

Science and Racket Sports Edited by T. Reilly, M. Hughes and A. Lees.
Published in 1994 by E & FN Spon ISBN 0 419 18500 3

player such as Monica Seles.

The coach who has an understanding of the biomechanics of stroke production and can integrate the above characteristics with appropriate stroke mechanics to develop techniques which suit the individual, has the potential to become a very effective coach. Consider the changes to the teaching of topspin stroke production when it became known that the ball was only on the strings during impact for a period of approximately four milliseconds. Coaches then realised that no volitional change in movement could occur (e.g. rolling the racket over the ball) during impact. Players were then encouraged to develop low-to-high racket pathways and maintain a vertical racket at impact so that topspin could be imparted to the ball.

Before discussing how current research information has helped the coach to assess technique it is important to review how findings on the utilisation of "elastic energy" in stroke production and general court movement, have influenced coaching philosophy.

2 The Utilisation of Elastic Energy in Tennis

"Prepare early" is a common phrase used by coaches in racket sports. The logic behind such a statement is that for the ball/shuttle to be hit at the appropriate time and not "late" requires this early preparation. The question that must be answered is the role that energy stored during the stretch cycle of the movement (backswing or preparatory movements) plays in the subsequent muscle shortening cycle of the activity (forwardswing or movement to the ball). The mechanics underlying the use of elastic energy in stretch-shortening cycle activities is based on the fact that as the muscles and tendons are stretched they store elastic energy. During the shortening phase when the movement is reversed the stretched muscles, tendons and tissue recoil back to their original shape. When this occurs, a portion of the stored energy is recovered and assists the movement forwards. Biomechanical research has shown that the use of elastic energy has generally resulted in augmentation of performance derived from prior stretch. Increases in jump height by 10.3% (Asmussen and Bonde-Petersen, 1974) and 16.7% (Komi and Bosco, 1978) have been reported because of the above phenomenon. The mean augmentation of performance derived from stretch in the bench press of 18.7% (Wilson et al., 1991) was similar to the 13.7% increase in velocity produced by Bober et al. (1980) for a seated pushing movement.

The recovery of this stored energy is dependent to a large extent on the time between the stretching and shortening movement phases. The longer the delay, the greater is the loss of elastic energy. Research by Wilson and his associates (1991) has shown that after a delay of approximately one second, 55% of the stored energy was lost; after two seconds 80% was lost and after a four seconds delay all stored energy was lost.

For maximum efficiency in stroke production, players must practice allowing the backswing and forwardswing phases to flow from one to the other with minimal interruption. This is often even more important for young players with only low levels of muscle strength who need the additional assistance provided by this energy to overcome the inertia of the racket, which is often placed in a position of poor mechanical advantage at the completion of the backswing.

Elastic energy is also used to help a player move quickly in a balanced posture to the ball. From a ready position the body must "unweight" itself by accelerating downward towards the court. Deceleration of the body then applies stretch to the muscles, tendons and tissue which results in the storage of elastic energy. This stored energy can then at least partially be used to assist the lower limb drive in moving the player to the vicinity of the next stroke. The timing of the split step relies heavily on the ability of the player to co-ordinate this event with the opponent's ball impact.

3 Mechanical Considerations and Stroke Production

Examples from the literature are given to show how biomechanics plays an important role in effective stroke production. A comprehensive analysis of the tennis literature up to 1988 can be found in Elliott (1989).

3.1 The grip and stroke production

"Firmness of grip is NOT the major contributing factor in controlling post-impact ball velocity" - many tennis coaches believe that firmness of grip by the hand on the racket at impact is an important factor in determining the effectiveness of a return. Studies featuring central impacts showed that the ratio of the velocity of the ball post-impact compared to the velocity pre-impact was independent of the level of grip pressure (Baker and Putnam 1979; Watanabe et al., 1979; Elliott, 1982). Liu (1983) used a mathematical model based on impact theory to provide analytical support for the previous experimental findings.

Hatze (1976) reported that an off-centre impact may be accompanied by an increase in recoil impulse, which need not be transmitted to the ball. Elliott (1982) while reporting that rebound ratios were reduced for off-centre compared to central impacts also showed that higher off-centre ratios were associated with an increase in grip pressure. Grabiner et al. (1983) demonstrated that post-impact ball velocity was not reduced in some off-centre impacts where the closing velocity between the racket and the ball was low. Therefore while a firm grip is not essential for central impacts it is an integral factor in off-centre impacts.

3.2 "Cushion grips reduce impact shock"

A study by Hatze (1992) showed that cushion grip bands statistically reduced impact shock and post-impact racket vibrations. "High performance tennis players vary the pressure of the hand on the racket for different groundstrokes" - the pattern of hand force loading in the one-handed backhand was shown to be different to that for the forehand (Knudson and White, 1989; Knudson, 1991). These authors suggested that hypothenar forces were critical gripping forces in the forehand prior to impact, while force in the thenar region of the hand was the primary gripping force in the backhand drive.

3.3 The influence of racket size on early skill development

"Young beginners must use a racket related to their physical characteristics" - research literature suggests that enhanced performance results when the physical characteristics of the player and the racket are optimised. Ward and Groppel (1980) investigated the influence of racket length on the stroke mechanics of the forehand drive of eight-year old children. These children swung a shorter racket (58.4 cm) with a higher horizontal velocity and a more vertical racket-face at impact than did children who were taught with a longer racket (68.6 cm). The path of the racket in the forwardswing phase of the stroke clearly showed that these subjects were unable to control the moment of inertia of the longer racket during this phase of the stroke. Elliott (1981) investigated the influence of racket length on the learning of tennis skills in sixty children aged 7 to 10 years. Two groups of children were matched for age, height, weight and manual dexterity and were taught over an 8 week coaching period. One group used a junior racket (66 cm, 310 g) while the other used a sub-junior racket (61 cm, 265 g). The group taught with the sub-junior rackets recorded superior results in the Hewitt revision of the Dyer tennis tests (Hewitt, 1965) and practical tests on the service, forehand drive and backhand drive when compared to the group taught using the junior rackets. Only in tests of volleying performance, where the moment of inertia of the racket was of lesser concern to the stroke, were the results not in favour of stroke production with the sub-junior racket. Both studies clearly demonstrated the need for racket size to be related to the physical characteristics of children.

3.4 The forehand

"The racket and shoulder alignment at the completion of the backswing are pointed beyond a perpendicular to the back fence" - high performance players using a multi-segment forehand rotated the shoulders a mean 10° beyond a line perpendicular to the back fence and positioned the racket 52° beyond this orientation at the completion of the backswing (Elliott et al., 1989a).

"The majority of elite players emphasise trunk rotation and use an open stance in forehand stroke production in preference to stepping into the ball" (Schonborn, 1992). Rotation of the trunk and lower limb drive increased racket-shoulder rotation over the forwardswing so that this forward movement was responsible for approximately 10% of final racket velocity at impact for a group of high performance players. The shoulders rotated through an angle of 95° from the backswing position so that at impact the alignment was almost parallel to the net (Elliott et al., 1989a).

"The angle at the elbow joint during the fowardswing changes to increase racket velocity and the racket trajectory in the modern forehand". Players who used a multi-segment forehand recorded a significantly higher maximum elbow flexion velocity of 3.3 rad/s and wrist flexion velocity (2.6 rad/s) at impact than those who used the "old style" single unit forehand (elbow: 0.6 rad/s; wrist: 1.4 rad/s). The multi- segment stroke is therefore characterised by movement of the individual segments of the upper limb (upper arm, forearm, hand) in an attempt to generate higher velocity (i.e., as in the service action). Whereas the "old style" forehand was generally thought to move more as a single segment. Players who used the multi-segment stroke were able to quickly change the racket-trajectory (0.3 rad to 0.8 rad upward movement) immediately prior to impact by this flexion velocity at the elbow joint (Elliott et al., 1989a). Higher resultant ball velocities were produced by the multi-segment group (34.5 m/s) compared to the single unit group (32.3 m/s).

"Any type of backswing (straight, looped, about the elbow) can be used with a multi-segment forwardswing" - coaches have often been told that a multi-segment forehand can only be hit using a looped backswing where the racket was rotated primarily about the elbow. In the study by Elliott et al. (1989a) all subjects used a looped backswing. However, observation of professional players shows that all types of backswings are used in preparation for a multi-segment forwardswing.

3.5 The backhand

"The racket and shoulder alignment at the completion of the backswing are pointed beyond a perpendicular to the back fence" - a mean rotation of the shoulder alignment 0.6 rad beyond a perpendicular to the back fence and a racket orientation 0.7 rad beyond this point were recorded for high performance players (Elliott et al., 1989b). Many professional players can be observed preparing for a backhand by positioning the racket almost parallel with the back fence.

"The elbow joint plays an integral role in the development of racket velocity in the backhand stroke" - high performance players filmed hitting a topspin backhand drive (Elliott et al., 1989b) or backspin backhand drive (Elliott and Christmass, unpublished observations) both used movement at the elbow joint to generate racket velocity for impact. Subjects hitting a topspin backhand extended the elbow joint from a mean angle of 2.1 rad at the completion of the backswing to 2.9 rad at impact. However, elbow joint angular velocity, which had recorded peak values 0.08 s prior to impact was minimal at impact.

Similar data were recorded for the backspin backhand where a mean elbow joint angle of 2.9 rad was recorded at impact. Elbow extension was identified as an important velocity generating aspect of the stroke accounting for approximately 25% of the racket velocity at impact. Elbow joint angular velocity in a similar manner to the topspin stroke was minimal during impact.

"The racket trajectory and racket-face angle vary for topspin and backspin strokes and for backspin strokes of varying height" - in the topspin backhand an initial upward trajectory of 0.3 increased dramatically to 0.8 rad immediately prior to impact and the racket-face at impact was perpendicular to the court for balls of approximately hip height (Elliott et al., 1989b). In the backspin backhand a mean downward trajectory of 0.4 rad for hip height impacts was reduced to 0.3 rad for shoulder height impacts. At impact the racket-face was bevelled more open for the lower stroke (0.2 rad) than was recorded for the higher impact (0.1 rad) (Elliott and Christmass, unpublished observations).

3.6 The service

"The height that the ball should be "pushed" should be to approximately the top of the racket if a player is to hit a relatively stationary ball". Beerman and Sher (1981) reported that when the ball was tossed 1.2 m above the racket, a height commonly reported in the literature, then the player has to make contact with a ball moving at approximately 5 m/s.

"A good leg drive will not only increase the displacement of the racket but may cause impact to occur off the ground". A mean maximum vertical shoulder velocity of 1.7 m/s during the leg drive produced a force at the shoulder that was eccentric to the racket-limb, thus causing a downward rotation of this limb as measured by a velocity of the racket of -5.8 m/s downward behind the back. This naturally created a larger loop behind the back (Elliott et al., 1986). A strong "leg drive" was shown to cause the body to leave the ground prior to impact in the majority of high performance players filmed (Elliott and Wood, 1983; Elliott et al., 1986).

"An UP and OUT action prior to and after impact is required to produce some forward rotation of the ball in the flat power serve" - a study of high performance 12 year olds, 15 year olds and adults showed that an "UP and OUT" movement of the racket about impact, although a characteristic of a mature service action, was not commonly found in the younger age categories (Elliott, 1983).

The so-called "flat serve" would therefore appear to be a misnomer for many highly-skilled players. The four adults filmed in this study were all able to perform a power serve with forward rotation (a combination of topspin and sidespin). This forward rotation was at least partially caused by a service swing where the racket moved in an upward trajectory immediately prior to impact and then continued to move forward and upward after impact. No significant ball rotation resulted from an impact where the racket moved in a straight line, both one frame prior to, and following impact, which was a characteristic of the 12 years group.

"The foot-up and foot-back service styles are characterised by different biomechanical techniques". The force curves caused by the feet pushing against the court for the foot-up and foot-back service techniques following the initial transference of weight were different in pattern. Vertical ground reaction force levels were larger throughout the drive phase prior to impact for the foot-up group than the foot-back group (Elliott and Wood, 1983). These larger forces resulted in a higher impact position and a better 'up and out' racket trajectory for the foot-up technique when compared to the other technique. Players who used the foot-back technique recorded larger horizontal forces and this technique may therefore be more conducive to rapid movement to the net. Ball velocities were similar for both techniques. Players may of course prefer to position the feet somewhere between the two extremes (back foot brought up to the front or left in initial ready position).

"The upper arm plays a very large role in the generation of racket velocity" - preliminary studies have shown that the upper arm plays a significant role in the generation of racket speed in the tennis serve (Deporte et al., 1990; Sprigings et al., 1993). Research data, admittedly from small samples, have shown that horizontal flexion of the upper arm contributes approximately 20%, while upper arm inward rotation contributes approximately 25% or more of final racket velocity.

3.7 The volley

"The length of the backswing varies for volleys hit at the service-line when compared to those closer to the net". The racket was positioned behind the hitting-shoulder for volleys played at the service-line by high performance players, while in volleys played closer to the net the racket was positioned relatively close to this shoulder. The racket was logically always displaced further behind the body for backhand volleys than for forehand volleys

(Elliott et al., 1988).

"The racket must move in the direction of the hit for an effective volley" - data from a group of high performance players when compared to proficient volleyers showed that the high performance group recorded greater wrist and tip of racket velocities when compared to the proficient group. The high performance players moved their racket forward and downward after impact while the proficient players moved their rackets in a "dishing action" where the racket-face opened and moved more in a downward trajectory (Elliott et al., 1988).

3.8 Approach shot

"The mechanics of the backspin and topspin forehand approach shots are significantly different". The mean upward trajectory for the racket-head of 0.5 rad for the topspin stroke was very different to the downward path of 0.3 rad towards the ball recorded for the backspin approach shot hit by high performance players. Further compensation occurred in the mean angle of the racket face at impact that was bevelled open by 0.1 rad in the backspin shot and closed by 0.1 rad in the topspin stroke (Elliott and Marsh, 1989).

4 Conclusion

Biomechanical information must therefore be used by coaches in a number of different ways. They need to integrate an understanding of the mechanical characteristics of each stroke with their own coaching philosophies in an endeavour to decide how each stroke should be taught. That is, having accepted that a good "leg drive" is an important mechanical characteristic of the service action, each coach must then decide HOW and WHEN to teach this technique to young performers. Coaches must also use biomechanical data to establish a range of acceptability when analysing selected aspects of stroke production. Information on the level of knee flexion in the service action of elite performers should be used as a guide in deciding whether a player needs more or less knee flexion to improve their technique and hopefully service effectiveness. Progressive coaches will therefore integrate mechanics into their coaching to develop stroke techniques which suit the individual player.

5 References

Asmussen, E. and Bonde-Petersen, F. (1974) Storage of elastic energy in skeletal muscle in Man. **Acta Physiol. Scand**.,91, 385-392.

Baker, J.A. and Putnam, C.A. (1979) Tennis racket and ball responses during impact under clamped and freestanding conditions. **Res. Quart**., 50, 164-170.

Beerman, J. and Sher, L. (1981). Improve tennis service through mathematics, **JOHPER**, 52, 55-56.

Bober, T., Jaskolski, E. and Nowacki, Z. (1980) Study on eccentric-concentric contraction of the upper body extremity muscles. **J. Biomech**., 13, 135-138.

Deporte, E. van Gheluwe, B. and Hebbelinck, M. (1990) A three-dimensional cinematographical analysis of arm and racket at impact in tennis in **Biomechanics of Human Movement: Applications in Rehabilitation, Sports and Ergonomics** (eds N. Berme and A. Cappozzo) Bertec Corp., Ohio, pp 460-467.

Elliott, B. (1981) Tennis racquet selection: a factor in early skill development. **Aust. J. Sports Sci.**, 1, 23-25.

Elliott, B. (1982) Tennis: the influence of grip firmness on reaction impulse and rebound velocity. **Med. Sci. Sports Exerc.**, 14, 348-352.

Elliott, B. (1983) Spin and the power serve in tennis. **J. Human Mov't. Stud.,** 9, 97-104.

Elliott, B.C. (1989) Tennis strokes and equipment in **Biomechanics of Sport** (ed K. Vaughan) CRC Press, Florida, pp 263-288.

Elliott, B. and Marsh, T. (1989) A biomechanical comparison of the topspin and backspin forehand approach shots in tennis. **J. Sports Sci.**, 7, 215-227.

Elliott, B. and Wood, G. (1983) The biomechanics of the foot-up and foot-back tennis service techniques. **Aust. J. Sport Sci.**, 3, 3-6.

Elliott, B. Marsh, T. and Blanksby, B. (1986) A three-dimensional cinematographic analysis of the tennis serve. **Int. J. Sport Biom.**, 2, 260-271.

Elliott, B., Marsh, T. and Overheu, P. (1989a) A biomechanical comparison of the multisegment and single unit topspin forehand drives in tennis. **Int. J. Sport Biom.**, 5, 350-364.

Elliott, B.C. Marsh, A.P. and Overheu, P.R. (1989b) The topspin backhand drive in tennis: a biomechanical analysis. **J. Human Mov't. Stud.,** 16, 1-16.

Elliott, B.C. Overheu, P. and Marsh, A.P. (1988) The service line and net volley in tennis: a cinematographic analysis. **Aust. J. Sci. Med. Sport**, 20, 10-18.

Grabiner, M.D. Groppel, J.L. and Campbell, K.R. (1983) Resultant tennis ball velocity as a function of off-centre impact and grip firmness. **Med. Sci. Sports Exerc.**, 15, 542-544.

Hatze, H. (1976) Forces and duration of impact and grip tightness during the tennis stroke. **Med. Sci. Sports Exerc.,** 8, 88-95.

Hatze, H. (1992) The effectiveness of grip bands in reducing racquet vibration transfer and slipping. **Med. Sci. Sports Exerc.**, 24, 226-230.

Hewitt, J.E. (1965) Revision of the Dyer backboard tennis test. **Res. Quart.**, 36, 153-157.

Knudson, D.V. (1991) Forces on the hand in the tennis one-handed backhand. **Int. J. Sport Biom.**, 7, 282-292.

Knudson, D.V. and White, S.C. (1989) Forces on the hand in the tennis forehand drive: applicaton of force sensing resistors. **Int. J. Sport Biom.**, 5, 324-331.

Komi, P.V. and Bosco, C. (1978) Utilisation of stored elastic energy in leg extensor muscles by men and women. **Med. Sci. Sports,** 10, 261-265.

Liu, Y.K. (1983) Mechanical analysis of racket and ball during impact. **Med. Sci. Sports Exerc.,** 15, 388-392.

Schonborn, R. (1992) Paper presented 6th I.T.F. East Asian Coaches Workshop, Indonesia.

Sprigings, E. Marshall, R. Elliott, B. and Jennings, L. (1993) A method for determining the effectiveness of arm segment rotations (3-D) in producing racket-head speed. **J. Biomech.** (In press)

Ward, T. and Groppel, J. (1980) Sport implement selection: can it be based upon authropometric indicators? **Mot. Skills Theor. Pract**., 4, 103-110.
Watanabe, T., Ikegami, Y. and Miyashita, M. (1979) Tennis: the effect of grip firmness on ball velocity after impact. **Med. Sci. Sports**, 11, 359-261.
Wilson, G.J. Elliott, B.C. and Wood, G.A. (1991) The effect on performance of imposing a delay during a stretch-shorten cycle movement. **Med. Sci. Sports Exerc.**, 23, 364-370.

17 A three-dimensional analysis of the tennis serves of National (British) and County standard male players

R.M. Bartlett, J. Piller and S. Miller
Crewe and Alsager Faculty, Manchester Metropolitan University, Alsager, UK

1 Introduction

There are certain qualities that determine the degree and level of success a tennis player can experience. The primary components of tennis playing success are good stroke mechanics, appropriate physiological capacities and appropriate psychological attributes. Each has its own relative importance to the tennis player and improvement represents the successful integration of those three factors in the competitive environment.

Of the skills that are performed during a tennis match, the serve has been reported by several authors as being the most important stroke (for example Elliott and Kilderry, 1983). The serve can often be a dominating factor in high level tennis, especially in the men's game, with many players ultimately using the stroke as a good weapon for success (Elliott, 1983). However, it is also a very difficult stroke to master. The serve is a stroke that has received considerable investigation in both the scientific and non-scientific literature. Much of the knowledge concerning the techniques of executing the various types of serve has been acquired from the writings of coaches and players, and hence the scientific value of such knowledge is questionable. Although the serve is difficult to analyse effectively without 3-D methods, few such studies have been reported. The majority of studies fail to report adequately the methodological procedures, including details of calibration techniques and subsequent digitisation and smoothing routines employed. There is a general lack of statistical analysis of findings and a complete neglect of the experimental errors incurred during both the filming and the digitisation processes.

As previously outlined, the effectiveness of the tennis serve in today's men's game is primarily dependant on the post-impact ball speed. A conceptual model of the service action was hence established to identify the factors which determine the speed of projection of the served tennis ball. The objectives of the study were to undertake a three-dimensional cinematographical comparison of the service action of British and county male tennis players, and to identify the major kinematic parameters which would result in a greater post-impact ball speed. These parameters included: the height of the ball toss and the height of the ball at impact; the timing of the movement of the back-foot forward; kinematics of the backswing and force-production phases, with particular reference to the knee and elbow joints; hip-shoulder separation angles; horizontal and linear segment end-point speeds; and body position at impact.

Science and Racket Sports Edited by T. Reilly, M. Hughes and A. Lees.
Published in 1994 by E & FN Spon ISBN 0 419 18500 3

2 Methodology

Twenty six national (British) and county male tennis players were filmed at various venues during the summer of 1990. Two phase-locked Photosonics 1PL cine cameras operating at 200 Hz, verified by an internal timing light, were used to film each player performing three first serves into a target area. The shutter opening on each camera was set to 160 degrees producing a corresponding exposure time of 1/450 second.

Each camera was fitted with a Schneider Kreuznach Variogon 1:2 - 18/90 zoom lens, mounted on a Kennett tripod and loaded with 120 m rolls of Eastman Ektachrome colour reversal video news film. The two cameras were positioned with optical axes approximately 90 degrees apart to obtain the most appropriate views of the subject and to ensure that all markers on the calibration frame were clearly distinguishable.

Joint centre markers, located with respect to bony landmarks, as recommended by Plagenhoef (1971), were used to aid in the location of the axes of joint movements during digitisation. Prior to filming each player was given unlimited warm-up time to complete his service practice and familiarise himself with the experimental environment.

A triaxial calibration structure containing markers of known spatial co-ordinates encompassing the field of movement of the service action was filmed for several seconds. This structure was then removed from the experimental area and the player filmed in the same area with identical camera positions.

One successful service action of each of seven top British (ranked within the British top 20) and 7 county (ranked lower than '0' on the VW rating system) right-handed male tennis players was analyzed. Following processing the films were projected by NAC analysis projectors onto a digitising tablet and digitised in sequence. Eighteen joint centres and six points on the racket were digitised using a TDS HR48 series digitising tablet interfaced to an Acorn Archimedes 440 computer running a cine digitising program (Bartlett, 1990). A DLT algorithm allowing for linear lens distortion was used for reconstruction of 3-D world co-ordinates from 2-D image co-ordinates. Removal of noise from the digitised data was effected by the use of a generalised cross-validated quintic spline smoothing technique implemented for the Archimedes by Bartlett (1990).

3 Results and Discussion

3.1 Movement of the back foot and the mass centre

A significant difference ($P<0.005$) between the two groups of players was observed regarding the timing of the movement of the back-foot forward during the backswing or preparation phase of the serve, which ended when shoulder girdle retraction and rightward rotation of the trunk had been completed (Anderson, 1979). The county players moved their back-foot forward on average one second prior to impact, whereas the British players initiated forward movement of the back-foot 0.60 seconds prior to impact. In spite of individual variations being observed within the two groups, the results of the present study indicate that the British players had a tendency to adopt the foot-back style, while the county group players were proponents of the foot-up technique. The high correlation found between the timing of the movement of the back-foot forward and the resultant ball speed at impact ($r=0.075$) tended to indicate that the foot- back service technique was more conducive to greater post-impact ball speeds.

During the force-production phase, from the end of the preparation phase to impact (Anderson, 1979), the British players recorded significantly greater ($P<0.05$) mass centre movement in the vertical direction, whereas the county players recorded significantly greater ($P<0.05$) mass centre movement in the horizontal direction. These latter findings tend to disagree with earlier observations of Elliott and Wood (1983). It therefore appears from the findings of the present study that the movement of the back-foot forward early in the preparation phase by the county subjects could have caused a reduction in the stability of the server by creating a small base of support.

3.2 Backswing (preparation) phase

During the backswing phase, individual differences both within and between groups were found regarding the minimum angular displacement values of the elbow joint. The mean minimum elbow angle of 1.3 ± 0.25 rad reported in the 3-D study of Elliott et al. (1986) was far higher than the mean value of 0.85 ± 0.25 rad obtained in the present investigation. Previous research has also observed that the elbow joint did not fully flex when the racket looped down the back, but rather the humerus rotated while in the abducted position to increase the movement of the racket behind the server's back. The biomechanical function of elbow joint flexion during the backswing phase is to reduce the racket's moment of inertia and to place the racket in a position behind the server's back for the subsequent elbow extension. Although the amount of arm rotation was not measured in the present study, it appears from the findings that too much elbow flexion, present in the majority of players, may have affected the potential for effective generation of racket momentum later in the kinematic chain.

Minimum knee angles of 1.94 ± 0.18 rad and 1.97 ± 0.24 rad were recorded for the British and county players respectively. The present mean knee angle of 1.96 ± 0.2 rad was again lower than the previous 3-D value of 2.22 ± 0.4 rad reported by Elliott et al. (1986). A conceptual model of the serving action, as well as previous research, would suggest that there is a optimal knee angle at maximum flexion for best generation and utilisation of the ground reaction forces. It could be speculated that too much or too little knee flexion would have caused insufficient transfer of the ground reaction forces and subsequently affected the sequential movement of other segments within the kinematic chain.

3.3 Kinematics of the hip and shoulder

Although the British players recorded greater linear velocity values compared to the county players at the hip, shoulder and end of racket, none of the differences between the two groups was found to be statistically significant. However, only three players produced their maximum velocity values for the downward movement of the racket as the hip had reached its maximum vertical velocity.

Similar trends were observed in the 3-D study by Elliott et al. (1986). These authors reported that those players who were classified by three professional coaches as having a good leg drive were able to achieve those maximum values for the downward movement of the racket as the hip had reached its maximum vertical velocity.

3.4 The force production phase

The rotation of the hips and trunk was followed by movement of the racket from the back scratch position to the point of impact. Although the duration of the preparation phase was identical for both groups (0.12 s), the British players were able to attain an increased speed of rotation of the right arm (British - 13.6 ± 2.4 rad/s; county - 11.5 ± 0.97 rad/s). This appeared to be a major factor contributing to the increase in racket momentum preceding impact.

Some correlation was found to exist between the minimum elbow angle and the angular velocity of the elbow at impact. This supports the earlier observation that the high degree of elbow flexion present in the backswing phase in the majority of players may have ultimately hindered the potential for effective generation of racket momentum later in the kinematic chain.

3.5 Segment end-point linear speeds

All players were seen to show a progressive increase in the resultant linear speeds of segment end-points from the shoulder joint to the end of the racket as the time of impact approached, with the British players producing greater mean speed values at the shoulder, elbow and wrist. The majority of players recorded their maximal speed values prior to impact: the more distal the joint, the closer the time of occurrence of maximal speed approached impact. A similar trend was also reported in the previous 3-D studies of Elliott et al. (1986) and Van Gheluwe and Hebbelinck (1983).

3.6 Ball movement

Individual variations in the ball toss were observed, with the mean ball impact position occurring 0.56 ± 0.30 m below the peak height of the ball toss. Although there is no perfect ball toss height, effective generation of racket head momentum will only be achieved if co-ordination exists between the service toss and the height of the ball at impact.

Similar mean values of 1.48 ± 0.10 and 1.41 ± 0.05 were calculated for the height of impact as a ratio to standing height for the British and county players respectively. The results are slightly lower than the previous mean value of 1.53 ± 0.04 reported by Elliott et al. (1986), which indicates the potential for increased leg drive for players in the present study.

A significantly ($P<0.05$) higher mean post-impact ball speed of 48.5 ± 4.1 m/s was found for the British players, compared to the mean value recorded by the county players of 40.3 ± 6.0 m/s.

3.7 Body position at impact

Front knee joint angles of 2.7 ± 0.29 rad and 2.9 ± 0.15 rad recorded by the British and county players at impact were lower than anticipated. A more extended knee joint could have resulted in an increase in the maximum lifting height and may have increased the potential for hip rotation owing to the increased length of lever arm and reduced moment of inertia. The British players recorded higher angular displacement impact values for the thigh to horizontal and right thigh to trunk angles, with the difference in the former measurement found to be statistically significant ($P<0.05$). The more extended trunk angle was linked with an increase in the hitting height, as a correlation was found to exist between the right thigh to trunk values and the impact position relative to standing height. Very similar mean elbow joint angles of 2.5 ± 0.21 rad (British) and 2.6 ± 0.10 rad (county) indicated that the upper limb of both groups was angled forward into the court at impact.

4 Conclusion

In conclusion, the increased hitting height, increased speed of rotation of the hitting arm and effective timing and speed of movement of the limbs appeared to be the major kinematic parameters which resulted in a significantly higher mean post-impact ball speed for the British players compared to the mean value recorded by the county players.

5 References

Anderson, M.B. (1979) Comparison of muscle patterning in the overarm throw and tennis serve. **Res. Quart.**, 50, 541.

Bartlett, R.M. (1990) The definition, design, implementation and use of a comprehensive sports biomechanics software package for the Acorn Archimedes computer, in **Biomechanics in Sports: Proceedings of the VIIIth International Symposium of the Society of Biomechanics in Sports** (eds M. Nosek, D. Sojka, W.E. Morrison and P. Susanka), Conex, Prague, pp. 273-278.

Elliott, B. (1983) Spin and power in tennis. **J. Human Mov't. Stud.**, 9, 97-104.

Elliott, B. and Kilderry, R. (1983) **The Art and Science of Tennis**, Saunders, New York.

Elliott, B. and Wood, G. (1983) The biomechanics of the foot-up and the foot-back tennis service techniques. **Austr. J. Sport Sci.**, 3, 3-5.

Elliott, B., Marsh, T. and Blanksby, B. (1986) A three-dimensional analysis of the tennis serve. **Int. J. Sport Biomech.**, 2, 260-271.

Plagenhoef, S. (1971) **Patterns of Human Movement: a Cinematographic Analysis.** Prentice Hall, Englewood Cliffs.

Van Gheluwe, B.V. and Hebbelinck, M. (1983) The kinematics of the service movement in tennis: a three-dimensional cinematographical approach, in **Biomechanics IX-B** (eds D. Winter, R. Norman, R. Wells, K. Hayes and A. Patla), Human Kinetics, Champaign, pp. 343-348.

18 A biomechanical analysis of the tennis serve, examining the effect of altering the foot fault rule

R. Higgins and A. Lees
Centre for Sport and Exercise Sciences, School of Human Sciences, Liverpool John Moores University, Liverpool, UK

1 Introduction

The game of tennis has dramatically changed over the last fifteen years in that it is now a game dominated by the serve. The increase in the speed of the serve has meant that aces and one or two shot rallies are now becoming commonplace. It is now accepted on the professional circuit that it is difficult to compete at the top level without a fast serve.

The International Tennis Federation now acknowledges that it must intervene to control the power produced as a result of technological advancements in equipment, greater levels of player's fitness, and improved stroke production. There are several ways in which this can be achieved. The non-playing time between points could be reduced from 25 to 20 seconds to allow the players less recovery time; the speed of tennis balls in flight could be reduced by lowering the pressure and different speeds of tennis balls produced for play on different surfaces; court dimensions could be altered (e.g. to create a service line behind the baseline to allow the opponent extra preparatory time to receive the ball, or to alter the dimensions of the service box) although this could prove costly to implement on an international scale. One suggestion favoured by the International Tennis Federation is to control the speed of the serve by altering the foot fault rule so that one foot remains in contact with the ground until the racket and ball have made contact.

The aim of this research was to examine the effect of ball pressure and the altered foot fault rule for controlling serving speed.

2 Method

Eight male tennis players (mean age 22.5 years) of top club or regional standard participated in the study. Each was filmed (video camera at 50 Hz with high speed shutter at 0.001 s) performing a series of flat first serves. The success of each serve was noted on a data collection sheet. A variety of pressurised (PRESS) and normal (NORM) tennis balls was used in random order although the subjects were not aware of this fact. The first ten serves were performed using the traditional foot fault rule (TRAD) and the second ten using the alternative rule (ALT). The subjects served from the right to left hand service box and the video camera was positioned to the

Science and Racket Sports Edited by T. Reilly, M. Hughes and A. Lees.
Published in 1994 by E & FN Spon ISBN 0 419 18500 3

right of the subjects. This allowed the entire movement of the subject and the initial flight of the tennis ball to be captured on film for future data analysis. The collection of data was repeated ten weeks later in order to examine the continuity and reliability of the subject's performance.

Data were obtained from the video recordings via a computerised video digitisation system. This enabled the average horizontal (VX), vertical (VY) and vector (VV) velocities and the angle of the tennis ball to the horizontal to be computed. The fastest two serves from each category were subsequently analysed in detail. This used a 13-segment whole-body model defined by 18 points. It was used to examine the displacement of the centre of mass in the horizontal and vertical directions and the velocity of the racket head, wrist, elbow and shoulder throughout the movement.

3 Results

3.1 The tennis balls

The characteristics of the tennis balls were established by two experimental investigations. The first (Table 1) involved the progressive static loading and unloading of each tennis ball with weights to compare the hysteresis energy lost during a deformation cycle. The second (Table 2) measured the rebound height of the tennis balls when dropped from a height of 1 m onto two types of surface (rubber and concrete).

Table 1. Tennis ball - energy lost in static loading (J)

Ball type	Loading	Unloading	Energy loss	
PRESSURISED	120.4	143.1	22.6	
NORMAL	129.6	146.2	16.6	P <0.01

Table 2. Tennis balls - rebound height (m)

ball type	Rubber	Concrete
PRESSURISED	51.25 +/- 1.04	57.81 +/- 1.43
NORMAL	65.5 +/- 1.87	73.78 +/- 2.16
	P < 0.01	P < 0.01

3.2 The serves

In session 1 (Table 3) significant differences were found between the two serves for the horizontal and vector velocities of the tennis ball; the velocities of the wrist, elbow and shoulder; and the horizontal displacement of the centre of mass at impact. The results produced during the traditional serve were greater for all the variables except the vertical velocity of the tennis ball and the angle that the ball created with the horizontal, both of which were smaller.

Table 3. Kinematic data at impact for session 1

Varaible	Serve TRAD	ALT	P	Ball type PRESS	NORM	P
Ball velocity and angle						
ball-VX (m/s)	44.55	42.76	0.04	3.77	43.53	0.78
ball-VY (m/s)	-5.68	-5.46	0.77	-5.80	-5.34	0.55
ball-VV (m/s)	45.08	43.18	0.04	44.28	43.99	0.75
ball ANGLE (deg)	-8.13	-7.21	0.14	-7.45	-7.88	0.48
joint and racket velocity						
WRIST (m/s)	10.16	9.33	0.00	9.79	9.70	0.71
ELBOW (m/s)	4.63	4.13	0.02	4.37	4.38	0.98
SHOULDER (m/s)	2.27	1.79	0.02	2.09	1.97	0.53
RACKET HEAD(m/s)	29.10	28.46	0.09	28.59	28.97	0.31
CM position relative to the baseline						
horizontal (m)	0.14	-0.08	<0.01	0.03	0.03	0.90
vertical (m)	1.22	1.12	0.20	1.13	1.21	0.34

Table 4. Kinematic data at impact for session 2

VARIABLE	Serve TRAD	ALT	P	Ball type PRESS	NORM	P
Ball velocity and angle						
ball-VX (m/s)	45.02	43.61	0.16	44.04	44.58	0.58
ball-VY (m/s)	-7.81	-7.83	0.94	-7.84	-7.80	0.91
ball-VV (m/s)	45.73	44.34	0.17	44.77	45.30	0.59
ball-ANGLE (deg)	-9.86	-10.02	0.36	-10.10	-9.95	0.70
joint and racket velocity						
WRIST (m/s)	9.90	8.93	<0.01	9.41	9.42	0.94
ELBOW (m/s)	4.26	3.39	<0.01	3.80	3.85	0.60
SHOULDER (m/s)	1.81	1.29	<0.01	1.54	1.56	0.87
RACKET HEAD(m/s)	28.85	27.83	<0.01	28.00	28.69	0.05
CM position relative to the baseline						
horizontal (m)	0.251	0.030	<0.001	0.116	0.150	0.82
vertical (m)	1.231	1.195	0.364	1.200	1.221	0.96

In session 2 (Table 4) no significant differences in ball kinematics were found between the traditional and alternative serves. Significant differences were obtained for the racket head and arm joint velocities and the horizontal displacement of the centre of mass with the traditional serve being faster and further over the baseline at impact. The resultant ball velocities produced by both types of serve were higher in session 2 than in session 1, although these were not significant. Conversely, the arm and racket head velocities had decreased, suggesting an improved striking technique during the latter session. The centre of mass at impact was further over the baseline in session 2 compared to session 1, again suggesting a small modification of the striking technique. The subjects were found to improve their serve success rate. In session 1, 65% of the traditional serves and 56% of the alternative serves were successful, compared to 70% and 62% for each serve respectively in session 2. These results further emphasise the improvement in technique made by the players.
There were no significant differences between the two types of tennis ball in either session.

4 Discussion and Conclusions

The results on the tennis ball characteristics show that the pressurised ball performed significantly differently to the normal ball both in terms of static loading energy loss and dynamic rebound height. The term 'pressurised' refers to the condition under which the ball is kept and not the absolute pressure of the ball. It is evident from these results that the 'pressurised' ball was lower in internal pressure than the normal ball. Despite these findings, there were no significant differences in the performance characteristics of each ball during the serve. It may be that during contact with the racket the properties of the strings and racket are more dominant than the properties of the ball. As the ball has effectively zero horizontal velocity at impact it has no energy to lose, and so energy is imparted by the racket and strings only. Ball pressure is an important factor in baseline strokes where the ball has some initial energy, and the speed of the racket is lower, but it is concluded that it has no effect on the serve.The traditional serve produced significantly higher post-impact ball velocities during session 1 by about 2 m/s, but by session 2 this difference had been reduced to 1.5 m/s, and was non-significant. The improvement in ball speed in session 2 can be attributed to improved technique, but a reduction of the difference between the two types of serve suggests that an adaptation to serve type can be made. This will reduce the effectiveness of the serve change as a method of controlling serve speed. It is concluded that a serve rule change would only have a marginal effect and its value should be questioned. Therefore it is recommended that other methods for controlling service speed should be considered.

19 A biomechanical analysis of the double

R.A. Stretch
Department of Human Movement Studies, University of Fort Hare, South Africa

1 Introduction

In the coaching of the batting technique in cricket, a task requiring a double- handed grip, the roles of the top and bottom hands have recently been the attention of lengthy discussions by cricket coaches. This has been brought about by the predominance of limited-overs cricket where batsmen are required to score runs, even off good deliveries. To do this the players have had to improvise and thus "work" the ball into the gaps in the field. Thus the aims of the study were to evaluate the variability of grip forces in a typical defensive and attacking stroke in cricket, and to determine whether any differences occur when batting against different types of bowlers on different types of pitches. The results of this study could be applied to other racket sports where the double-handed grip is used.

A number of biomechanical and tennis authorities (Bunn, 1972; Plagenhoef, 1971; Hatze, 1976; Broer and Zernicke, 1979) believe that grip firmness is one of the most important factors in hitting a tennis ball effectively. However, the tennis instructional literature does not clearly explain the forces on the hand when playing double-handed strokes. Furthermore, despite extensive research into grip forces on the hand when playing the forehand drive, a detailed description of the double-handed grip forces has not been reported.

2 Methods

A standard size short-handle Slazenger cricket bat was instrumented to respond to grip forces applied by both the top and bottom hands during the execution of the stroke. The forces for each hand were measured by force sensors linked to a silicon rubber tube positioned around the bat handle. The voltage frequencies from the force sensors were amplified and converted from analogue to digital impulses for on-line storage, retrieval and analysis. The subjects used in the first experiment were fourteen male provincial cricketers. Each batsman batted against a medium-paced bowler on a turf pitch. Sufficient time was given for the batsman to adjust to the experimental bat and condition. The grip force data from 0.75 s before to 0.25 s after impact were extracted for analysis. The group means were obtained every 0.05 s, as well as 0.02 s pre- and post-impact. In the second experiment the procedure was repeated with two of the subjects batting against a medium-paced and a spin bowler on artificial and turf pitches.

Science and Racket Sports Edited by T. Reilly, M. Hughes and A. Lees.
Published in 1994 by E & FN Spon ISBN 0 419 18500 3

A three-way analysis of variance was used to examine whether inter- subject differences occurred, while a two-way analysis of variance was used to examine whether the batsmen showed similar grip force patterns for the forward defensive stroke and the drive off the front foot and whether any differences occurred when playing on different surfaces against different types of bowlers. Any differences, so identified, were treated to post hoc analysis by the Tukey method in order to identify where these differences occurred.

3 Results and Discussion

In the first experiment significant differences ($P < 0.01$) for the intra-subject means of the top and bottom grip force patterns for the forward defensive stroke and the drive for the full time period were observed for the fourteen subjects. However, little variations during the early stages (up to 0.15 s prior to impact) of the downswing for both the forward defensive stroke and the drive, as well as during the latter parts of the follow through (from 0.10 s to the end) in the forward defensive stroke were observed for both hands (Fig. 1).

In the execution of the forward defensive stroke the grip forces measured in the top hand increased with the peak force being attained 0.02 s prior to impact. The grip force patterns for the top hand showed forces 0.02 s before impact of 129.2 ± 41.63 N, which reduced slightly to 127.11 ± 29.33 N at impact and 110.9 ± 22.22 N at 0.02 s post-impact. The grip forces relaxed rapidly up to 0.10 s after impact, after which a slight plateau and a more gradual relaxing of the grip forces occurred. This was the result of the player generating the necessary grip forces to regain control of the bat after impact.

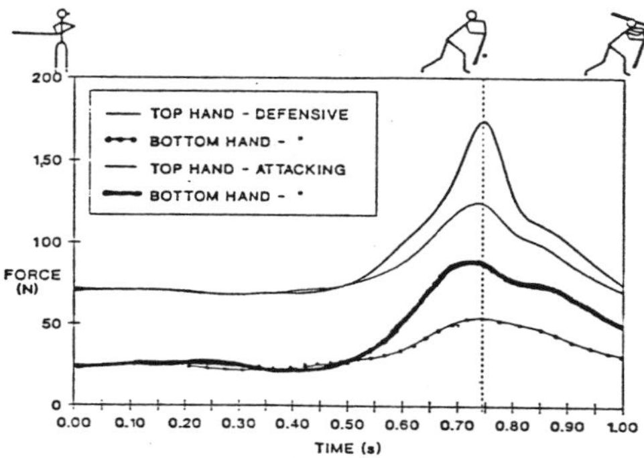

Fig. 1. Grip force patterns when batting on a turf pitch against a medium- paced bowler (n = 14).

The grip force patterns for the bottom hand in the forward defensive stroke showed a similar pattern to the top hand with the exception that the forces were smaller (54.07 ± 16.93 N 0.02 s prior to impact), with the peak force (73.9 ± 37.92 N) reached at impact. The forces 0.02 s post-impact (65.5 ± 26.88 N) were greater than those 0.02 s pre-impact as a result of the bat being driven into the hand by the momentum of the ball impacting the bat. After impact a similar pattern as for the top hand occurred, with a rapid relaxation of the bottom hand, followed by a slight plateau and a more gradual relaxing of the grip force as the necessary hand forces were generated to regain control of the bat after impact.

Contrary to the coaching literature, the results of this study show that in the forward defensive stroke, the bottom hand reinforces the top hand at impact, thus providing greater control of the ball, a factor paramount in playing the forward defensive stroke. The grip forces for the bottom hand reach a peak at impact and 0.02 s after impact which could be a result of the batsman tightening his grip to ensure complete control of the bat at impact. This finding concurs with that of Elliott (1982) who noted that the firmness of the grip is important for stroke control in tennis. These forces could, however, be exaggerated by the force of the ball impacting on the bat which in turn is forced against that part of the hand in contact with the posterior part of the bat handle.

The initial part of the grip pressure pattern for the drive off the front foot (Fig. 1) was very similar to that of the forward defensive stroke as the batsman only makes his final stroke selection based on ball flight information (Abernethy and Russell, 1984; Gibson and Adams, 1989). The grip force of the top hand increased with peak forces of 158.4 $\pm$ 41.12 N, being reached 0.02 s before impact, reducing to 155.6 $\pm$ 51.3 N at impact and 125.7 $\pm$ 28.54 N, 0.02 s post-impact. This relaxation continued up to 0.05 s post-impact and was followed by a slight increase in grip force as the necessary hand forces were generated to regain control of the bat after impact. This was then followed by a more gradual relaxing of the grip force as the bat was swung through to finish up high in front of the batsman. As in the forward defensive stroke some of the increased forces in the hand were to control the inertia of the bat. However, the top hand plays the dominant role in the stroke and would need to grip the bat firmly in order to control the stroke (Greig, 1974; Reddick, 1979; Andrew, 1987; M.C.C., 1987). The grip force patterns for the bottom hand when playing the drive off the front foot showed a similar pattern to the top hand with the exception that the forces were smaller and the peak force (87.5 $\pm$ 32.19 N) was reached at impact. The forces at 0.02 s before impact were 83.9 $\pm$ 32.26 N, while the forces at 0.02 s post-impact were 82.4 $\pm$ 28.62 N. After contact a similar pattern occurred as for the top hand. A rapid relaxation of the bottom hand occurred (up to 0.05 s post-impact), followed by a slight increase in grip force as the necessary hand forces were generated to regain control of the bat after impact. This was then followed by a more gradual relaxing of the grip force as the bat was swung through to finish up high in front of the head.

The differences between the grip force patterns of the top and bottom hands for the forward defensive stroke and the drive were fairly constant throughout the early part of the stroke. At 0.10 s prior to impact the difference in the drive increased as the top hand applied more force. After impact the difference again increased as the bottom hand relaxed during the forward defensive stroke. This prevented the bat from being pushed forward resulting in the ball being hit up in front of the batsman.

As far as the study is applicable to the double-handed grip forces in tennis, it may be possible to extrapolate the following from these results. Firstly, when playing a powerful double-handed stroke a firm grip, with the bottom hand reinforcing the top hand just prior to and at impact, is recommended. At impact this grip will provide optimum racket head velocity, maintain control of the racket and impart ample force to the ball by effectively linking the forces generated by the body's kinetic chain, to the ball. Secondly, these findings in cricket would suggest that when playing touch shots such as the drop shot, players should loosen their grip as this would assist in decelerating the racket head velocity, thus adding control to the stroke.

In the second experiment, when batting against medium-paced bowlers on an artificial pitch, smaller forces were generated by the top hand when playing the drive than in experiment one. Peak forces were reached after impact (Fig. 2). The force patterns for the bottom hand before and at impact were similar to those when batting on turf, whereas greater forces during the follow through were demonstrated when batting on the artificial pitch. In the execution of the forward defensive stroke similar force patterns for the top hand were again demonstrated, as in the stroke played on turf. The bottom hand showed similar forces at impact; however the peak forces were greater and occurred 0.05 s after impact.

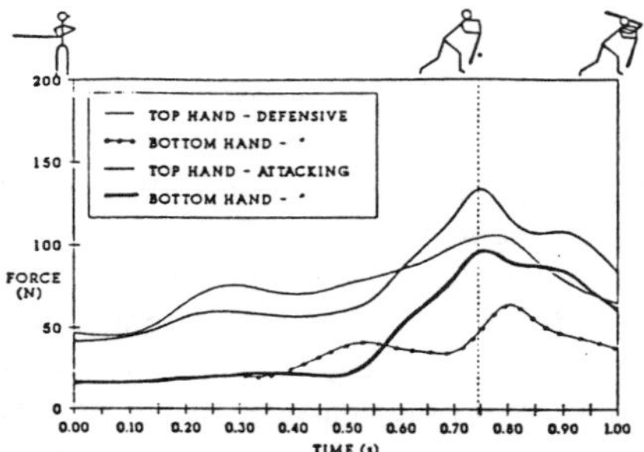

Fig. 2. Grip-force patterns when batting on an artificial pitch against a medium-paced bowler (n = 2).

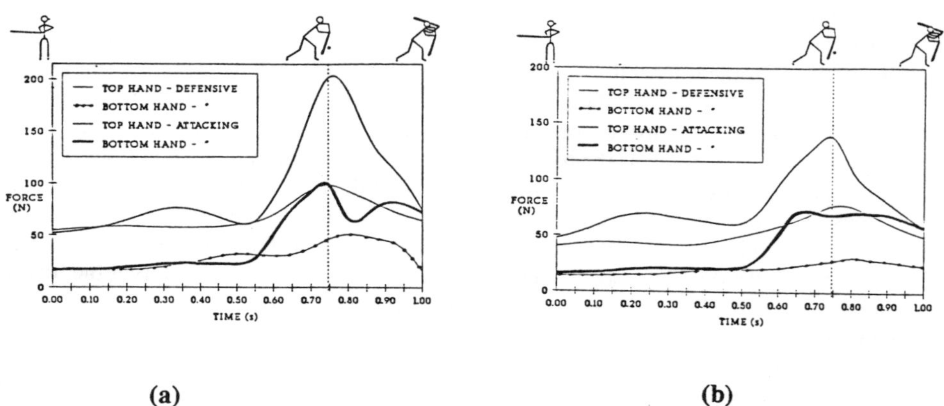

(a) (b)

Fig. 3. Grip-force patterns when batting against a spin bowler on (a) a turf pitch and (b) an artificial pitch (n = 2).

The drive played on the turf pitch against a spin bowler (Fig. 3a) showed greater forces, with the peak forces occurring after impact for the top hand as opposed to experiment one. A similar grip force pattern was demonstrated for the bottom hand except that after impact a slight re-gripping of the bat occurred as the necessary hand forces were generated to regain control of the bat and to control the inertia of the bat during the follow through. The forward defensive stroke showed similar, although smaller, grip force patterns for both hands.

When playing the drive against a spin bowler on an artificial surface (Fig. 3b) the top hand demonstrated a similar, although smaller, grip force pattern than when batting on turf with the exception that the peak forces were reached 0.02 s prior to impact. The grip-force pattern for the bottom hand differed greatly, with the peak forces being reached 0.10 s prior to impact and maintaining a plateau until the completion of the follow through. During the execution of the forward defensive stroke a similar grip force pattern was demonstrated for the top hand, with the bottom hand showing very little change in grip forces throughout the stroke.

As far as the study refers to the double-handed grip forces in tennis, it may be possible to extrapolate the following from these findings. When playing on slower surfaces it may be necessary to increase the grip forces in order to play a powerful double-handed stroke. Similarly, against a ball with a slower approach velocity, it may be necessary to increase the grip forces on the racket to ensure that control of the racket is maintained and to link effectively the forces generated by the body's kinetic chain to the ball in order to impart optimal forces to the ball.

4 Conclusions and Recommendations

From the results on cricket batting under the various experimental conditions, the results would tend to confirm certain aspects of the tennis instructional literature as the grip-force pattern for the top hand in the drive in cricket was similar to that found at the top of the hand in the tennis drive (Knudson, 1988). When playing on fast surfaces such as grass, wood or concrete, strokes need to be shorter and biomechanically more efficient for players to be successful as the pace of the game of tennis has increased greatly due to the improvements in rackets (Braden, 1993). This has possibly led to more players using double-handed strokes, particularly for the return of serve as it helps to control and keep the return more stable. Further, by using a double-handed stroke it is possible to play the return of serve earlier, particularly against the high-bouncing top-spin serve. This enables the player to be more aggressive while reducing the margin of error (Smith, 1993). Further, in the double-handed stroke the non-dominant hand enables the player to manoeuvre the racket head at the last instance enabling the stroke to be disguised (Groppel, 1984) or to be played later as the non-dominant hand enables the player to "make contact a bit further back" (Smith, 1993; p. 42). When playing on the slower surfaces such as clay, the player should grip the racket more tightly in order to balance the forces on the racket as it is swung rapidly forward, thus ensuring optimum summation and transfer of forces through the body. This movement culminates in the hand giving impetus to the racket in order to generate optimum power and control at impact.

This study revealed the variability of grip forces in the typically forward defensive stroke and the drive off the front foot in cricket, as well as the differences that occur when batting against medium-paced and spin bowlers on turf and artificial pitches. Some of the findings in cricket batting have been extrapolated to indicate possible advantages of using the double-handed stroke in tennis. However, each technique has specific characteristics that are conducive to optimal performance. It is therefore recommended that further research on impact loading in tennis should document the actual forces on the hands when utilizing the double-handed grip in a variety of tennis impact conditions. This would enable coaches and players to have a complete understanding of the grip force requirements of the double-handed stroke.

The author wishes to thank the Centre for Science Development for their financial support of this study.

5 References

Abernethy, B. and Russell, D.G. (1984) Advance cue utilisation by skilled batsmen. **Austr. J. Sci. Med. Sport,** 16 (2), 8-10.

Andrew, K. (1987) **Skills of Cricket,** Crowood Press, Marlborough, Wilts.

Braden, V. (1993) Use a compact swing. **Tennis,** 28 (10), 47.

Broer, M.R. and Zernicke, R. (1979) **Efficiency of Human Movement,** W.B. Saunders, Philadelphia.

Bunn, J.W. (1972) **Scientific Principles of Coaching** (2nd ed.), Prentice-Hall, Englewood Cliffs, NJ.

Elliott, B.C. (1982) Tennis: the influence of grip tightness on reaction impulse and rebound velocity. **Med. Sci. Sports Exerc.**, 14, 348-352.

Gibson, A.P. and Adams, R.D. (1989) Batting stroke timing with a bowler and a bowling machine: a case study, **Austr.J. Sci. Med. Sport**, 21 (2), 3-6.

Greig, T. (1974) **Greig on Cricket**, Stanley Paul Co. Ltd., London.

Groppel, J.L. (1984) **Tennis for Advanced Players and Those Who Would Like to be,** Human Kinetics Publishers Inc., Champaign, Illinois.

Hatze, H. (1976) Forces and duration of impact, and grip tightness during the tennis stroke. **Med. Sci. Sports,** 8, 88-95.

Knudson, D. V. (1988) **An analysis of grip forces and three-dimensional accelerations in the tennis forehand drive,** D.Phil Thesis, University of Wisconsin, Madison U.S.A.

M.C.C. (1987) **The M.C.C. Cricket Coaching Book,** 5th edition, William Heinemann Ltd, London

Plagenhoef, S. (1971) **Patterns of Human Motion: A Cinematographic Analysis,** Prentice-Hall Publishers, Englewood Cliffs, New York.

Reddick, T. (1979) **Play cricket the right way,** Seven Seas Publications, Cape Town.

Smith, S. (1993) Return serve two-handed, **Tennis,** 28 (10), 42.

20 Three-dimensional cinematographical analysis of the badminton forehand smash: movements of the forearm and hand

H.P. Tang*, K. Abe, K. Katoh and M. Ae
**Toyama Prefectural University, Toyama, Japan*
University of Tsukuba, Tsukuba City, Japan

1 Introduction

In the game of badminton, the smash is a power stroke used to gain a point advantage. The movements of the forearm and hand not only transmit the energy produced from the arm swing to racket head, but also produce a great velocity of racket head by its rotation. Hence the forearm and hand make important actions for transmitting and producing the power in the badminton smash motion.

Analyses of the upper limb movement in the smash have been done in some qualitative investigations with cinematography (Adrian, & Enberg, 1971; Poole, 1970; Tang, 1992). Gowitzke and Waddell (1979) analyzed the performances of elite players by studying 16 mm film which recorded their movements. The film analysis revealed that a major proportion of the forces acting on the forehand produced from medial rotation of the humerus at the shoulder joint and

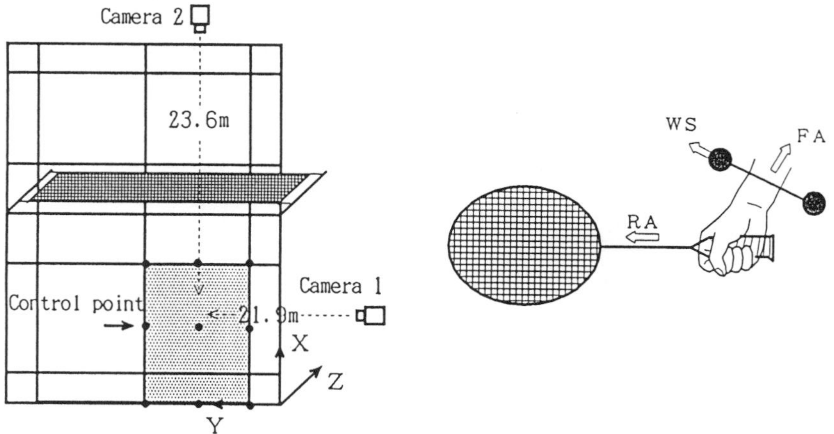

Fig.1. Schematic drawing of experimental setup and reference frame for detecting the motion of forearm.

Science and Racket Sports Edited by T. Reilly, M. Hughes and A. Lees.
Published in 1994 by E & FN Spon ISBN 0 419 18500 3

pronation of the forearm at the radio-ulnar joints. The players showed little or no "classical" wrist involvement.

This study was designed to analyze quantitatively the jumping forehand smash motions of elite players based on three-dimensional kinematic data, and to get insight into the basic badminton smash technique.

2 Methods

Jumping smashes of four male elite players were filmed with two high speed cameras(Photo-Sonics Inc. 16-1PL) operating at 250 Hz with exposure time of 1/1500 and 1/1250 s. Fig. 1 shows the schematic drawing of the experimental setup and reference poles for detecting the motion of the forearm and hand. The nine jumping smashes were selected for the analysis, and were digitized from the take-off of the jump to the end of the swing in the air. Thirty three-dimensional coordinates for the segment endpoints and racket were computed by a Direct Linear Transformation Method (Walton, 1979). Small reference poles were fixed on the forearm of the swing arm of the subjects to detect their movements of the radio-ulnar joint and wrist joint(Fig. 1, Sakurai, et al., 1993). The four angle changes were obtained throughout the smash motion:

(a) pronation/supination angle at the radio-ulnar joint;

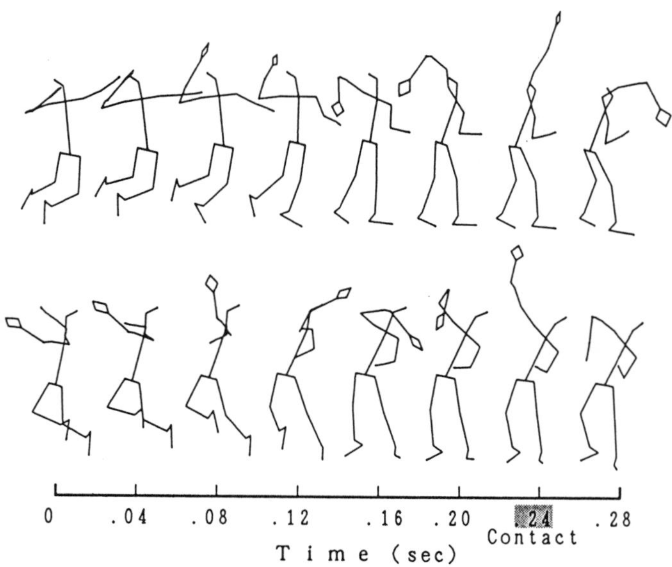

Fig.2. Side and front views of jumping smash motion (the average value of nine performances).

(b) radial flexion/ulnar flexion angle at the wrist joint;
(c) palmar flexion/dorsi flexion angle at the wrist joint;
(d) racket angle(the angle between the forearm and racket shaft).

3 Results

Fig. 2 shows side and front views of the jumping smash motion. Fig. 3 shows the averages of the angles for the pronation and supination, ulnar flexion and radial flexion, dorsi-flexion and palmar flexion and racket angle.

At approximately 0.108 s the wrist (J1) started its radial flexion gradually from a position of slight ulnar flexion, and reached its maximum position (-23.6°) of radial flexion at 0.192 (0.048 s before contact) s. Then the wrist moved rapidly from the radial flexion to ulnar flexion immediately before the contact.

At approximately 0.084 s the wrist (J2) started its dorsi-flexion gradually from a position of slightly palmar flexion, and reached its maximum position (32.8°) of dorsi flexion at 0.204 (0.036 sec before contact) s. Then the wrist moved rapidly from dorsi flexion to palmar flexion through the contact.

The radio-ulnar joint (J3) supinated rapidly from a supinated position at 0.188 s, and reached its peak value (93.4°) of supination at 0.220 (0.020 s before contact) s.

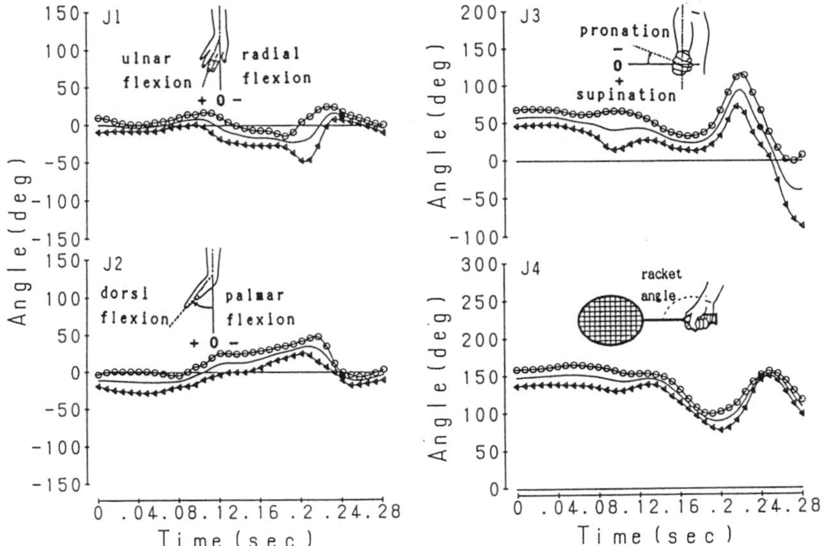

Fig.3. Averages of the angles (N=9, O & ▼: SD, ●: point of contact).

Then the joint continued to pronate rapidly through the contact and follow-through.

At approximately 0.144 s, racket angle reduced rapidly from 139.2° to almost a right angle at approximately 0.200 (0.040 s before contact) s, then increased rapidly through the contact.

The average values at contact were 12.4°, -7.2°, 42.8° and 147.0° of the ulnar flexion, palmar flexion, supination and racket angle respectively.

4 Discussion

4.1 Rapid pronation

The hand movements at the wrist joint and the forearm movement at the radio-ulnar joint seemed to contribute to produce great velocities of the racket head, because the rotations of pronation of the radio-ulnar joint, ulnar flexion and palmar flexion of the wrist either occurred rapidly immediately before the contact or continued to occur rapidly through the contact. The range of rotation of pronation, ulnar flexion and palmar flexion until the contact were 50.6°, 36.0° and 40.0°, and respective times required for rotating the angles were 0.020 s, 0.048 s and 0.036 s. Then, the pronation occurred the greatest range in the shortest time in the three rotations. The results showed that pronation of the radio-ulnar joint was the important joint action on forehand smash.

4.2 Motion in opposite direction

Preliminary to three motions were motions in the opposite direction; e.g., supination rotation of the radio-ulnar joint, radial flexion and dorsi-flexion of the wrist were detected. These motions in the opposite direction would be useful to extend the range of the motion in each joint angle. The results also appeared to be related to intrinsic muscle properties, that greater power can be exerted by stretching-shortening cycle of the muscles.

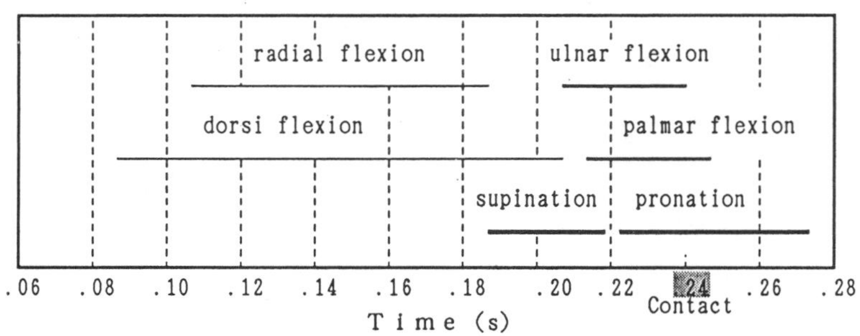

Fig.4. Timing of smash motions of the radio-ulnar and wrist joint(N=9).

4.3 Timing

Fig. 4 shows the timing of the radio-ulnar and wrist joint rotation in smash motions. The order of time of the last joint rotation starting immediately before contact was ulnar flexion, palmar flexion and pronation. Respective times required for the rotation until contact became shorter in turn of late occurring. The results showed that the faster the rotation, the later the rotation occurred and the shorter was the rotation time. The interval for the three joint rotations to occur was about 0.008 s. This kind of chain and continuous movement of different joints, with different freedom in the same joint may accelerate the racket head efficiently.

4.4 Mechanism of smash

Two machines used in the smash motion are associated with the kinetic link model. These mechanisms are the lever and the wheel-axle (Kreighbaum and Barthels, 1990). For the lever-system, a bigger racket angle (approximately 180°) has the potential of giving a higher contact point and a faster linear velocity by virtue of the palmar flexion and the arm swing. The bigger racket angle has a contrary effect on the decrease of the linear velocity of pronation by reducing the radius of the rotation. On the other hand, for the wheel-axle system, a smaller racket angle (approximately 90°) has the potential of giving a faster linear velocity by virtue of the pronation. But the smaller racket angle has a contrary effect too on the decrease of the height of the contact point and the linear velocity of palmar flexion by reducing the radius of the rotation.

The result showed that the average racket angle was 147.0° between 90° and 180° at contact. This value may be a suitable choice between the height and the speed at contact in practical play.

5 References

Adrian, M.J. and Enberg, M.L. (1971) Sequential timing of three overhead patterns. **Kinesiology Review**, AAHPER, Washington, DC.

Gowitzke, B.A. and Waddell, D.B. (1979) Qualitative analysis of the badminton forehand smash as performed by international players. **National Symposium on the Racket Sports**, Univ. Illinois. pp. 10-25.

Kreighbaum, E. and Barthels, K.M. (1990) **Biomechanics** (Third edition), Burgess Publishing Company: Minnesota, pp. 611-636.

Poole, J.R. (1970) A cinematographic analysis of the upper executing two basic badminton strokes. **Ph. D. dissertation**, Louisiana State University, Baton Rouge, Louisiana.

Sakurai, S. Ikegami, Y. Okamoto, A. Yabe, K. and Toyoshima,

S. (1993) A three-dimensional cinematographic analysis of upper limb movement during fastball and curveball baseball pitches. **J Appl Biomech.**, , 9, 47-65.

Tang, H.P. Kazuyoshi, A. Koji, K. Minayori, K. (1992) Three-dimensional cinematographic analysis of the badminton forehand smash. **Bulletin of Toyama Prefectural University**, 2, 40-44.

Walton, J.S (1979) Close-range cinephotogrammetry: Another approach to motion analysis. in **Science in biomechanics cinematography** (eds J. Terauds), Academic Publishers, Del Mar, pp. 69-97.

Part Four
Racket Sports Equipment

21 An ergonomic evaluation of the shoe-surface interface in badminton

N. Smith and A. Lees
Centre for Sport and Exercise Sciences, School of Human Sciences, Liverpool John Moores University, Liverpool, UK

1 Introduction

During recent years much attention has been paid to the interface between sports shoes and surfaces. The majority of research conducted has been connected with running, and the little related to racket sports has been associated with tennis shoes (e.g. Stackoff and Kaelin, 1989). Badminton involves a variety of fast, lunging movements, creating high stresses and demands on the footwear of players. While it is evident that high forces will act on the shoe to distort, deform and destroy it, these forces have not been quantified. A quantification of such forces would be of value to both the player and the shoe manufacturer. The aims of this study were i) to analyse the movements in badminton using notational analysis techniques and ii) to quantify the shear (or horizontal friction) forces acting on the shoe using force platform methods. A combination of these methods allows an estimate to be made of the stresses and demands on the footwear of a player.

2 Methods

The actions made during badminton were first classified into thirteen basic types from a qualitative analysis of badminton match-play. Five complete matches involving international and county standard badminton players were videotaped. Notation was performed from pre-recorded videotapes of badminton match-play due to the speed of the game. A hand notation system was employed to obtain the average frequency counts of each of these basic actions during a game.
To quantify the ground reaction forces in each movement, eight subjects (6 male, 2 female, mean age 21.8 years) of county and high club standard were asked to perform each action on a Kistler force platform with both their racket side and non-racket side foot. The platform was covered with a wafer thin layer of plasticine in order to obtain imprints of the foot during each of the actions so as to establish foot position. Subjects were given plenty of opportunity to practice the movements so that they were realistic. Data were sampled at 200 Hz. Informed consent was obtained from each subject.

Science and Racket Sports Edited by T. Reilly, M. Hughes and A. Lees.
Published in 1994 by E & FN Spon ISBN 0 419 18500 3

From the data of number of actions per game, and the force magnitudes directed within segments of the shoe, it was possible to estimate the force loading around the shoe for an average game.

3 Results

Results from notation analysis took the form of frequency counts of each of the thirteen designated actions. From these data mean frequencies per game of each action were calculated and are given in Table 1.

Table 1. Average frequency of key actions per game

Action	Frequency	Action	Frequency
Lunge	71	Lunge to side	12
Smash	27	Drop	11
Lunge to forehand	20	Lunge to backhand	7
Clear	22	Jump Smash	3
Start	22	Kill	1
Drive	3	Jump	1
Block	24		

The force platform study produced a horizontal force diagram (Fig. 1). This gave a series of force vectors representing the horizontal force acting on the sole of the shoe. The magnitude of the accumulated force or ‘stress’ and the number of counts within successive 30 degree segments around the shoe were computed. The segment with the greatest number of counts gave the predominant direction of the force. Generally this covered two or three segments. The accumulated force for the action was recorded for each subject performing an action, and the mean force (N) per action determined by dividing the accumulated force by the number of counts made during the action. This was then divided by body weight to give a mean force value in body weight units. This and the force direction acting on the shoe are given in Table 2. The total stress on each shoe (the racket side and non-racket side) was computed from the average force per segment (in body weight units) for each action multiplied by the frequency of actions per game. This calculation yielded the data in Table 3.

Table 2. Mean forces and predominant direction of force for key actions

Action	Mean Force	Direction	Action	Mean Force	Direction
Lunge	0.698	FL	Lunge to side	0.695	F
Smash	0.758	L	Drop	0.685	L
Lunge to f/h	0.723	FL	Lunge to b/h	0.721	F
Clear	0.705	L	Jump Smash	0.744	RL
Start	0.483	RL	Kill	0.708	F
Drive	0.676	F	Jump	0.474	FL
Block	0.096	VARIED			

F=Front FL=Front Lateral f/h = forehand
L=Lateral RL=Rear Lateral b/h = backhand

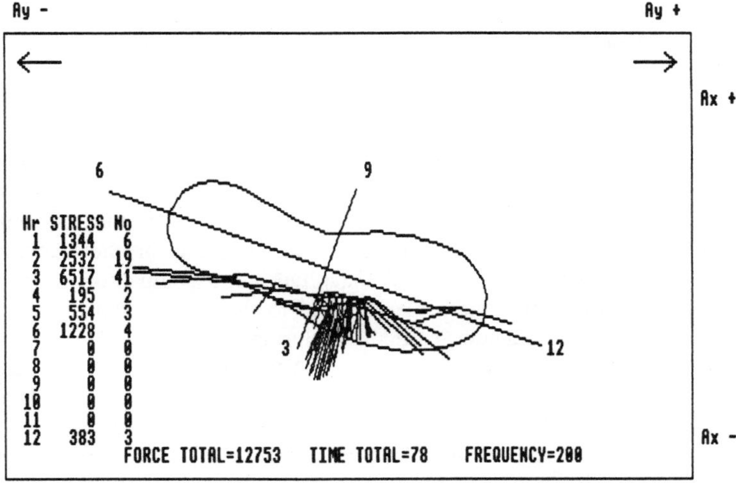

Figure 1. The horizontal shear force vectors acting on the shoe for a 'landing from a jump' action. The inset gives the segments clockwise from the front of the shoe, the accumulated force or 'stress', and the number of force readings in each segment. Force (N) and number of samples taken during the action are given below, together with the sampling frequency.

Table 3. The total stress on the badminton shoe (in body weight)

segment of shoe	racket side	non-racket side
1	23.56	2.00
2	5.59	0.66
3	4.94	0.70
4	12.05	0.68
5	16.48	2.49
6	5.37	4.49
7	1.69	16.24
8	0.31	15.73
9	0.49	16.99
10	2.16	12.37
11	15.66	5.77
12	40.80	2.17
TOTAL	129.10	80.29

4 Discussion and Conclusions

These data illustrate that the majority of actions are those in which the player is stretching to play a shot. These are generally described as a lunge. The stress put on the shoe depends largely on the particular type of action and the direction of movement. Most of the actions apply horizontal forces in the region of 0.5 - 0.7 body weight, or just over half body weight. These forces are determined not only by the action but also by the frictional characteristics of the shoe-floor interface and the ability of the body to sustain forces of this magnitude. In a companion study, Lees and Hurley (1993) showed that the forces applied to the ground can lead to high forces in the lower limb musculature, particularly during a lunge.

The forces tend to be directed towards the front and front lateral portion of the shoe for the racket side and the lateral and rear lateral for the non-racket side. There is therefore an asymmetry in the stress imposed on the badminton shoe. This may dictate an asymmetrical construction technique for right and left handed players in order to promote the longevity of the shoe.

5 References

Lees, A.and Hurley, C. (1993) **Forces in a badminton lunge**. Communication to the First World Congress of Science and Racket Sports, Liverpool. 9-13th July.

Stackoff, A. and Kaelin, X., (1989) **Technical and biomechanical criteria of the court shoe,** in **The Shoe in Sport** (eds B. Segesser and W. Pforringer), Wolfe, London, pp 77-86.

22 Computer aided design of rackets

H. Sol
Vrije Universiteit Brussel (V.U.B.), Brussels, Belgium

1 Introduction

Designing rackets requires a thorough understanding of the relations between the **playing properties** of a racket (from a player point of view) and the objective **mechanical** properties (from an engineering point of view). The most important playing properties are:

- Performance or rebound efficiency ("racket power")
- Movability (the ease to move the racket)
- Control (the ability to place a ball exactly where you want it)
- Comfort (to reduce body fatigue and possible injuries)

The mechanical properties include a long list of **mass** related properties (total mass, balance, inertia, percussion centre,..), **damping** related properties (string damping, frame damping, local artificial damping, grip damping...) and **stiffness** related properties (resonant frequencies, mode shapes, bending stiffness, torsion stiffness..).

Changing a mechanical parameter rarely modifies only one particular playing property. It usually influences **all** the playing properties, some for the better others for the worse. The relation between some playing properties and mechanical properties can be complex and therefore a racket designer needs an access to advanced computer simulations to do a good job.

Most of the better modern rackets are made of fibre reinforced plastics, the so-called "composite materials". The different cross- sections of the blade, the throat and the handle of a racket made in composite material are closed thin-walled sections. The walls are formed by laminates of the fibre reinforced plastics. The composition of the laminates and the geometry's of the different cross- sections can vary from place to place in the racket. The computation of the mechanical properties of the cross-sections is very complex and it is quite impossible to design cross- sections without the help of modern computer programs.

This paper briefly describes how some computer programs can be used at different stages of a design cycle. In the following chapter, the relations between the "playing properties" and some important mechanical properties of rackets will be discussed.

Science and Racket Sports Edited by T. Reilly, M. Hughes and A. Lees.
Published in 1994 by E & FN Spon ISBN 0 419 18500 3

2 Mechanical properties and their relation with playing properties

The mechanical parameters of a racket can be divided into three groups:

2.1. Geometrical properties.
2.2. Rigid body properties.
2.3. Vibration properties.

The next paragraphs will briefly describe these properties and mention their relations with playing properties like power, control, movability and comfort.

2.1 The geometrical properties

The geometrical properties include the global racket geometry's and the cross- section geometry's at different positions of the racket.

The global racket dimensions (total racket length, length and width of the blade, string area,...) for modern rackets have evolved towards more or less fixed sizes and are sometimes limited by sport federation rules. The blade and throat geometry's of rackets are adapted to specific game demands (badminton, tennis, squash,...) and change sometimes due to fashion or commercial impulses. Often the blade geometry is typical for a certain racket manufacturer and acts as a kind of personal trade mark.

The geometry and dimensions of the sections at different positions of the racket are constantly changing. They are the subject of many patents of different manufacturers.

The global racket geometry and the geometry at different positions of the cross-sections determine the rigid body and vibration properties and are of paramount importance for the all playing properties of the racket. The selection of the geometry's and the computation of their impact on the different properties of the racket must therefore be executed with great care.

2.2 The rigid body properties

The rigid body properties of a racket are determined by the distribution of the **mass** over the racket. The most important rigid body properties are:

- The total mass of the racket
- The position of the centre of gravity ("balance")
- The mass inertia's ("swing weight" and "polar moment of inertia")
- The percussion centre and percussion zone

The total mass or **weight** of a racket is probably the best understood mechanical property. A large total mass increases the power and control of a racket but decreases the movability and the comfort.

The position of the centre of gravity, often called **balance** of a racket, characterises the **type** of racket. A centre of gravity located towards the top produces an offensive racket with increased power, while a low centre of gravity makes the racket more comfortable and more suitable for a baseline player.

The **swing weight** or out of plane mass inertia of a racket is the resistance against variations of rotational ("swing") speed (for example, the rotational speed varies from zero to maximal speed during the service stroke). A large swing weight increases the power and control but reduces the movability and comfort.

The **polar moment inertia** of a racket is the resistance of the racket against variations of rotational speed around the longitudinal axis (e.g. due to off-centre hits). A large polar moment of inertia increases the stability and thus the control of the racket. Some manufacturers add concentrated masses at both sides of the longitudinal axis of the racket blade in order to increase the polar moment of inertia of the racket.

The (main) **percussion centre** (See Fig.1) is the position in the blade of the racket where an impact of a ball causes no re-percussion in a selected **pivot point** position in the handle of the racket (e.g. for a tennis racket, this position is selected at 7.5 cm from the handle end). The human hand also defines a certain grip zone in the handle of the racket (e.g. for a tennis racket, a grip zone between 0 cm and 15 cm can be taken). Every position in the grip zone (or "**pivot zone**") corresponds with a different percussion centre in the blade and thus forms a "**percussion zone**" in the blade (See Fig. 2).

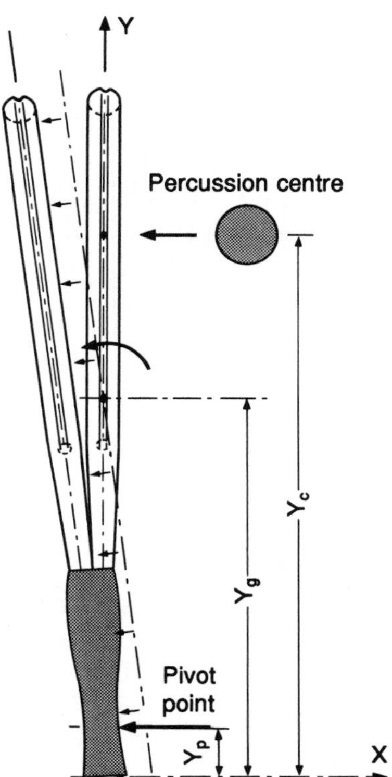

Figure 1. Main centre of percussion and corresponding pivot point.

A comfortable racket will have its main percussion centre where the ball is hit most often (e.g. in the middle of the blade) and will have a large percussion zone.

It is known that a centre of gravity towards the head causes a small percussion zone. In contrast, a low centre of gravity causes a large percussion zone and thus a comfortable racket.

The rigid body properties of a racket can be calculated with a specialised computer program "RIGID", which is developed at the Vrije Universiteit Brussel (V.U.B.). This computer program requires the mass properties and positions of each cross- section as INPUT values.

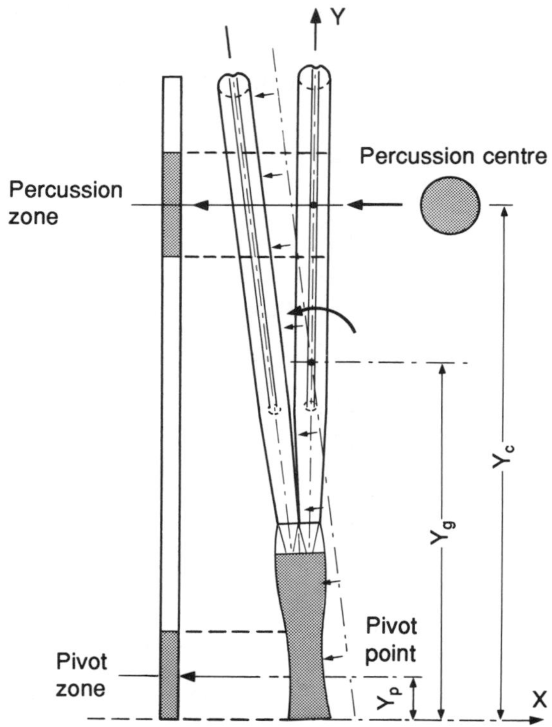

Figure 2. Pivot zone and corresponding percussion zone.

The mass properties of the cross- sections can be computed with another specialised computer program (also developed at the V.U.B.), called "PROFILE". This program requires the material properties and the geometry's of the cross- sections as INPUT values.

2.3 The vibration properties

After a racket is hit by an impact, the racket vibrates for a while in the hand of the player. The vibration behaviour is dependant on the position and amplitude of the impact and also on the vibration characteristics of the racket.

An arbitrary vibration response of a racket after an impact can be composed with an infinite series of **mode shapes**, each multiplied with a time dependant contribution factor. The contribution factors depend on the position and type of the impact. Mode shapes are elementary vibration patterns that can be considered as the vibration "fingerprints" of the racket. Figure 3 shows some typical mode shapes of a tennis racket.

In each mode shape, the racket vibrates a number of times every second around an equilibrium position. The number of vibration periods in one second is expressed in Hertz (Hz). A racket with a fundamental bending mode shape of 130 Hz, for example, will vibrate in that mode 130 times in one second, meanwhile showing the typical deformation pattern of a bending mode shape (Figure 3.a).

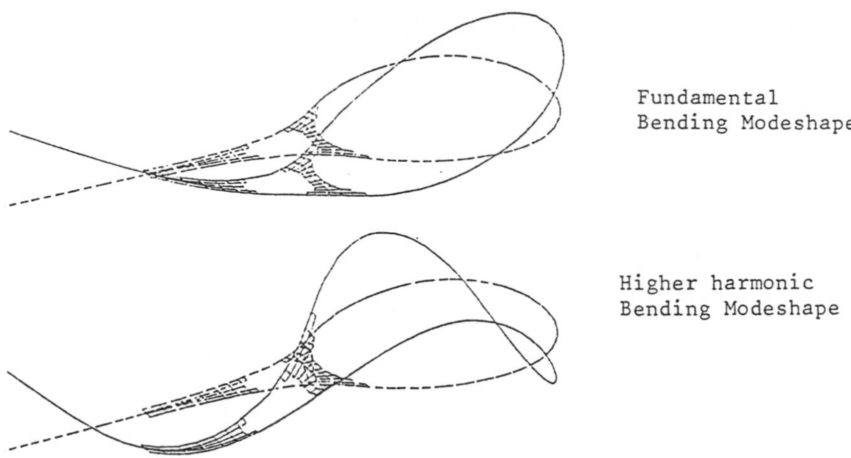

Figure 3. Some mode shapes of a tennis racket.

The frequency of vibration of each mode shape is also called **resonant frequency**. The higher the resonant frequency is, the more complex the mode shape will be. The fundamental bending mode shape is the most simple one and - fortunately for the racket designer- this mode shape dominates the vibration behaviour of a racket.

Modifications of the mass or stiffness distribution of the racket will change the mode shapes and thus the vibration behaviour of a racket.

The stiffer the racket, the higher will be the resonant frequency of the first bending mode shape. The stiffer the racket, the more power and control it has, but the less comfort. The magnitude of the resonant frequency of a racket tells a lot about the character of a racket. Unfortunately, a lot of manufacturers, tennis players and coaches are not familiar with the word "resonant frequency" and therefore it is not yet commonly used.

Having a closer look at the first fundamental mode shape, one can notice that there are two lines on the vibration pattern where the amplitude is zero (one is situated in the blade, the other in the handle). These lines are called **nodal lines**. If a ball hits a racket on the nodal line in the blade, the resulting vibration will very low. Therefore, a well-designed racket should have this nodal line going through the middle of the racket blade.If the player grips a racket in the nodal line through the handle, he won't suffer much from the vibration. So, a comfortable racket must have that nodal line at the location of the hand grip (See Figure 4).

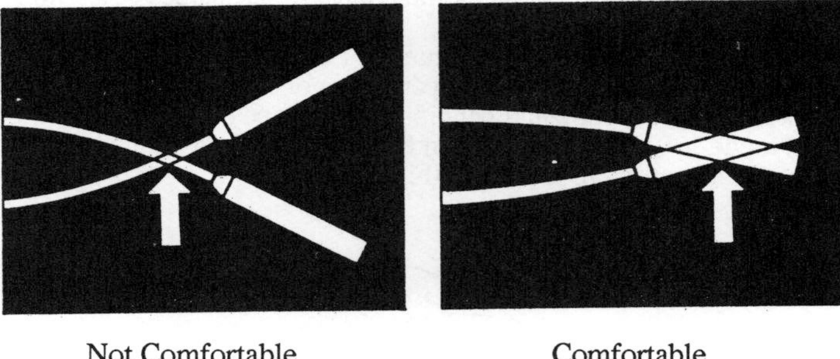

Not Comfortable Comfortable

Figure 4. Nodal line (handle) of the fundamental bending mode shape.

The vibration properties of a tennis racket can be computed with special computer programs called "finite element" programs.

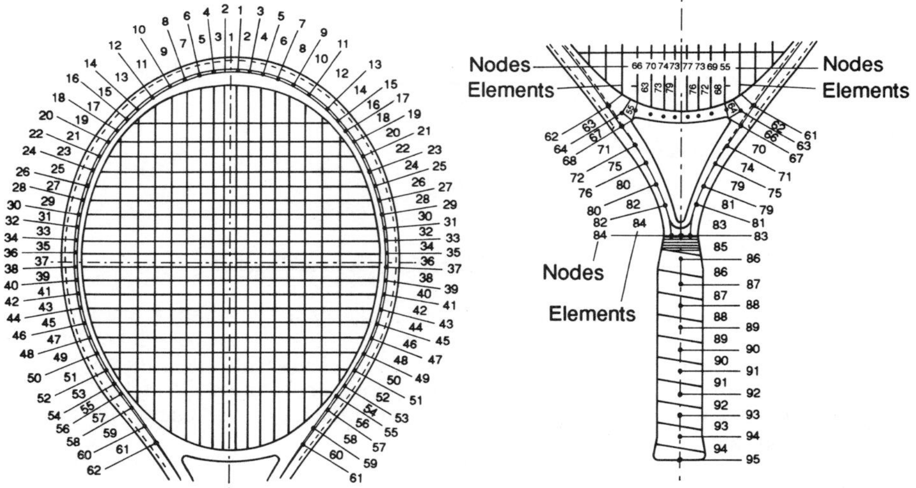

Figure 5. Finite element model of a tennis racket.

The numerical model of a tennis racket that must be developed for a finite element program is divided into a number of beam elements. The beam elements are connected to one another by so-called nodes. Figure 5 shows a finite element model of a tennis racket using 94 beam elements and 95 nodes.

The stiffness and mass properties of each beam element and the co-ordinates of the nodes are the INPUT values for a finite element analysis. The stiffness and mass properties of each element are computed with the program "PROFILE". Figure 6 gives an example of a graphical output of the program "PROFILE".

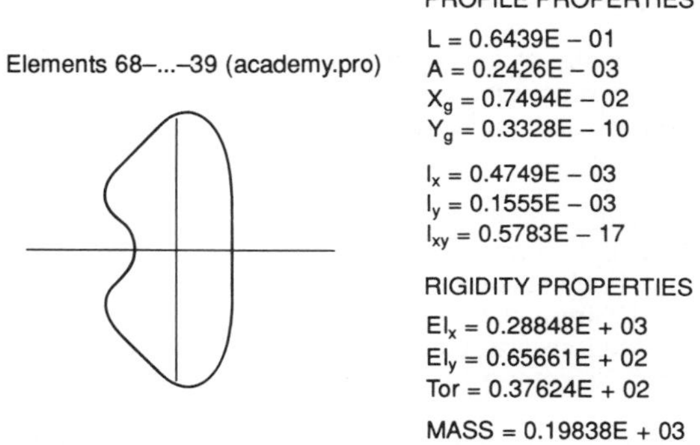

Figure 6. Cross- section properties computed by the program "PROFILE".

Another vibration property of a racket is its **damping behaviour**. Without going into much detail, it can be said that an increased damping of the racket frame increases the comfort, the control and the power of the racket. An increased damping is the only mechanical property that improves **all** the playing properties! Some manufacturers therefore add a device in the handle of the racket to increase the damping.

3 Computer aided design (C.A.D.) of a racket

3.1 Global geometry design

A design cycle starts with the definition of the global geometry of the racket (total racket length, shape and dimensions of the string area, racket throat geometry,...). This geometry is inspired by experience, fashion, marketing strategy, artistic inspiration, and so on. Computer aided design (C.A.D.) programs, executed on modern computers, are able to visualise the designed racket with three-dimensional colour plots on a graphical screen. The designer can modify interactively the geometry. The result is shown immediately on the computer screen and can be discussed with the marketing and the product managers.

3.2 Cross-section geometry design

At a next stage of the design cycle, the cross-section geometry's are developed. The stiffness and mass properties of the cross-sections can be computed with the program "PROFILE" and are stored in a "cross-section's database". The material properties for the computation of the profile properties are stored in a "material property data base". The data for these databases are generated with experiments on test specimen (torsion, tensile and bending tests).

3.3 Rigid body property's design

After the definition of the global racket geometry's and the composition of a cross-section's database, the rigid body properties of the racket can be computed and critically analysed. It is physically impossible to produce an "ideal" racket with a maximum for **all** the playing properties (power, control, movability and comfort) because increasing or optimising a specific property (e.g. power) often decreases another (e.g. comfort).

Examples - Increasing the total mass increases the power but reduces the movability.
- A higher centre of gravity increases the power but reduces the comfort (smaller percussion zone).
- A bigger swing weight increases the power, but reduces the movability of the racket.

The designer must make a choice for the "**nature**" of the racket. He can make, for example, a "medium weight powerful" racket or a "light weight comfortable" racket and then tune the rigid body properties of the racket in that sense.

The program "RIGID" immediately computes the new values of the rigid body modes if other cross- sections are selected or modified. It is also possible to add concentrated masses at different positions of the racket frame to improve the rigid body properties.

The designer can thus interactively change the cross- sections of the racket or/and add concentrated masses until the desired rigid body properties are obtained. Figure 7 shows an example of a graphical result output of the program "RIGID".

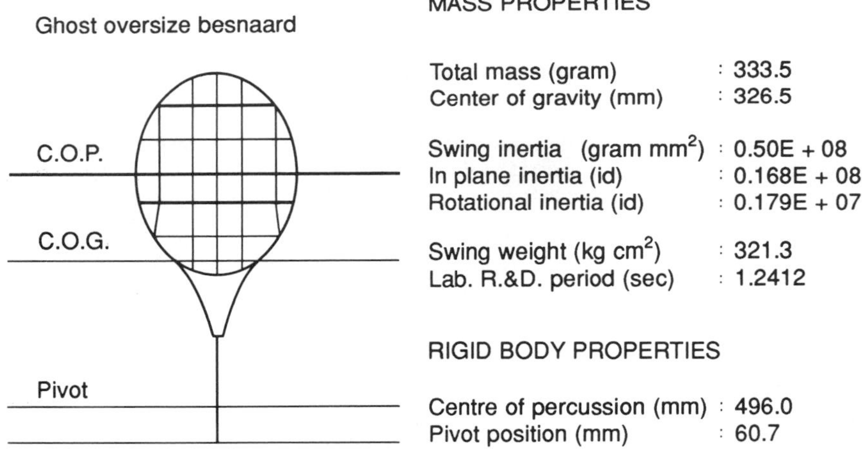

Figure 7. Computed rigid body properties by the program "RIGID".

3.4 Vibration behaviour design and failure control

Once the obtained rigid body properties are satisfactory, the designer can enter into the last design stage: the verification of the vibration properties and failure control of all the cross- sections due to the forces generated by the string tensions and the impact forces. The vibration behaviour and the distribution of forces on the racket frame can be computed with a finite element program. The designer must verify if the vibration behaviour is in agreement with the "nature" of the racket that is being developed. Next, the designer must check if the computed forces in the different cross-sections are allowable. This can be performed again with the program "PROFILE", that checks if the allowable stresses are not exceeded in the composite laminates according to an appropriate failure criterion. If, during this stage, the mass distribution should be altered, the rigid body properties (previous step) should also be verified again!

3.5 Prototype production

If all the computational results are satisfactory, the next step is the actual production of a series of prototypes of the racket. Computer aided design of a racket in combination with a good database of material properties allows nowadays very accurate predictions. The predicted computer results are therefore usually very close to the actual properties of the produced prototypes.

The enormous advantage of computer aided design is that the properties of the new racket are accurately predicted so that disappointments (and therefore the necessary production of a new, expensive, prototype mould) are avoided.

4. Testing

4.1 Laboratory tests.

All the rigid body and vibration properties can be checked on the prototypes. The necessary equipment to measure experimentally all the properties - even the vibration behaviour - is nowadays easy to handle, accurate and not expensive.

4.2 Player tests.

The final and most important evaluations are the player tests. Organising good player tests requires a lot of experience and is therefore reserved to specialists. The questions directed to the players have to be clear and simple to allow an unambiguous interpretation. If necessary, the racket can undergo some final adaptations according to the comments of test players.

5 Conclusion

A racket manufacturer that really wants to design a racket according to desired playing properties can not avoid the use of computer programs. The relations between the playing properties and the mechanical properties of a racket must be well understood. Computer aided design, if properly applied by an experienced designer, improves the product quality and saves both time and money.

6 References

Brody, H. (1988) **Tennis Science for Tennis Players**. University of Pennsylvania Press, Philadelphia.

23 Computer aided prediction of the vibration and rebound velocity characteristics of tennis rackets with various physical properties

Y. Kawazoe
Saitama Institute of Technology, Saitama, Japan

1 Introduction

The performance of the tennis racket in terms of the coefficient of restitution is closely related to impact phenomena. Nevertheless, there are a number of unclarified points regarding the impact phenomenon and the optimum design of tennis rackets (*Groppel*, 1987).

In this paper, the vibration of a racket-frame and the rebound velocity of a ball when it hits the strings of rackets with various physical properties, such as the frame stiffness, mass distribution and the string tension, are predicted using a simple impact model. The model is based on the idea that the contact duration, which has a strong influence on the racket-frame vibration and is not much affected by the frame stiffness, is determined by the natural period of a whole system composed of the mass of a ball, the non-linear stiffness of a ball and strings, and the reduced mass of racket at the impact point on the string face. The rebound velocity of the ball can be derived by considering the main sources of energy loss during impact, such as the instantaneous deformation of the ball and strings, rotation of the racket and vibration of racket-frame ($Kawazoe, 1989, 1992, a - e$).

2 Approximate Non-linear Impact Analysis and the Prediction of a Ball Rebound Velocity

The coefficient of restitution e_{BG}, when the racket head is firmly clamped in the collision between a ball and strings, is closely related to the energy loss due to the instantaneouse deformation of the ball and strings. If the vibration of the racket frame is neglected, the impulse could be approximately described as Eq.(1) using the mass m_B of a ball, the reduced mass M_r of a racket at the hitting point on the string face, and the ball velocity V_{Bo} before impact ($Kawazoe, 1992a, e$).

$$\int F(t)dt = V_{Bo}(1 + e_{BG})m_B/(1 + m_B/M_r) \ . \tag{1}$$

Assuming that the contact duration, which is not much affected by the frame stiffness accoding to the experiment, is determined by the natural period of a whole system composed of the mass of a ball, the nonlinear

Science and Racket Sports Edited by T. Reilly, M. Hughes and A. Lees.
Published in 1994 by E & FN Spon ISBN 0 419 18500 3

stiffness K_{GB} of a ball and strings, and the reduced mass of racket, the contact duration between the ball and the racket might be

$$T_c = \pi {m_B}^{1/2}/(K_{GB}(1 + m_B/M_r))^{1/2} \ . \tag{2}$$

The stiffness K_{GB}, however, has a strong non-linearity and its value changes during impact also depending on the impact velocity ($Kawazoe, 1992a$). In order to make the analysis simpler, the equivalent force F_{MEAN} can be introduced during impact time T_C ($\int F(t)dt = F_{MEAN}T_C$). Accordingly, the relationship between F_{MEAN} and corresponding K_{GB} is represented as Eq.(3) from Eq.(1) and Eq.(2).

$$F_{mean} = V_{Bo}(1 + e_{BG}){m_B}^{1/2}{K_{GB}}^{1/2}/(\pi(1 + m_B/M_r)^{1/2}) \tag{3}$$

On the other hand, each curve of restoring forces F_B, F_G and F_{GB} vs. the deformations of a ball, strings and the compound system of ball and strings can be determined respectively. This is so as to satisfy a number of experimental data using the least square method assuming that a ball with concentrated mass deforms only at the side in contact with the strings. Also, the curves of the corresponding stiffness K_G, K_B, and K_{GB} can be derived by differentiation of the restoring forces with respect to deformation ($Kawazoe, 1992a$). Thus, the relationship between F_{GB} and K_{GB} can be derived using the least square method as Eq.(4) by eliminating the deformation graphically from the above two relations.

$$F_{mean} = func.(K_{GB}) \tag{4}$$

From Eq.(3) and Eq.(4), the parameters K_{GB} and F_{MEAN} against the impact velocity V_{Bo} (when the pre-impact velocity of racket $V_{Ro} = 0$) can be derived. Also, the contact duration T_C can be determined against the impact velocity V_{Bo} from Eq.(2) ($Kawazoe, 1992a$).

The force-time curve of impact is approximated as a half-sine pulse shown on the left in Fig.11. Its mathematical expession is

$$F(t) = F_{max} sin(\pi t/T_c)(0 \leq t \leq T_c) \tag{5}$$

where

$$\int F(t)dt = F_{MEAN}T_C, \qquad F_{max} = \pi F_{mean}/2 \tag{6}$$

The fourier transform of Eq.(5) is shown on the right in Fig.11 and represented as Eq.(7), where f is the frequency ($Kawazoe, 1992a$).

$$S(f) = 2F_{max}T_c \mid cos(\pi f T_c) \mid /[\pi \mid 1 - (2fT_c)^2 \mid] \tag{7}$$

The amplitude of racket vibration due to impact can be simulated by applying the impact force to the experimentally identified racket vibration model ($Kawazoe, 1989, 1992c$). When the impact force $S_j(\omega_k)$ applies to the arbitrary point j on the string face, the amplitudes X_{ijk} at the arbitrary point i of the racket are expressed as

$$X_{ijk} = r_{ijk}S_j(\omega_k) \tag{8}$$

where $\omega_k = 2\pi f_k$, r_{ijk} denotes the residue of k-th mode, and $S_j(\omega_k)$ is the impact force component of k-th frequency ω_k in the frequency region (*Kawazoe*, 1992*a*). When the hitting position and the pre-impact velocity are given, the vibration of the racket can be simulated by using Eq.(7) and Eq.(8). The energy loss due to the racket frame vibration can be derived from the amplitude distribution of the velocity and the mass distribution along a racket frame when a ball collides with a hand-held tennis racket (*Kawazoe*, 1992*c*, *e*).

The rebound velocity of a ball when a ball strikes the string face can be derived, considering the main sources of energy loss during impact (*Kawazoe*, 1992*e*). If the longitudinal mass distribution of racket frame is assumed to be uniform, the energy loss ΔE_1 due to racket-frame vibrations can be calculated. Another energy loss ΔE_2 due to the collision between the ball and strings with the reduced mass of racket at the hitting point could also be derived using the measured coefficient of restitution e_{BG}. Accordingly, the coefficient of restitution e_r with respect to the relative velocities corresponding to the total energy loss $\Delta E(=\Delta E_1 + \Delta E_2)$ is given by

$$e_r = (1 - 2\Delta E(m_B + M_r)/(m_B M_r V_{Bo}^2))^{1/2} \quad (9)$$

The coefficient e of the post-impact velocity relative to the pre-impact velocity of a ball is given by

$$e = (1 - 2\Delta E(m_B + M_r)/(m_B M_r V_{Bo}^2))^{1/2} - m_B(1 + e_{BG})/(m_B + M_r) \quad (10)$$

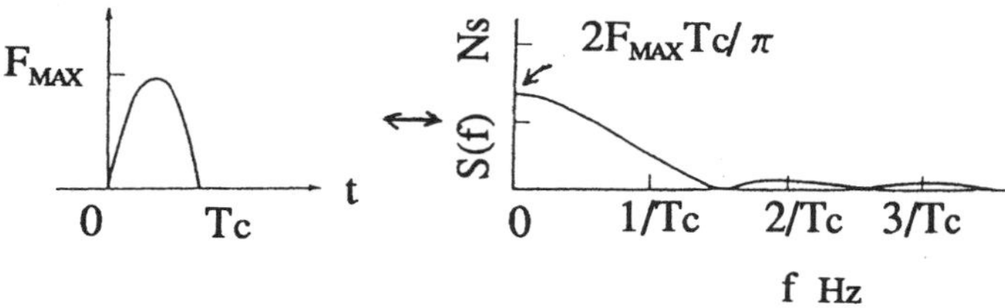

Fig.1 Shock shape and its spectrum during ball/racket impact.

3 Results and Discussion

The calculated contact time agrees well with the measured one during actual forehand strokes. Also, the measured distribution of the coefficient e on the string face (impact velocity: 26.4 m/s) and the calculated one (30.0 m/s) showed good agreement. It tends to be maximized along the longitudinal axis of the racket and peaks close to the throat due to the mass distribution of a racket (*Kawazoe*, 1992*e*).

Figure 2 shows the predicted post-impact vibrations of rackets with various physical properties when a ball hits the top, the centre and the

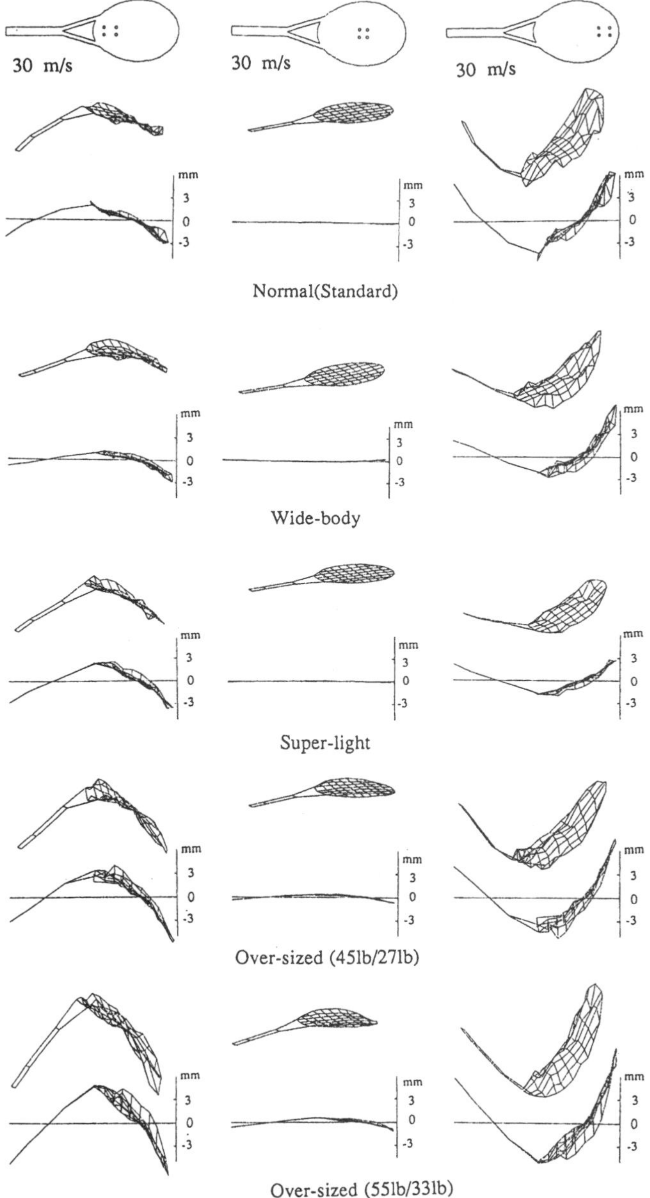

Fig.2 Predicted amplitude of the racket frame vibration immediately after impact when a ball hits the racket (near, center, top) at a velocity of 30 ms^{-1}.

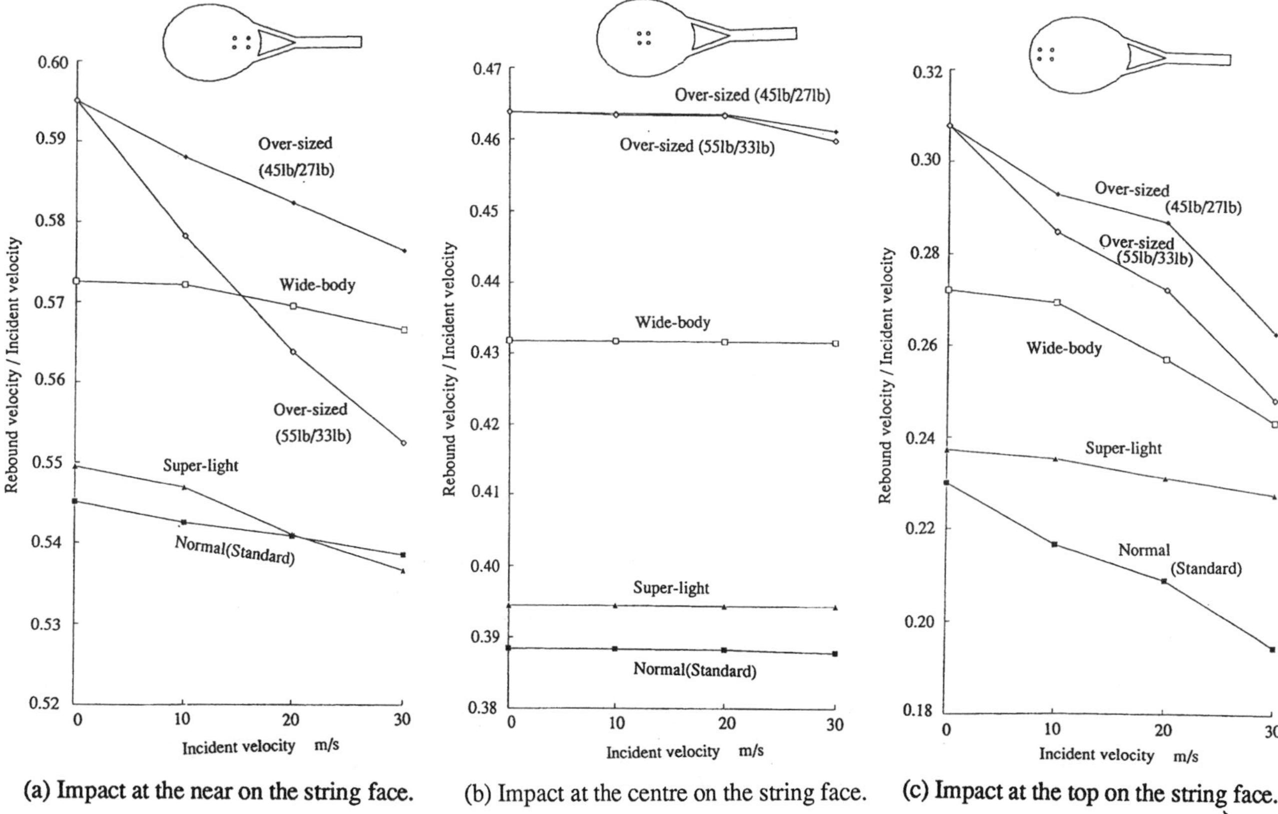

Fig.3 Predicted rebound velocity against incident velocity when a ball strikes rackets with different physical properties at the near, centre, and top on the string face.

near on the string face at a velocity of 30 m/s respectively. The rackets tested are Yamaha's EX-II (360 g,length 680 mm,area 100 in^2, centre of gravity from the grip end: 308 mm, 1st vibration mode: 122 Hz), a PROTO-02 (370 g, centre of gravity: 317 mm, 215 Hz), a PROTO-EX110 (366 g,685 mm,110 in^2, centre of gravity:325 mm,132 Hz) strung loosely, a PROTO-EX110 strung tightly, and a EOS100 (290 g, 680 mm, centre of gravity: 350 mm, 171 Hz). It is seen that the amplitude of racket vibration is very small when a ball hits the centre, whereas it is large when a ball hits the off-centre (the top or the place close to the throat) on the string face. The amplitude of vibrations with the wide body racket is rather small compared with the normal one. The amplitude of the super-light and top-heavy racket is small at the top, whereas the amplitude with the over-sized racket is large at the near on the string face. If strung tightly, the amplitude of vibration increases remarkably in the off-centre impact.

Figure 3 shows the predicted coefficient e against the impact velocities when the ball strikes the racket with different physical properties. It is seen that each racket has its own characteristics with respect to the rebound velocity. The rebound coefficient with PROTO-02 (wide body) and EOS100 (super light and top-heavy) are not affected by an increase of impact velocity at the top and higher than that with the normal one. The super-light and top-heavy racket decreases gradually in rebound coefficient with an increase of impact velocity at the near on the string face. Although the rebound coefficient with PROTO-EX110 (over-sized) strung loosely is the highest among them, it decreases with an increase of impact velocity. If strung tightly, it decreases remarkably in the off-centre impact due to the energy loss caused by the vibration of racket-frame.

4 References

Groppel,J.L., Shin,I.S., Thomas,J.A. and Welk,G.J.(1987) The effect of strings type and tension on impact in midsized and oversizsed tennis racqets, Int. J.Sport Biomech., 3, 40-46.

Kawazoe,Y.(1989) Dynamics and computer aided design of tennis racket. Proc.Int.Sympo. on Advanced Computer for Dynamics and Design'89, 243-248.

Kawazoe,Y.,(1992a), CAE of tennis rackets with impact phenomena (Prediction of racket response and a view of restitution in racket-ball impact). Trans.JSME, 58, 2467-2474.(in Japanese)

Kawazoe,Y.(1992b) Analysis of coefficient of restitution duringa nonlinear impact between a ball and strings considering vibration modes of racket frame. JSME *D&D* '92 Symposium, pp.77-82.(in Japanese)

Kawazoe,Y.(1992c) Impact phenomena between racket and ball during tennis stroke. Theoretical and Applied Mechanics, 41, 3-13.

Kawazoe,Y.(1992d) Ball/racket impact and computer-aided design of rackets, Int.J. Table Tennis Sci., 1, 9-18.

Kawazoe,Y.(1992e), Approximate Nonlinear Analysis of Impact in Tennis, Proc. Int. Symp. on Impact Engineering'92, 473-478.

24 The effectiveness of damping material in reducing impact shock in the tennis forehand drive

R. Tomosue, K. Sugiyama, K. Yoshinari and K. Yamamoto
University of Tokyo, Tokyo, Japan

1 Introduction

The impact shock and post-impact vibration transfer in tennis have been hypothesized to contribute to upper extremity injuries. To reduce the transmission of the impact force to the hand, a damping material or a cushion grip band has now been used. Although study of the effectiveness of a grip band has now been reported (Hatze, 1992a, 1992b), how a damping material reduces the impact force has not been measured.

The purposes of this study were to measure the vibrations of a racket handle and the wrist joint during actual hitting in a tennis forehand drive and to quantify the effectiveness of a damping material in reducing impact shock and vibration transfer.

2 Methods

Seven Dunlop tennis rackets with different frame body width, face area, flexibility and string tension, and two Dunlop tennis rackets with a damping material were selected for the present study (Table 1). The damping material is a soft and light vibration absorbing device (double-layered sponge) designed for attachment to the two main strings near the throat of the racket (Figure 1). All rackets had the same weight and grip size.

To record the vibrations, two accelerometers (A & D Engineering, INC. Tokyo) were used; one was fixed to the racket handle (at 12cm from the end of each handle) and the other over the Lister tubercle. A Fast Fourier Transform Analyzer (Ono Sokki; CF-350, Tokyo) was used to record and to store simultaneously vibration traces from both sources.

The vibration amplitude was defined as the difference between the positive and negative peaks immediately following impact (Figure 2). To determine whether the vibration amplitude was significantly different among the rackets tested, a two-tailed Student's t-test was used.

A skilled male player was used as a subject; he gave informed consent. He was requested to hit flat forehand drives down the centre of a tennis court which was laid out in a gymnasium. A ball machine was used to propel new tennis balls towards him. This procedure was repeated five times for each racket. When the subject did not hit the ball at the centre of the strings, the trial was repeated in order to obtain consistent results.

Science and Racket Sports Edited by T. Reilly, M. Hughes and A. Lees.
Published in 1994 by E & FN Spon ISBN 0 419 18500 3

Table 1. Characteristics of the rackets tested

	Body width (mm)	Face area (cm^2)	String tension (N)	
A1	30	645	267	
A2	30	742	267+40	
B1	20	645	267	* without
C1	26	645	267	damping
A3	30	645	156	material
D1	26	645	267	
E1	21	542	267-44	
D2	26	645	267	* with damping
E2	21	542	267-44	material

Previous research has shown that the vibration amplitudes at the wrist joint and the racket handle in off-centre impacts showed 1.9-3.1 times and 1.3-1.6 times those of centre impacts, respectively (Tomosue et al., 1991).

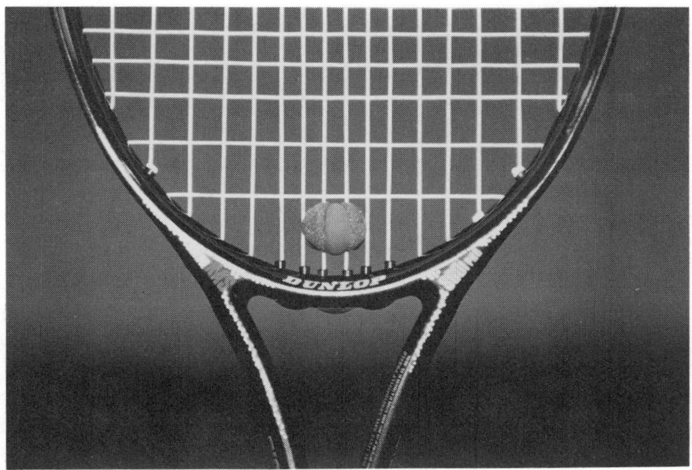

Fig.1. Damping material.

To avoid the influence of the intra-subject variations, not only impact point location but impact velocity and racket positions were determined using a high speed video camera (200Hz).

3 Results and Discussion

A typical record of the vibrations is shown in Figure 2. The vibration amplitudes of the wrist joint were so small as to be one-tenth of that of the racket handle. The high frequency vibrations were evident only from the racket handle.

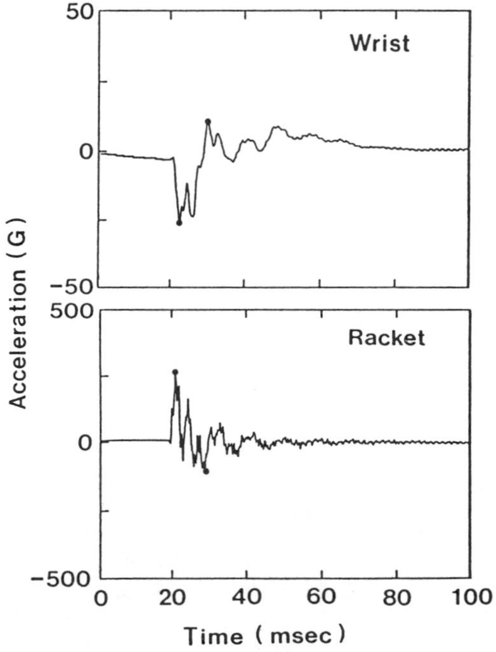

Fig.2. Recording of vibrations

The mean amplitudes for seven rackets without the damping material are presented in Figure 3. When comparing the oversized racket (A2) with its counterpart (A1), the former produced significantly greater ($P<0.05$) amplitude only for the wrist joint. When comparing the wide body racket (C1) with its counterpart (B1), the former produced significantly greater ($P<0.05$) amplitude only for the racket handle. String tension and flexibility did not affect the vibration levels. An interaction of face area, frame body width and flexibility was evident. However, the differences between any of the racket conditions were comparatively small. When comparing the oversized racket, the wide body racket, the low string tension racket and the still racket with their counterparts, there were no significant differences in their vibration responses for either the racket handle or the wrist joint. The mean amplitudes for the rackets with the damping material and the same rackets without a damping material are presented in Figure 4. The effect of a vibration device is evident. The damping material significantly reduced the amplitude in the racket handle (racket D1-D2: 364.0 ± 30.5 g to 273.6 ± 29.1 g ($P<0.01$), racket E1-E2: 596.6 ± 77.9 g to 432.8 ± 45.0 g ($P<0.01$)) and in the wrist

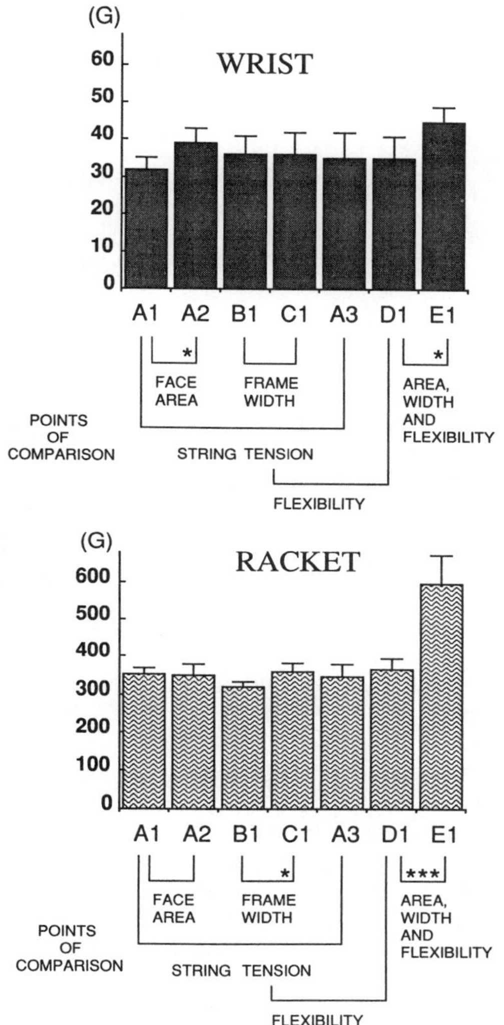

Fig.3. Vibration amplitude for the rackets without a damping material. Each bar represents the mean ± SD for five strokes. *:P<0.05, ***:P<0.001.

joint (racket E1-E2: 45.5 ± 4.0 g to 38.1 ± 3.3 g (P<0.05)). A non-significant trend of smaller amplitude in the wrist joint for the racket with the damping material (racket D1-D2: 35.0 ± 6.3 g to 31.0 ± 5.0 g) was observed. One possible explanation for lower vibration levels recorded from the rackets with damping material is that the double-layered sponge appreciably reduced the amplitude of the string vibrations, which had an apparent effect on the frame vibrations.

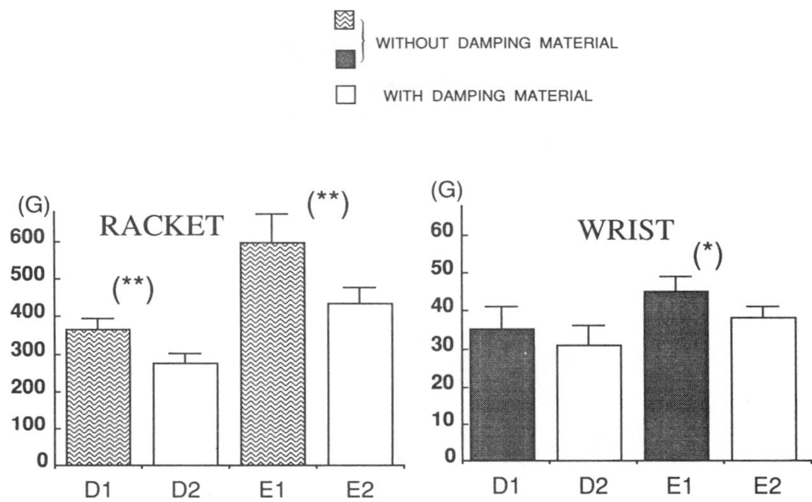

Fig.4. Vibration amplitude for the rackets with and without a damping material. Each bar represents the mean ± SD for five strokes. *:P<0.05, **:P<0.01

Many elements are involved in the vibration studies such as initial amplitude, damping time and frequency. These elements have been examined under various clamping conditions as a source of adverse loading on the arm as a result of impact (Brody, 1987, 1989; Hatze, 1976, 1992). The present study was an experimental examination of the effect of damping material on the vibration amplitude in an actual stroking condition. If the maximal amplitude of vibration is strongly related to inducing over use injuries, there may be a positive effect for a tennis player when using the damping material.

4 References

Brody, H. (1987) Models of tennis racket impacts. **Int. J. Biomech.,** 3, 293-296.

Brody, H. (1989) Vibration damping of tennis rackets. **Int. J. Biomech.,** 5, 451-456.

Hatze, H. (1976) Forces and duration of impact, and grip tightness during the tennis stroke. **Med. Sci. Sports Exerc.,** 8, 88-95.

Hatze, H. (1992a) The effectiveness of grip bands in reducing racquet vibration transfer and slipping. **Med. Sci. Sports Exerc.,** 24, 226-230.

Hatze, H. (1992b) Objective biomechanical determination of tennis racket properties. **Int. J. Biomech.,** 8, 275-287.

Tomosue, R., Mutoh, Y., Yoshinari, K. and Kawazoe, Y. (1991) Measuring the vibrations of a racket handle and the wrist joint in the tennis forehand drive. **Proceedings of XIIIth Int. Congress on Biomech.** Perth, 138-139.

25 Ball dyanamic characteristics: a fundamental factor in racket dynamic optimization

M. Caffi and F. Casolo
D.S.T.M. – Politecnico di Milano, Milan, Italy

1 Introduction

Experimental tests on tennis equipment were carried out in order to validate an analytical model (Casolo and Ruggieri, 1991) for ball-racket impact and to optimize the values of the parameters involved. These tests demonstrated the predominant effect of the ball's behaviour, that most of the energy lost during the impact phase is dissipated by the ball.

The ball impact phase was defined as the portion of the tennis stroke which starts from the first contact of the ball with the strings and ends with the first instant of the rebound in which the ball is no longer in touch with the racket. This phase generally lasts 3-7 milliseconds. The design of models of strings and racket systems should include the characteristics of the ball. For example, as an extreme case, if the ball were rigid and not deformable, the increase of the string tension, which improves the racket precision, would not cause a proportionate increase of the ball rebound velocity, which, on the contrary, is verified for standard balls. Despite this fundamental role of the characteristics of the ball, very few scientific works have been published on tennis balls and very poor tests are suggested for their homologation.

The aim of this work is to provide a better understanding of the influence of some mechanical parameters of the impact of the tennis ball and the racket.

2 Material and Methods

An appositely designed air gun (Fig.1 and Fig.2) enables the ball to hit the target at a pre-set velocity, that can be changed by means of a set of conic inserts (Fig.3) from 5 to 80 m/s. A three-axis aiming system and a laser pointer enabled positioning of the impact point easily and precisely. Two laser barriers (Fig.4), obtained by multiple reflections of two laser beams, enabled measurement of the speed of the ball both before and after the impact on the target. An electronic device, which was based on a clock (10 Mhz) armed and disarmed by a simple logic circuit, measured the lag of time between the first and the second barrier interruption and transmitted the digital value of the velocity to a computer serial port.

Fig. 1. Ball and racket testing equipment: 1) Air gun; 2) Laser pointer; 3) Speed measuring device; 4) Velocity display; 5) Rigid frame; 6) Racket head holder; 7) Frame for whole racket test.

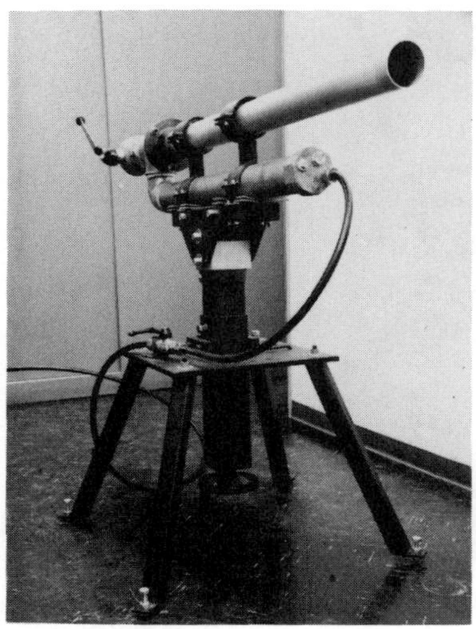

Fig. 2. Air gun.

Fig. 3. Gun's conic inserts.

Various targets were available: a rigid frame (Fig.5) was either fixed on a plain wall as a mark or used to support the racket head so that the string effect could be taken into account. A special frame was also available in order to test the response of the whole ball-racket system, ball, strings and racket, just before the impact a release system freed the racket, on which a body equivalent mass (Casolo and Ruggieri, 1991) could be mounted.

Fig. 4. The laser apparatus for the measurement of pre-impact and rebound velocities.

Fig. 5. The rigid frame for the tests on the plane wall and on the constrained racket head.

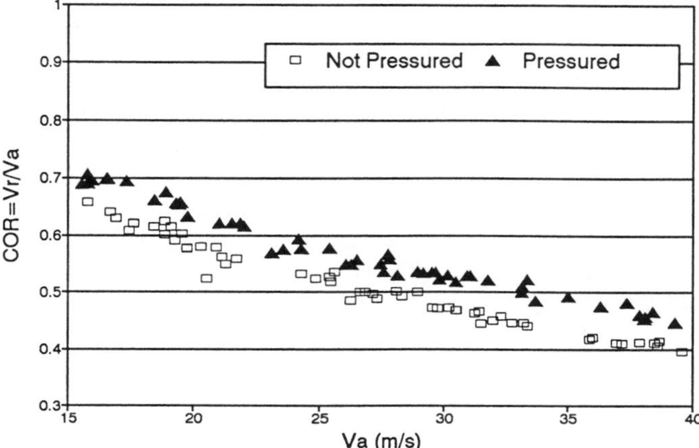

Fig. 6. Rebound test for two kinds of ball: pressured and not pressured -Vr ball rebound velocity, Va pre-impact velocity.

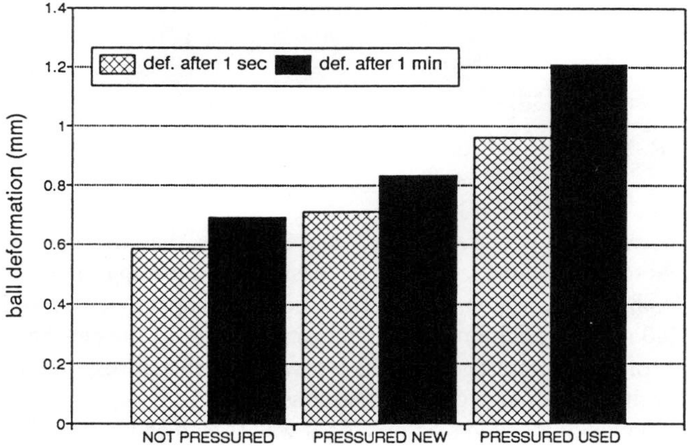

Fig. 7. Average results of loading tests (40 N) for three kinds of balls.

3 Results and Discussion

Ball rebound tests on a rigid wall clearly showed how the impact velocity affects the impact efficiency. For all types of balls that were tested, the coefficient of restitution of the impact

(COR) decreases as the pre-impact velocity increases (Fig.6).

The COR parameter is widely used in current practice to compare tennis rackets and is defined as the ratio of post-impact ball velocity to the relative velocity of the ball before impact with respect to the target. Therefore, in general, COR does not represent the mechanical efficiency of the impact because it does not take into account the racket velocity after the impact and the elastic energy stored in its frame. Only in particular cases, when the target cannot move during the impact, is COR directly related to the impact efficiency. This condition is verified in all the experiments described here.

Static loading tests are not adequate to compare the characteristics of different balls. Fig.7 shows the results of a compression test obtained by applying a force (40 N) on the ball. The ball deformation in the loading direction was measured after 1 s and after 60 s and the average values of three homogeneous groups of balls are displayed. Fig.8 shows the average results of COR tests for the same groups of balls on the rigid wall.

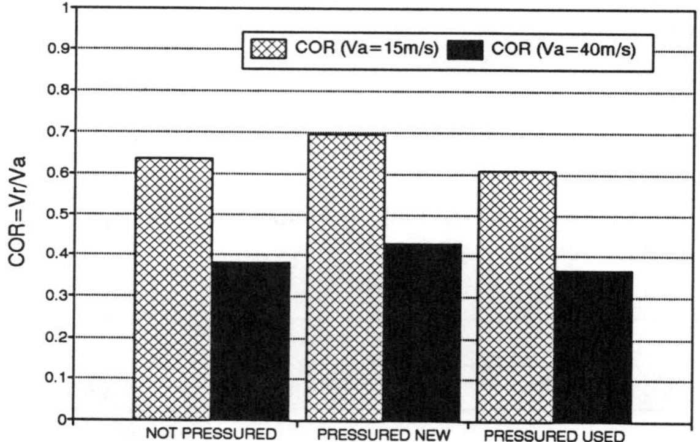

Fig. 8. Average COR for three kinds of ball against a rigid wall measured for Va=15 m/s and for Va=40 m/s.

The comparison between the two graphs (Fig.7 and 8) shows that the ball stiffness cannot be directly correlated to the rebound speed. As an example, the group of non-pressurized balls -the stiffest at the loading tests- were not the most efficient at impact, neither at low (15 m/s) nor at high speed (40 m/s). In addition, Fig.6 demonstrates that for the new balls tested in the laboratory, the COR of the non-pressurized balls is lower than the corresponding value of pressurized balls, for the whole range of velocities considered.

A simple theoretical model of ball impact on a rigid wall (Leigh and Lu, 1992) can help to understand the effect of the mechanical parameters on the impact.

$$m\ddot{x} + c\ddot{x} + kx + hx^3 = 0 \quad (*)$$

It takes into account: the ball elastic constant (k), the damping coefficient (c), the effect of the internal pressure (h), and the ball mass (m). Preliminary checks of the results obtained using the parameters values suggested by Leigh and Lu (1992) or measured by Brody (1979, 1990) seem in agreement with the experimental results (Fig.9).

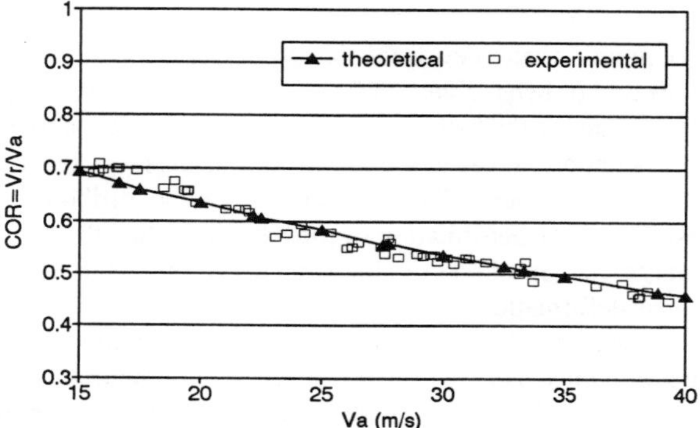

Fig. 9. Comparison of experimental and theoretical COR of the impact of tennis balls on rigid wall.

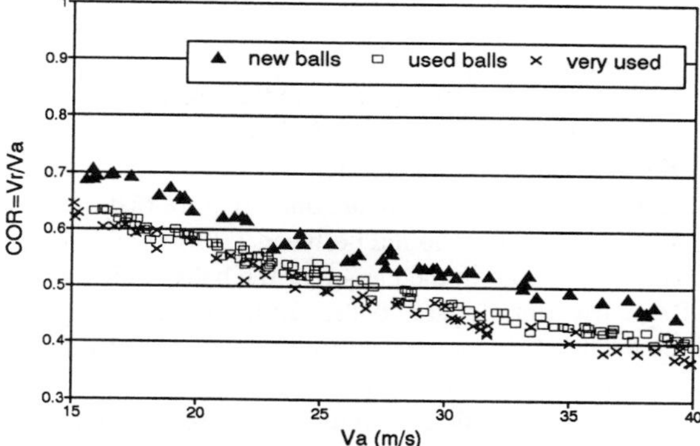

Fig. 10. Effect of the ball wearing on Vr/Va.

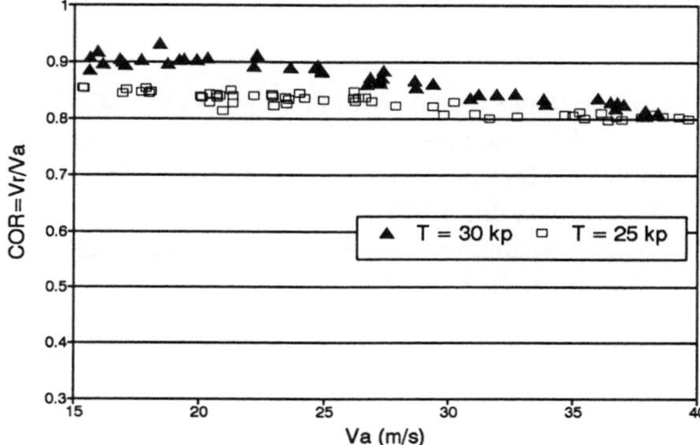

Fig. 11. Ball impacts on a constrained racket head: Vr/Va for string tension approximately 250 N and 300 N.

Another series of tests showed (Fig.10) the influence of ball wear. As expected, used balls have a slower rebound than new ones. It is interesting to note that balls only used for thirty or forty strokes do not behave very differently from those used much more.

The final test required impact of the ball with the racket head fixed on the rigid frame. This set-up enabled an evaluation of the influence of the strings on the impact (Fig.11). The increase of the rebound efficiency (Fig.6 and Fig.11) can be attributed to string deformation. This allows a lesser deformation of the ball, and while the ball deformation involves the loss of a large portion of energy, the strings, on the contrary, return most of the energy stored by their deformation.

Fig.11 shows, as expected, that lower string tension means higher rebound speed of the ball. Another interesting inference can be drawn from these preliminary data: the higher the impact velocity, the lower the influence of the differences in string tension on the rebound efficiency.

4 Conclusions

Although there is little evidence of previous research in this area, the knowledge of the ball behaviour at impact is very important in order to design or to choose rackets, strings and balls. The main factor affecting the rebound efficiency of the ball is the pre-impact velocity. The rules of the international tournaments only require that a ball dropped from 2.54 m (corresponding to Vr=7 m/s) will rebound between 1.35 m and 1.47 m high. This allows the organizer of a tournament freedom in the choice of the balls, and can therefore favour a certain kind of play. Regularly homologated balls, can have in fact very different behavior at the normal playing velocity. Therefore more strict rules must be introduced in order to test balls at real playing conditions (Va = 5 - 45 m/s).

Lower string tension allows higher rebound velocity, when the impact velocity is not extremely high, because it allows a lesser deformation of the ball (even if it may reduce the precision).

5 References

Brody, H.(1979) Physics of the tennis racket. **Am. J. Physics.,** 47, 482-487.

Brody, H.(1990) The tennis-ball bounce test. **The Physics Teacher**, Sept..

Casolo F. and Ruggieri, G.(1991) Dynamic analysis of the ball-racket impact in the game of tennis. **Meccanica**, 26, 67-73.

Leigh D.C. and Lu W. (1992) Dynamics of the interaction between ball, string, and racket in tennis, **Int. J. Sport Biomech.**, 8, 181-206.

Part Five
Sports Medicine

26 Elbow injuries in tennis

P.A.F.H. Renström
Department of Orthopedics & Rehabilitation, University of Vermont, Burlington, Vermont, USA

1 Introduction

Tennis is played today by millions of people around the world. Towards the end of the 70's, more than 40 million Americans played tennis (U.S. News and World Report, 1979). Top-level tennis is played in more countries around the world than almost any other sport. Tennis is played by all age groups, as it is a sport which in general does not produce severe medical problems. Some of the major problems in tennis occur, however, in the elbow region exemplified by the so-called tennis elbow. Pain near the lateral epicondyle of the humerus was described by Runge (1873), and was called "writer's cramp." Later it was called "washer women's elbow." As it also occurred in tennis, it soon was called "tennis elbow" (Morris, 1883). It should, however, be remembered that only five percent of people suffering from tennis elbow relates the injury to tennis. This injury is more common in industry and activities of daily living and occur in other racket sports. There are, however, many other injuries that may occur in the elbow region related to tennis. The different injuries causing elbow pain and their diagnosis, treatment and rehabilitation will be discussed below.

2 Functional Anatomy of the Elbow

The stability of the elbow is provided by the collateral ligaments, but also by the bones and their articulations and the muscles and tendons. The medial ulnar ligament is well developed and forms three distinct bands: the anterior oblique, a small transverse, non-functional ligament and the posterior oblique ligament (Fig. 1). The anterior oblique ligament is very strong and is taut through the entire arc of elbow flexion and is the primary constraint of valgus stress of the elbow. The posterior oblique ligament is taut in flexion and lax in extension and does not play a primary role in elbow stability. The lateral-collateral ligament is not clinically important as it has only a few non- functional weak fibres.

The anconeus muscle appears to provide lateral support, as does the forearm extensor

Science and Racket Sports Edited by T. Reilly, M. Hughes and A. Lees.
Published in 1994 by E & FN Spon ISBN 0 419 18500 3

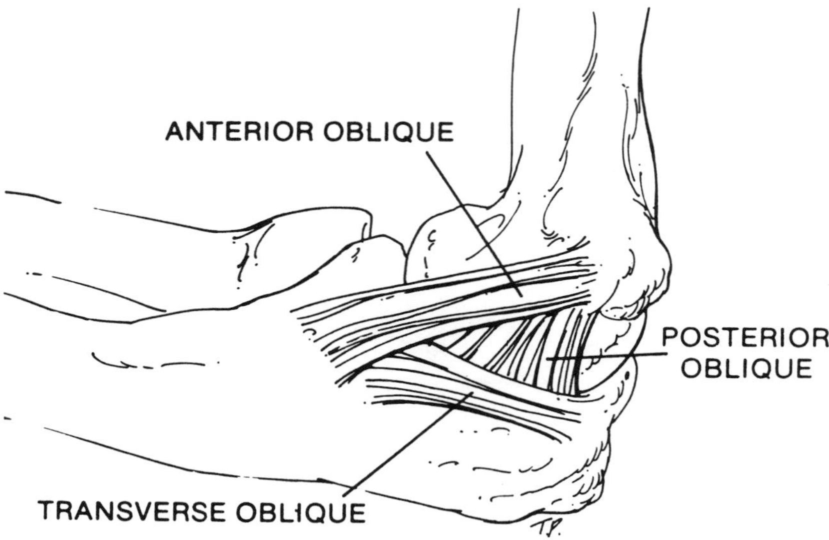

Figure 1. Collateral ligaments on the medial side of the elbow. (From Tullos HS, Bryan WJ: Functional Anatomy of the Elbow. In Injuries to the Throwing Arm: Zarins B, Andrews JR, Carson WG., W.B. Saunders Company, 1985, pp. 191.)

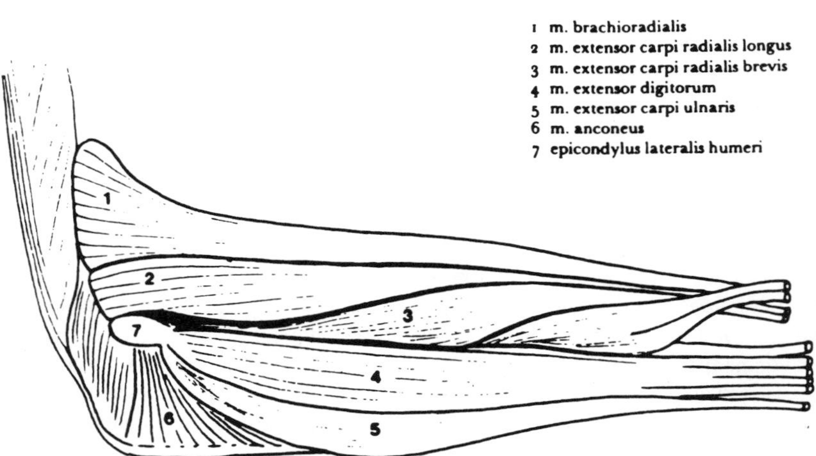

Figure 2. Origin of wrist and finger extensor muscles on the lateral side of the elbow. (From Winkel D, Fisher S, Vroege C: Wede Delen Aandoeningen Van Het Bewegingsapparaat. Deel 2: Diagnostiek (in Dutch). Utrecht, The Netherlands: Bohn, Scheltema en Holkema, 1984, pp. 159-161.)

muscles. The extensors carpi radialis brevis and longus, digitorum communis, digiti minimi and carporadialis originate at the lateral epicondyle and are mainly wrist extensors (Fig. 2). The three primary flexor muscles of the elbow are the biceps brachii, the brachioradialis and the brachialis. The most important pronator muscles of the elbow are the pronator teres and the pronator quadratus. The triceps is the only effective extensor of the elbow.

The radial nerve runs anterior lateral of the elbow and divides into the posterior interosseous nerve and the lateral cutaneous nerve of the forearm, and especially the former can be entrapped. The medial nerves remain anterior of the elbow in its course and pass between the two heads of the pronator muscle and can also become entrapped. The ulnar nerve goes through the triceps fascia, as it approaches the cubital tunnel on the medial posterior aspect where it can be compressed and cause distal problems.

The elbow is a joint which can be moved about a longitudinal and transverse axis. Flexion-extension is provided by the humeral-ulnar joint. The rotational motion is provided by the unique articulation of the radius with the capitellum portion of the humerus so that forearm pronation and supination can be carried out.

The normal range of motion of the elbow is flexion and extension 0 to 145 degrees with a functional arc of 0 to 130 degrees. Constraints to elbow extension and flexion can be seen in Figure 3. Pronation and supination can be carried out with 70 degrees of pronation to 80 degrees of supination. The axial rotation is around the centre radial head to the centre of the distal ulna.

There is a valgus carrying angle of 10-15 degrees in full extension and 8 degrees varus in full flexion (Fig. 4). The internal rotation is 5 degrees during early flexion and external 5 degrees during terminal flexion.

3 Injuries to the Elbow

Injuries can occur in the elbow depending on the type of activity. In tennis they are most commonly localized to the lateral epicondyle such as the lateral epicondylitis. Tennis can also cause medial epicondylitis and extensor overload can cause posterior tennis elbow.

3.1 Lateral epicondylitis - lateral elbow tendinosus - tennis elbow:

Lateral elbow tendinosus is most common in tennis players of 35 to 50 years of age. This group is often characterized by a high activity level and they often play tennis three times per week or more of at least 30 minutes or greater per session. It has been shown that 45 percent of the athletes who play tennis daily, or 20 percent of those who play twice a week, may at certain stages suffer from lateral elbow tendinosus. Frequency of play has a direct relationship with pain. The more frequently a person plays, the greater the incidence of pain (Carroll, 1981; Priest et al., 1980). Players of higher ability, which means players that play longer and practice more, have more commonly a history of elbow pain.

Persons most likely to sustain lateral elbow tendinosus are those that have demanding techniques and inadequate fitness levels. It is well established that faulty technique is one of the most common causes for lateral elbow tendinosus, especially a faulty

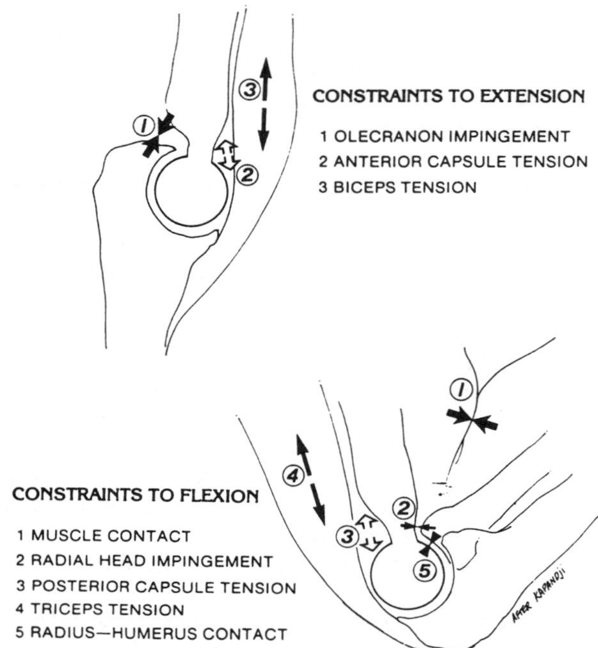

Figure 3. The constraints to elbow extension and flexion. (From Tullos HS, Bryan WJ: Functional Anatomy of the Elbow, in Injuries to the Throwing Arm: Zarins B, Andrews JR, Carson WG., W.B. Saunders Company, 1985, pp. 192.)

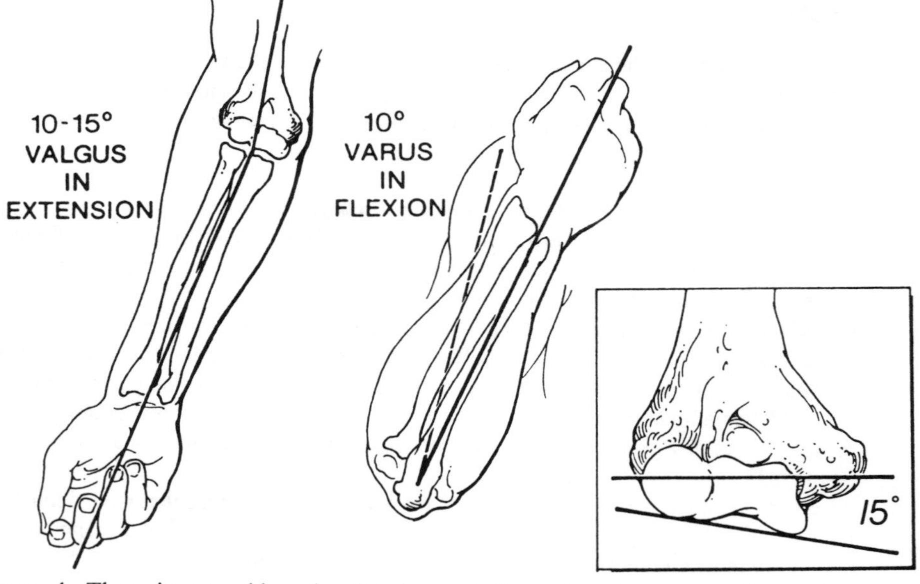

Figure 4. The unique trochlear slop (15 degrees) allows the elbow to pass from valgus to varus positions as flexion proceeds. (From Tullos HS, Bryan WJ: Functional Anatomy of the Elbow. In Injuries to the Throwing Arm: Zarins B, Andrews JR, Carson WG., W.B. Saunders Company, 1985, pp. 194).

backhand. The serve is also associated with elbow pain. Studies have shown an association of tennis elbow with repetitive hobbies such as house decorating, gardening and knitting and industrial activities involving wrist motions of different kinds (Kamien, 1988).

In a study of average players, Priest et al. (1980) found that 31% of a group of 2,633 players suffered elbow pain at sometime during their career. Thirty-seven percent of 84 top-level players had elbow pain in a study by Priest et al. (1980), which can be compared to 22% of 41 players in a study by Gerber (1987). In top-level players, however, the clinical observation is that they more commonly have elbow pain localized to the medial side.

Table 1. Origins and insertions of wrist- and finger-extending muscles [adapted from Snijders, C.J., Vokers, A.C.W., Mechelse, K. and Vleeming, A. (1987): Provocation of epicondylalgia lateralis (tennis elbow) by power grip or pinching. **Med. Sci. Sports Exerc.,** 19, 518].

Muscle	**Origin**	**Insertion**
ECRL (Extensor carpi radialis longus)	Lateral supra-condylar ridge of the humerus Lateral inter-muscular septum	Dorsal surface of base of metacarpal 2
ECRB (Extensor carpi radialis brevis)	Common extensor origin at the lateral epicondyle Fascia covering the common extensor origin Inter-muscular septum (often fused with ECRL)	Dorsal surface of base of metacarpal 3
ECU (Extensor carpi ulnaris)	Common extensor origin covering fascia Posterior border of the ulna	Medial side of base of metacarpal 5
EDC (Extensor digitorum communis)	Common extensor origin covering fascia Inter-muscular septa	Extensor hood over metacarpophalangeal joints 2 to 5 Dorsal surface of proximal inter-phalangeal joints 2 to 5
EDM (Extensor digitorum minimi)	Common extensor origin covering fascia	Extensor hood of 5

Pathology

The pathoanatomy of lateral elbow tendinosus related to tennis involves primarily extensor carpi radialis brevis and secondary extensor digitorum communis (Nirschl, 1992). Figure 2 shows the anatomical relations near the lateral epicondyle. The bellies of the relevant muscles are all located in the forearm, while the long tendons bridge the elbow and wrist joints, and insert on the metacarpals, or phalanges (Table 1). The lateral epicondyle of the humerus forms a common origin for at least parts of all the extensors of the wrist and fingers.

The pathology represents a degenerative process that is secondary to tensile overuse fatigue, weakness and possibly avascular changes. Goldie (1964) reported granulation tissue in the subtendinous space as being the cause of the problem. Microscopic tendon tears of the extensor origin were first reported by Coonrad and Hooper (1973), and later confirmed by Nirschl and Pettroni (1979) to be present in extensor brevis tendon. The likely sequence of events is: "avascular compromise, an altered nutritional state, and forced overload cause angiofibroblastic changes and ultimate rupture of these vulnerable tissues." There are usually no inflammatory cells present. The term tendinosis has, therefore, been replacing the term tendinitis. This means that tennis elbow should be called lateral elbow tendinosis.

Tendinosis can appear at multiple sites in approximately 15 percent of the patients. It is then called Mesenchymal Syndrome which occurs in patients who may have a systemic and generalized tendinosis (Nirschl, 1992).

Symptoms

The onset of symptoms can be sudden or gradual. In most instances, there is no predisposing activity that can be found. Sometimes there is a history of repetitive activity or overuse, such as playing tennis intensively at a training camp, or going back to tennis activity after a period of no activity. Lateral elbow tendinosus is characterized by pain and often weakness localized to the lateral part of the elbow. Sometimes this pain can radiate distally or not-so-commonly more proximally.

There is palpable tenderness over the lateral epicondyle. This tenderness is mostly localized over the extensor brevis tendon insertion, which is slightly on the anterior aspect of the epicondyle. "The coffee cup test," which means picking up a full cup of coffee, will produce localized pain at the lateral epicondylar area. This test is more or less pathognomonic for lateral epicondylitis (Coonrad and Hooper, 1973). There is pain with resistance stress tests by dorsi-flexion of the wrist, or the middle finger, localized to the elbow confirming the area of abnormality. According to Nirschl (1992) involvement of the extensor carpi radialis brevis is typical for tennis players. This involves pain at the elbow on resistance stress test by dorsi-flexion of the wrist. When lateral elbow tendinosus is caused by industrial work, it seems, according to the author's experience, that extensor digitorum communis is mostly involved. This can also generate a positive middle finger test, i.e. pain at the elbow on resistance at dorsi- flexion of the middle finger. In other words, it seems clinically that there may be two different aetiologies in lateral elbow tendinosus with somewhat different locations of the problem.

Table 2. Pathological stages of tendinosis

Stage I:	Temporary irritation (? chemical inflammation)
Stage II:	Permanent tendinosis - less than 50% tendon cross section
Stage III:	Permanent tendinosis - greater than 50% tendon cross section
Stage IV:	Partial or total rupture of tendon

R. Nirschl: Elbow tendinosis/tennis elbow. Tendinitis II: Clinical considerations. **Clinics in Sports Medicine,** 11(4):851, October 1992

An accurate diagnosis of tendinosis includes an evaluation of the magnitude of pathological change, which is helpful as a prognostic predictor, as well as formulating the treatment protocol. Nirschl (1992) has developed a staging of tennis elbow tendinosus (Table 2). The patient's description of time and intensity of pain is the best guideline to evaluate the amount of problems. A grading system concerning the tendinosis phases of pain is outlined in Table 3.

Table 3. Tendonosis phases of pain

Phase I:	Mild pain after exercise activity, resolves within 24 hours
Phase II:	Pain after exercise activity, exceeds 48 hours, resolves with warm-up
Phase III:	Pain with exercise activity that does not alter activity
Phase IV:	Pain with exercise activity that alters activity
Phase V:	Pain caused by heavy activities of daily living
Phase VI:	Intermittent pain at rest that does not disturb sleep Pain caused by light activities of daily living
Phase VII:	Constant rest pain (dull aching) and pain that disturbs sleep)

R. Nirschl: Elbow tendinosis/tennis elbow. Tendinitis II: Clinical considerations. **Clinics in Sports Medicine,** 11(4):851, October 1992

Aetiology - Age and Sex

Epidemiological studies have identified age as a contributing factor associated with the occurrence of tennis elbow, with onset more common after age 30 (Nirschl, 1992). Incidence of tennis elbow by age group is seen in Table 4 (Kamien, 1989).

Results concerning the incidence of tennis elbow between sexes is somewhat conflicting. Hang and Peng (1984) found no statistical difference between male and female tennis players; this has been supported by Allman (1975). Grouchow and Pelletier (1979) and Priest et al. (1980) found that women were affected more often than men.

Strength and Flexibility

Inadequate strength, primarily of the forearm muscle, is considered to play a role in causing tennis elbow (Kulund et al.,1979), as well as inadequate wrist flexibility. This is because a tight wrist will affect the muscle flexibility of the forearm, which may result in lateral epicondyle tendon strain.

In tennis players these are statistically significant increases in forearm muscle, girth and grip strength, and decreases in the range of motion of playing extremities. The increase in forearm girth is approximately twice that of the upper arm (Priest et al., 1974). Strikingly and statistically significant increases in the humerus bone were found for nearly all of the dimensions in the playing arm. The significance of this is not known.

Playing time

Increased playing time has been shown to increase the incidence of tennis elbow up to 3.5 times for people over the age of 40. The players who play more than 2 hours a day are more susceptible than those who play less than 2 hours a week (Grouchow and Pelletier, 1979). Priest et al. (1980) found that the incidence of elbow pain increased with playing frequency.

Table 4. Incidence of tennis elbow by age group
Kamien M: The incidence of tennis elbow and other injuries in tennis players at the Royal Kings Park Tennis Club of Western Australia from October 1983 to September 1984. **Australian Journal of Science and Medicine in Sports,** 21(2),18-22, 1989.

Tennis Elbow	10-19	20-29	30-39	40-49	50-59	60+	Total
Men							
In last year	1	2	3	8	7	0	21
> 1 year ago	0	2	10	21	32	24	89
Never	11	2	17	23	11	13	77
Women							
In last year	1	0	3	2	0	0	6
> 1 year ago	0	1	9	12	8	2	32
Never	7	3	12	10	2	1	35
Total	20	10	54	76	60	40	260

It has been shown that the number of people who have had tennis elbow during their careers increased with the number of years they had played. Priest et al. (1980) experienced an influence of experience of the prevalence of elbow pain and the presence of a history of elbow pain. Hang and Peng (1984) found that increased playing experience was associated with a lower incidence of tennis elbow for those players under 40 years of age. Players over 40 years of age who had played tennis for many years had a higher incidence of tennis elbow. Increased incidence of tennis elbow among the better tennis players is probably due to increased playing time rather than a deficiency in their ability. Inexperienced players more often use improper stroke techniques, and are more prone to miss-hit the ball. Either of these, or the combination of the two, result in greater mechanical stress on the elbow joint (Bernhang et al., 1974; Nirschl, 1973).

Motions involved

Tennis elbow is generally combined with an improperly executed backhand stroke technique (Weber, 1976; VonBiehl and Scmitt, 1978; Biener, 1979; Grouchow and Pelletier, 1979; VonKramer and Schmitz-Beating, 1979; Kulund et al., 1979; Priest et al., 1980; Carroll, 1981). Out of 75 percent of players with tennis elbow, 40 percent have reported the use of a faculty backhand in combination with muscle weakness (Priest et al., 1980). Fifty percent of female and 30 percent of male professional tennis players with tennis elbow problems get lateral epicondylitis by overuse of the forehand and/or backhand. The player with a faulty backhand can often compensate with the use of a forehand grip or a fist-like grip with the thumb extended behind the handle for more power (Roy and Irvin, 1983). The faulty backhand stroke usually starts high with a high back swing with the body weight on the back leg. The power is generated at the wrist and elbow. As the elbow extends, the wrist strongly hooks into ulnar deviation, which is a motion commonly used for opening doors, chopping wood, and so on. The combination of the extended elbow and the ulnar hooking of the wrist causes the extensor mass, especially the deep extensor carpi radialis brevis to rub and roll over the lateral epicondyle and the lateral head. Microtears are present, and as a result of the rubbing, rolling and the microtears, a painful elbow evolves. In an attempt to heal the damage, granulation tissue forms, which can swell, stretch and become painful. Adhesions can also form between the annular ligament and the joint capsule. The pain worsens from the constant strain of the faulty backhand.

Twenty-five percent of the players in a study by Priest et al. (1980) identified the serve as the most painful tennis stroke. Overhead stroke, and especially the serve, caused pain in 29% of players with elbow pain. Epidemiological studies have linked the serving action with injuries to the elbows (Allman, 1975; Nigg and Denoth, 1980; Priest et al., 1980).

Rackets and tennis elbow

Factors of importance for the racket are torsion and centre of percussion - the sweet spot. The centre of percussion can be defined as the point on the racket which, when hit, will keep vibrational impact from being transferred to the hand; and consequently will maximize the energy available to the ball. One primary goal when designing a racket would be to have as large a sweet spot as possible. Secondly, it would be desirable to have the sweet spot as powerful as possible, with the delivery power as uniform as possible from the centre of the sweet spot to its outer edge. These goals are achieved differently, and result in various designs of rackets and frames. Modern frame designs have made it possible to enlarge the sweet spot and increase its power.

There is a popular belief that tennis elbow is the result of transmitted vibration caused by hitting heavy tennis balls. This view is supported by the eight years experience of an English Sports Medicine Clinic, which found upper limb injuries to be more frequent in tennis players than in badminton players (Chard and Lachmann, 1986). The role of vibration is still unclear.

Considerably worse strain has been seen occurring on the forearm muscles from hitting balls off centre along the vertical axis of any racket (Brody, 1979). These off-centre

Table 5. Occurrence of tennis elbow by composition, size and weight of racquet, grip size, tension and type of strings.
Kamien M: The incidence of tennis elbow and other injuries in tennis players at the Royal Kings Park Tennis Club of Western Australia from October 1983 to September 1984. **Austr. J. Sci. Med. Sports** 21(2):18-22, 1989.

		Tennis elbow	
	In last year n=27 %	**Past history n=121 %**	**Never n=112 %**
Racket Material			
Wood	22	13	28
Aluminum	30	49.5	28
Graphite	18.5	13	24
Composite	18.5	13	15
Other	11	8	5
Racket Size			
Standard	22	23	38
Mid-size	45	30	42
Oversize (Jumbo)	33	47	20
Racket Weight			
Light	11	19	24
Light medium	30	28	33
Medium	33	35	18
Don't' know	26	32	25
Grip Size			
Correct	55	50	49
Small	4	9	11
Large	30	29	26
Not Sure	11	12	14
Type of Strings			
Gut	33	26	21
Synthetic	67	74	79
Tension of Strings			
Tight	44	37	50
Moderately tight	52	60	44
Low tension	4	3	6

impact vibrations have been shown to be best absorbed by oversized rackets (Elliott et al., 1980). Hang and Peng (1984) formed the impression that the frequency of tennis elbow is lower in players using an oversized racket. Kamien (1989) suggested that tennis elbow may result from using an oversized aluminum racket. In interviews, some players in his study blame oversized aluminum rackets for the cause of their elbow pain, while other players gave it credit for their cure (Kamien, 1989). Occurrence of tennis elbow by composition, size, weight of racket, grip size, tension and type of strings is shown in Table 5.

Tennis elbow is more likely to occur in players who use a heavy racket than in players who use a light racket (Weber, 1976; Kulund et al., 1979). Other studies indicate that the weight of the rackets does not influence the incidence of tennis elbow (Grouchow and Pelletier, 1979; Carroll, 1981). The heavier the racket, the greater the momentum. The heavier and stiffer rackets increase the muscle force that is required during the swing of impact; while also increasing the stress on the elbow (Nirschl, 1973). It is recommended that recreational players should use evenly balanced light rackets.

Racket materials may be a factor in the incidence of tennis elbow (Weber, 1976; Von Biehl and Schmitt, 1978; Grouchow and Pelletier, 1979; VonKramer and Schmitz-Beuting, 1979; Carroll, 1981). Metal rackets have been considered to be too stiff to absorb the shock waves transmitted at ball impact. Bernhang et al. (1984) found that tennis players who use aluminum rackets are afflicted with tennis elbow almost twice as much as players who use wooden rackets. Other studies have been inconclusive over this point (Nirschl, 1992; Bernhang et al., 1974; Peng, 1978). Priest (1976) found, on the other hand, that wooden rackets are more apt to produce symptoms than aluminum or steel rackets. Frames made of fibreglass, different composite materials, and so on, are supposed to reduce the vibration with increasing stiffness; however, definite evidence for this does not exist.

Grip size

Several studies have been done to correlate the incidence of tennis elbow to different grip sizes. Some have indicated that too large (4 and 5 inches) or too small (4.25 inches) a grip is associated with a very high incidence rate of tennis elbow (Hung and Peng, 1984). Grouchow and Pelletier (1979) have found that for players over 40 years of age, those who used a large grip size, had an incidence rate of over six times that for those who used a smaller grip size. It is not immediately evident, however, that the grip size relates to the pathology of tennis elbow. Bernhang et al. (1974) compared hand size with grip size, calculating whether a grip size was correct or incorrect for that player. No association was found between the incidence of tennis elbow and the use of a grip which is too large or too small for the player's hand. Adelsberg (1986) used EMG's to study muscle activity generated in the forearm and shoulder muscles of a player using different size grips ranging from 4.25 to 4.75 inches (10.8 to 12.1 cm.). It was concluded that the force change in the muscles was not significant enough to suggest the need for a change in racket grip size. Bernhang et al. (1974) concluded that using the largest grip size that is comfortable is an effective prophylaxis against developing tennis elbow. Further verification of this point in his study is required. A player can determine his grip size by measuring from the proximal palmar crease to the top of the ring finger along the medial side of the ring finger.

Strings

Strings are either made of gut or nylon. Gut is manufactured from the smooth muscle portion of sheep or beef. Gut provides better control, higher ball velocities, lower levels of vibration transmission to the hand, and improved playing characteristics according to player evaluation (Groppel and Nirschl, 1986). In addition, tests measuring ball velocity favoured gut string over synthetic string when strung at the same tension.

Elliott (1988) concluded that ball velocities following impact were superior in rackets with gut string. The looser the strings are, the higher the post-impact ball velocity. This may be of some importance in tennis elbow treatment. The stringing patterns can also vary and can be trampoline, fishnet, or pulley-like.

How does string tension affect control? One effect is that an increase in string tension causes the ball to flatten out during impact. A second is that a trampoline effect occurs at low string tensions, where the ball is on the racket face for a longer period of time. At higher tensions, the ball is on the racket face for a shorter period of time. Therefore, if a ball is hit off-centre, the racket will have more time to rotate during impact, sending the ball in an errant direction. This provides less control and also higher rotational accelerations. A recommendation is that a racket should not be strung too tightly, usually between 50-55 pounds of tension in order to avoid tennis elbow. In general, more tightly strung rackets will give better control, whereas looser strung rackets will give more force. However, the tension in the strings will decrease within a short time. Gut string is rather resilient when freshly strung, whereas nylon strings will last longer and is more economical.

Balls

Heavy balls should be avoided, as well as dead, wet or pressureless balls. Use of these will increase the impact against the tennis racket whereby increasing the risk of tennis elbow.

Courts

The condition of the court can also be a factor in the incidence of tennis elbow. In Carroll's (1981) review some players cited irregularities in the court as possible factors in the development of their tennis elbow. These irregularities caused the ball to bounce unexpectedly and, consequently, the stroke was incorrectly timed, and resulted in strain due to the faulty technique. On the other hand, a slow court decreases the velocity of the ball, thereby minimizing the impact and torsional forces during impact. It is for this reason that the use of slow courts is suggested for patients with tennis elbow problems.

Background -- vibration and muscle activity

Several studies have been conducted to study the level of vibration in the hands and arms of those who work with hand held power tools. It has been found that for high frequencies (above 100 Hz), vibration entering the hand will remain in the hand and fingers; whereas lower frequencies (less than 70-80 Hz for finger grip and 20-50 Hz for palm grip) tend to transmit vibration up the arm (Suggs et al., 1977; Cundiff, 1974, Reynolds et al., 1982). As Cundiff (1974) explained, "the tissue between the hand surface and the arm is not stiff enough to drive the arm except at low frequencies." In each of these studies, the transmissibility was obtained by mounting accelerometers to the tool and to the hands and arms of the operator, whereby a transfer function was measured.

A racket vibration test was conducted by Carroll (1981). His study included seven rackets of different sizes and materials. With each racket he studied frequency, amplitude, amplitude decay and the effect of the ball's position at impact. He found that the level of each of these would vary depending upon the material of the racket, the frame stiffness, the racket weight and how the racket was gripped (i.e. subject's hand, vice, etc.). Brody (1989) compared the oscillations of a hand-held tennis racket with a clumped tennis racket. It was concluded that the hand-held racket showed vibrational modes similar to those of free rackets, while being very different from clamped rackets. He stated that "a free racket's lowest frequency of oscillation is about 100 to 175 Hz, which is similar to the higher frequency of the clamped racket." However, Brody (1989) conducted another study comparing tennis racket vibration damping in hand-held rackets with freely suspended rackets. In this, he found that hand-held rackets clamped out racket vibration a magnitude shorter than freely suspended rackets. Two other important points were mentioned in his study, one being that the time required to clamp the amplitude of oscillations to hold its value is dependent upon how tightly the racket is gripped. This, assuming that the frequency of this oscillation is about 100 Hz, agrees with Reynolds et al. (1982) who found that grip force most likely does not affect transmitted vibration beyond the wrist for frequencies much lower than 10 Hz.

The other important point in Brody's study is that the vibrations of a tennis racket which are the most annoying are caused by the first harmonic mode of oscillation. The frequency of this mode is from about 120 to 200 Hz. The highest magnitudes to occur at low frequencies are around 1 Hz. According to MacKay (1983) muscle resonance is between 20 to 25 Hz and elbow resonance is between 0.5 and 1.0 Hz. In view of this and the information from the hand power tool studies, it has been theorized that low frequency vibrations travel up the arm and this event is a contributing factor to the cause of tennis elbow. In our unpublished studies, however, the vibration transmitted from the racket reaches the hand, but is low when it reaches the elbow (Renström, Thesis, unpublished data). It seems that most of the vibration stays at hand level. Similar findings have recently been published by Henning et al. (1992) who used miniature accelerometers at the wrist and elbow in 24 tennis players in a similulated backhand stroke to study vibration. Amplitudes, integral and Fourier components were used to characterize vibration. They found more then four-fold reduction in acceleration amplitude and integral between wrist and elbow. Off-centre impacts resulted in approximately three times increased acceleration values. Increased racket head size was found to reduce arm vibration. In summary, they found that hitting close to the centre of the racket phase, a better skill level of the players and increased resonance frequency of the racket were identified as the main factors for a reduction of acceleration of the wrist and elbow.

Due to the discussions of the effects of racket vibration, vibration dampeners have been developed. Although these dampeners work well for damping string vibration, they do not aid in damping harmful frame vibration caused by off-centre shots (Brody, 1989).

It has also been of interest to study the affects of hitting the tennis ball off centre. As a result of the torque produced by mis-hits, there is an increase in both the amplitude and frequency of vibration (Carroll, 1981; Elliott, 1988). Bernhang et al. (1974) showed an increase in EMG activity as well for off-centre shots. For these reasons it is believed that oversize rackets, with larger sweet spots, may produce lower vibrational levels and higher rebound velocities (Elliott, 1988).

In summary, it seems that the vibration from the racket stays at the level of the hand. It seems that mis-hits, which produce racket torsion and result in increased lower arm muscle activity, most likely are a main contributor to the tennis elbow pain syndrome. Vibration most likely does not cause tennis elbow, but may aggravate the condition once a player has the injury.

Concepts for treatment

The treatment should follow the healing response and stimulate healing. The healing includes three phases: 1) acute inflammatory phase; 2) collagen and Grouund substance production phase; 3) maturation and remodeling phase.

The relief of pain and limitation of inflammation in the first acute phase can be carried out with rest, protection, ice, compression and elevation. Rest is defined as absence from abuse, but this does not mean that pain free activities cannot be carried out. Sometimes modalities and antiinflammatory medication can be helpful.

Exercises: The goal during the second phase is to stimulate promotion of healing to enhance the proliferative invasion of fibroblasts and collagen deposition. This can be done by exercises including stretching and strengthening. The stretching involves dorsiflexion of the wrist with the arm extended in the elbow and the lower arm pronated to reach maximum effect. This should be done several times a day, as the effect of stretching is rather short. The strength training can be carried out with a light weight doing repeated wrist motions. Endurance training can be carried out with many repetitions and low resistance. General body conditioning is important.

Braces: The hinged elbow brace was described by Ilfeld and Field (1966), the proximal forearm band by Froimsen (1971) and the counterforce brace by Nirschl (1974). Grouuchow and Pelletier(1979) found some beneficial effect of braces in his epidemiological study. Counterforce bracing, which constrains key muscle Groups for maintaining muscle balance, has been shown by Grouppel and Nirschl (1986) to decrease in the angular acceleration of the wrist and elbow during the serve and of the elbow during the backhand. The Group used surface EMG during motion, which is a controversial technique. An air-filled bladder (Aircast, Inc.) (Figure 5) has been developed as a counter-pressure element and has been studied by Snyder-Mackler and Epler (1989). They found that this constrictive band caused a significant reduction in integrated EMG of the extensor carpi radialis brevis and the extensor digitori communis when compared with controlled values and a standard band. The decrease in integrated EMG effected by the bands was more marked in the extensor digitorum than in the extensor carpi radialis brevis. This could be a result of the location, relative depth, or cross-section area of the muscles under the band. More research is needed to confirm the effect of braces for the treatment of tennis elbow. Clinical experience, including the author's, indicates, however, that the use of tennis elbow braces is a valuable complementary tool in the treatment of tennis elbow. The elbow bands can be combined with heat retaining neoprene sleeves to add the positive effects of heat in stimulating healing.

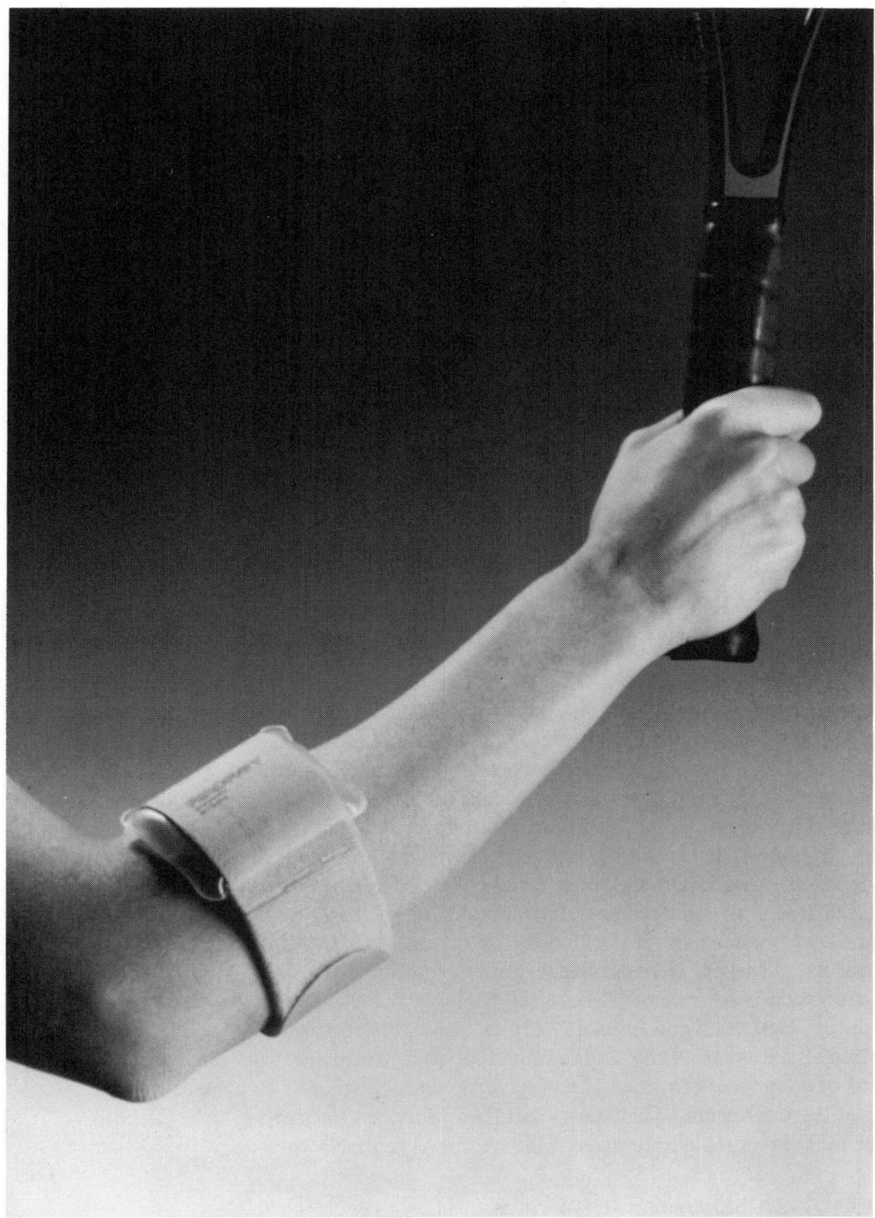

Figure 5. A tennis elbow brace with localized pressure is often helpful.

Modalities: There is no agreement for which treatment is most appropriate for this common condition. LaBelle et al. (1992) reviewed 185 articles published since 1966 to assess the scientific evidence of methods of treatment for epicondylitis of the elbow. Out of the 185 articles, 78 discussed treatment. Only 18 randomized were controlled studies. These 18 papers were graded for scientific validity, as an attempted meta-analysis. The mean score of the 18 articles was only 33% for a range of 6% to 73%. As a minimal of 70% is required for a valid clinical trial, the authors concluded that there was insufficient scientific evidence to support any of the current methods of treatment for epicondylitis.

Haker (1991) showed in double blind studies that in general the acupuncture technique applied to acupuncture points related to the elbow is the method of choice in the treatment of lateral epicondylitis. She also found that steroids may be recommended in severe cases. Low energy laser and pulse ultrasound were not effective.

Failed healing is considered to occur if there are chronic symptoms of phase four tendinosis pain or greater, exceeding a duration of one year. If there is poor response to a quality rehabilitation programme, if there is a history of persistent pain of grade four or greater, or if the patient has not been able to return to an acceptable quality of life, failed healing is suspected.

Surgery is, in these cases, sometimes indicated. During surgery it has been found that the tissues involved in tennis elbow is extensor carpi radialis brevis in 100 percent. Extensor digitorum communis and especially the anterior edge is involved in 35 percent and there is an osteophyte formation of the lateral epicondyle in 20 percent (Nirschl, 1992).

The surgery consists of identification of the pathological tissue which is resected. The attachment of normal tissues should be maintained and the normal tissues protected. There should then be quality post-operative rehabilitation. The elbow is protected at 90 degrees for one-week in a counterforce elbow immobilizer. Strength and endurance resistant exercises usually start at three weeks after surgery. Modified sports technique patterns are often initiated starting at six weeks after surgery. Eighty-five percent experience complete pain relief and return to full strength after surgery.

Failed surgery can be caused by iatrogenic harm which includes detached and unhealed extensor aponeurosis, detached or lax radial collateral ligament, relaxed or unhealed orbicular ligament, invaginated scar with subluxation of scar over the radial head, exuberant scar replacement of the extensor aponeurosis (Nirschl, 1992). The final reason for failed surgery is inappropriate patient selection.

There is a recurrence rate of 18-66% (Nevolos, 1980; Clarke and Woodland, 1975) in the literature, Gerberich and Priest (1985) had only 25% recurrence after 19 months. This group also found that the degree of pain prior to treatment is the most important predictor of complete recovery. The greater the pain, the more likely the complete success of the treatments. This means that there is a need for treating cases early to elicit the most favourable outcomes of the treatment regime.

Differential diagnosis to lateral epicondylitis

Cervical nerve root compression of C6 and C7, as well as cervical osteoarthritis may cause lateral elbow pain and mimic lateral tennis elbow. This is, however, something that is rare and is seen in the elderly.

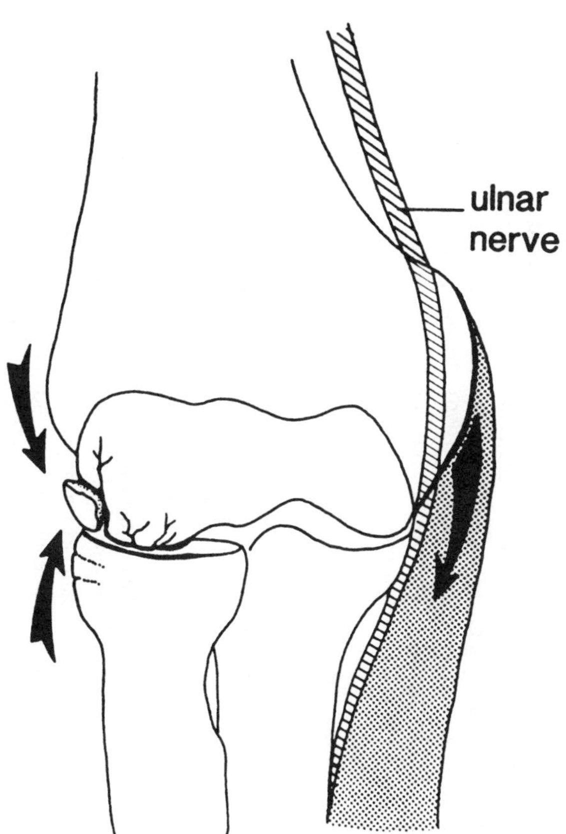

Figure 6. A. Serving motion showing valgus overload; B. Valgus overload results in medial tension and lateral compression. (From Hunter SC: Little Leaguer's Elbow. In Injuries to the Throwing Arm: Zarins B, Andrews JR, Carson WG., W.B. Saunders Company, 1985, pp. 229).

The radial nerve and posterior interosseous or superficial radial nerve branches are vulnerable to compression from distal to the level of the lateral head of the triceps through the arcade of Frohse. A point tenderness with this nerve entrapment is usually localized directly over the area of nerve entrapment, EMG and nerve conduction studies may be helpful in differentiation of which motor segment is involved. Pain on resistive extension and testing of the long finger are sometimes associated with findings of posterior interosseous nerve compression (Werner, 1979). Werner reported that this injury is present in 5% of the cases with lateral elbow pain, but the author's clinical experience finds this to be less common and most likely below 1%.

3.2 Medial epicondylitis - Medial elbow tendinosus - "Thrower's elbow" and "Golfer's elbow"

The primary pathological changes involved in medial tennis elbow are present in the origin of the pronator teres, palmaris longus and flexor carpi radialis close to the attachment to the medial epicondyle. Occasionally pathological changes also occur in the flexor carpi ulnaris.

The aetiology of medial tennis elbow is the same as in lateral tennis elbow. There are technical errors. The player can hit the ball hard with too much over top-spin on the forehand stroke, or a hard first flat serve or overhead stroke. The basic principles for treating medial tennis elbow are the same as treating the lateral tennis elbow.

The prognosis for healing for medial tennis elbow is, however, worse and the healing time is much longer than for the lateral side. It can sometimes take 6-12 months before return to tennis. The patients should be told this so that their expectations are realistic. In a study of 53 patients, 43 were conservatively treated, but only 15 were good. Out of 10 surgically treated patients, only 3 felt they were good.

3.2.1 Valgus stress overload syndrome

Through an extensive serve or even more through a pitching motion, there is a tremendous valgus stress upon the elbow causing distraction and tension of the medial aspect of elbow and compression of the lateral aspect (Figure 6). Compression of the lateral compartment, which often occurs in the so-called cocking phase can result in fracture of the capitellum or deformation of the radial head. An associated problem can be chondromalacia, synovitis, osteophytic spurs and loose fragments. In the medial compartment there can be additional strain and rupture and valgus instability of the elbow can occur.

<u>Elbow instability</u>

The valgus stress overload syndrome can give medial tension which means tension of the medial-collateral ligaments (Figure 1).

The medial-collateral ligament (MCL), especially the anterior band, is of great importance for elbow stability and is composed of two parts. Morrey et al. (1981) found that the origin of the anterior band is posterior to the axis of elbow rotation. The origin of the posterior band is just posterior to the above. The increased distance from origin to insertion of this ligament with flexion is from 0 to 120 degrees. The posterior portion of the MCL contributes little to valgus stability. The radial head contributes on the other hand significantly to stability at 0, 45 and 90 degrees of flexion, but the MCL is the most important stabilizer except at full extension. The anterior band is the major stabilizer from 20 to 120 degrees of flexion. When the patients have medial-collateral ligament instability, there is pain on the medial side of the arm during throwing or serving. There is a sensation of elbow opening or giving way. There is a valgus instability with the arm flexed 30 degrees which can be confirmed on stress radiographs.

The pathophysiology involves edema and inflammation or scar formation within the ligament. There can also be calcific densities within the scar or ossifications within the ligament. Ruptures can also occur. These changes can be verified on an MRI.

The treatment includes rest and ice and generally rehabilitation with strengthening exercises as the main focus. Surgery is indicated if failure with conservative therapy is present after 6 months and occasionally in acute ruptures.

Ulnar neuritis

The majority of nerve lesions in athletes can be described as neuropraxias, which is the mildest form of nerve injury. It is characterized by a conduction block along a nerve where all nerve elements axons and connective tissue remain in continuity (Sicuranza and McCue, 1992). Prognosis for complete recovery is good if irreversible and organ damage has not occurred owing to long-standing compression. Severe injuries can be axonal injury and distal axon degeneration without disruption of the supporting sleeve of connective tissue, or complete nerve disruption, which is rare in athletes.

The peripheral nerves in athletes can be injured by compression, tension (traction) or a combination of both (Szabo and Gilberman, 1987). Acute compression nerve damage occurs when any heavy force compresses a nerve against an unyielding structure, e.g. ulnar compression at the wrist of bicyclists. Chronic nerve compression, which can cause irreversible damage with loss of axon, and nerve fibrosis can occur in the wrist in form of carpal tunnel syndrome.

Peripheral nerves are also susceptible to stretch injury. Nerves may stretch up to 20% before damage occurs. Valgus extension overload during serving, as well as pitching, creates significant tensile overload on the medial elbow ligament structures, and compressive loads laterally. The medial tension of the ulnar nerve, can elongate 4.7 mm during extension to full flexion. It can be moved 7 mm medially by the triceps. These tensile loads also affect the ulnar nerve as it crosses through the cubital tunnel, causing nerve irritation and compression. The nerve may become unstable as the elbow is flexed.

Ulnar nerve entrapment was found in 60% of surgical cases of medial tennis elbow (Nirschl, 1992). These entrapments were found distal to the medial epicondyle at the medial and muscular septum, as a nerve enters the flexor carpi ulnaris (Kulund et al., 1979). The nerve entrapment may be secondary to elbow instability, spurs, synovitis and more proximal compression.

The symptoms are often pain or numbness down into the little finger region, i.e. ulnar nerve innervated regions. The diagnosis is set by history and palpation tenderness over the medial epicondyle, or just posterior of the medial epicondyle, as well as pain on palmar flexion of the wrist against resistance.

The treatment consists of rest, ice and immobilization in the acute phase. Anti-inflammatory medication can be of value. Strengthening and stretching programmes should start as early as possible. In a chronic phase, the nerve can be treated surgically with transposition of the nerve beneath the flexors and decompression for at least 5 cm distal to the epicondyle.

Ulnar nerve problems are in the author's opinion probably more common in tennis then earlier observed. Damage to this nerve should be suspected in tennis players with long-lasting elbow problems on the medial side.

Osteochondritis dissecans

Osteochondritis dissecans is an injury to the articular cartilage and the bone. It usually occurs on the anterolateral surface of the capitellum because of the compression secondary to the valgus stress. An osteochondritis dissecans occurs most commonly in men in their second decade. This injury causes pain and limitation of extension, swelling and locking. Osteochondritis dissecans is traumatic and often of vascular aetiology. A simple excision of the fragmented portion of the capitellum and drilling of the base of the lesion to help the bleeding bone give satisfactory results and can be done through the arthroscope.

Loose fragments can also occur, often secondary to osteochondritis dissecans. They can also be composed of cartilaginous or fibrous tissue. These loose bodies can be exercised through arthroscopy.

3.3 Posterior tennis elbow tendinosis

During the serve motion there is an aggressive elbow extension during the follow-through phase (Fig. 7). The olecranon can impinge with the posterior aspect of the humerus and cause problems. Triceps tendinosis can occur. Osteophytes can form on the olecranon by forced hyperextension of the olecranon into the olecranon fossa, or by shear forces between the olecranon and the olecranon fossa secondary to the valgus movement placed on the elbow during the serve.

The pathology of the posterior compartment can be evaluated through arthroscopy with a posterior lateral portal. The osteophytes are usually located on the posterior medial aspect of the olecranon. The treatment is usually conservative, but occasionally surgery is needed.

Arthroscopy

Arthroscopy is more and more commonly used for diagnosis and treatment of many elbow injuries. By avoiding a large capsular excision, many of the problems of post-operative scarring and capsular contraction of the elbow can be avoided. The indications for arthroscopy are presented in Table 6.

Elbow arthroscopy (Figure 8) should be performed slowly and deliberately by experienced sports medicine surgeons. Usually a 3-4 mm, 30 degree angle arthroscope provides optimal visualization of the elbow: 1.6 mm flexible arthroscopy is today available and can sometimes be used. The most common portal is the anterolateral portal, 2 cm distal and 3 cm anterior of the lateral epicondyle. The lateral and posterior antebrachial cutaneous nerves must be avoided. The instrument should be directed toward the centre of the elbow with the elbow flexed at 90 degrees at all times. The arthroscopic instruments pass within a mean distance of 4 mm of the radial nerve regardless of the flexion or extension of the elbow when the elbow is not extended with

Figure 7. In the follow-through phase in the serve, hyperextension of the elbow is common. The hyperextension during the serve can cause compression of the olecranon against the humerus.

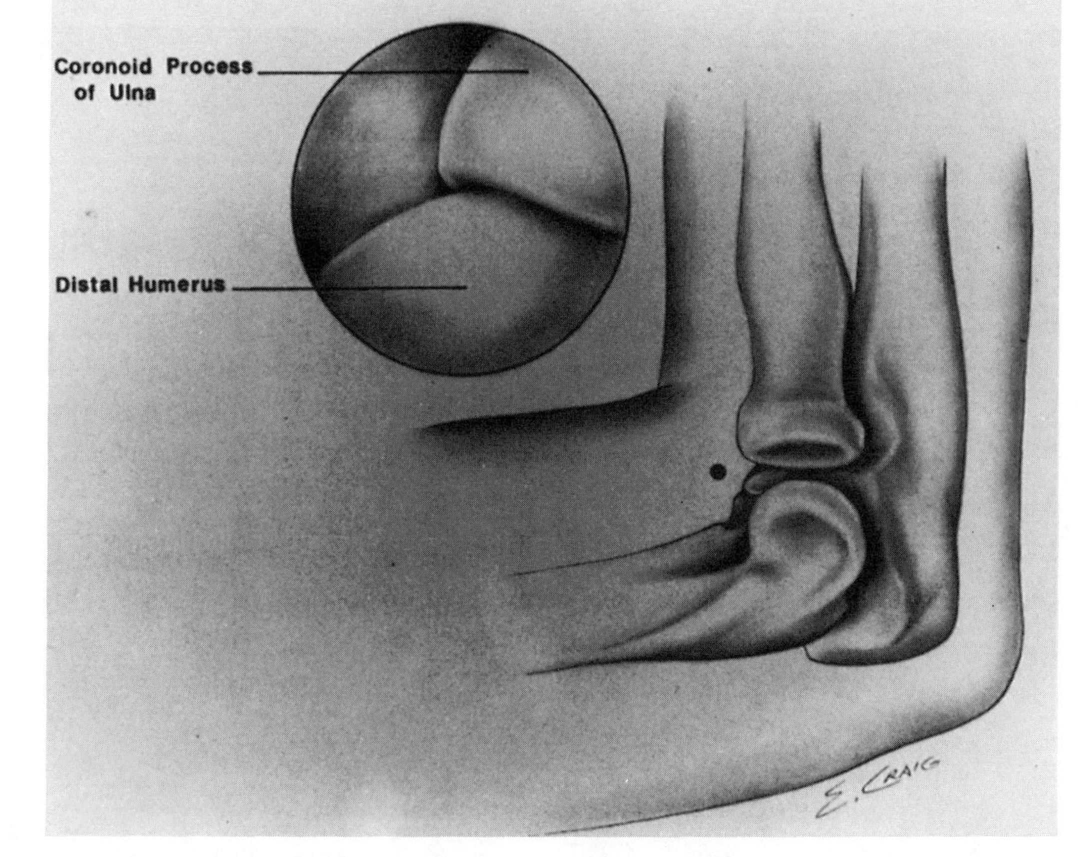

Figure 8. Arthroscopy is a helpful tool in the treatment and diagnosis of elbow injuries.

fluid. However, when 35 to 40 cc of fluid is inserted into the elbow capsule, the radial

Table 6. Indications for arthroscopy

1. Extraction of loose bodies
2. Evaluation and treatment of osteochondritis dissecans of the capitellum
3. Evaluation and debridement of chondral or osteochondral lesions of the radial head.
4. Debridement and lysis of adhesions of post-traumatic, or certain degenerative processes about the elbow.
5. Partial synovectomy, rheumatoid disease.
6. Partial excision of humeral or olecranon osteophyte.

nerve moves an additional 7 mm anteriorly. The maximum distention of the elbow should be maintained at all times, particularly when established in initial arthroscopic portals.

When doing the anteriomedial portal, 2 mm distal and 1 cm anterior to the medial epicondyle, the radial head and the capitellum can well be visualized. The medial antebrachial cutaneous nerve should be avoided.

The posterolateral portal is carried out 3 cm proximal to the olecranon superior and posterior to the lateral epicondyle. The olecranon fossa and tip of the olecranon can be seen as well as the distal humerus. It should be remembered that this portal is established with the elbow at 20 to 30 degrees of flexion.

4 Conclusions

Elbow injuries in tennis players are not uncommon. When they occur they are often of overuse character and can often be chronic and give long-lasting problems.

The most common injury is the so-called tennis elbow, which remains an enigma and a great clinical problem as still little is known about its pathophysiology and aetiology. It seems that a tennis player's chance of eventually getting a tennis elbow are more than 1 in 2, and this means that more focus should be directly towards prevention. It seems that the type of racket, grip, and so on, are not important in producing tennis elbow, but these factors are most likely important in the rehabilitation after tennis elbow and to avoid reinjury. Factors such as using gut string, low string tension, light balls and pain free strokes may allow return to competitive tennis earlier. The natural history for tennis elbow is good and most patients will get better in respect of treatment used. Exercises that promote healing and a forearm brace are key factors in the treatments and return to tennis. The healing time of overuse syndromes in the elbow is long. Tennis elbow may cause pain for between 1 week and 18 months with a mean of about 36 weeks. Because of the long treatment time and limited treatment alternatives, these problems continue to be frustrating for both the patient and the doctor. The key to successful treatment is also a correct diagnosis and, therefore, the treating doctor must be aware of the available differential diagnosis.

5 References

Adelsberg, S. (1986) The tennis stroke: An EMG analysis of selected muscles with rackets of increasing grip size. **Amer. J. Sports Med.,** 14,139-142.

Allman, F.L. (1975) Tennis elbow: Etiology, prevention and treatment. **Clin. Orthop.**, 3,308-316.

Bernhang, A.M., Dehner, W. and Fogarty, C. (1974) Tennis elbow: A biomechanical approach. **Amer. J. Sports Med.,** 2,235-260.

Biener, K. (1979) Unfalle in verschiedene Sportarten. Sozial - und Praeventivmedizin 24, **4,** 277.

Brody, H. (1987) **Tennis Science for Tennis Players.** University of Pennsylvania Press, Philadelphia, PA.

Brody, H. (1979) Physics of the tennis racket. **Amer. J. Physics.,** 47, 482-487.

Brody, H. (1989) Vibration damping of tennis rackets. **Int. J. Sports Biomech.,** 5, 451-456.

Carroll, R. (1981) Tennis elbow: incidence in local league players. **Brit. J. Sports Med.,** 15, 250-256.

Chard, M.D. and Lachmann, S.M. (1986) The pattern of injuries in racquet sports - a sports injury clinic study. **Brit. J. Sports Med.,** 20, 182.

Clark, A.K. and Woodland, J. (1975) Comparison of two steroid preparations used to treat tennis elbow, using the hypospray. **Rheum. Rehab.,** 14(1), 47-49.

Coonrad, R.W. and Hooper, W.R. (1973) Tennis elbow: its course, natural history, conservative and surgical treatment. **J. Bone Joint Surg.,** 55, 1177-1182.

Cundiff, J.S. (1974) Energy dissipation in human hand-arm exposed to random vibration. **J. Acoust. Soc. Am.,** 59, 212-214.

Elliott, B.C. (1988) Biomechanics of the serve in tennis. A biomedical perspective. **Sports Med.,** 6, 285-294.

Elliott, B.C., Blanksby, B.A. and Ellis, R. (1980) Vibration and rebound velocity characteristics of conventional and oversized tennis rackets. **Res. Quart. Exerc. Sport,** 51, 608-615.

Froimson, A.I. (1971) Treatment of tennis elbow of the forearm support band. **J. Bone Joint Surg.,** 53A, 193.

Gerber, C. (1987) Tennisellbogen Ein anderes ätiologisch-therapeutisches Konzept. **Schweiz Ztschr. Sportmed.,** 35, 13-197.

Gerberich, S.G. and Priest, J.D. (1985) Treatment for lateral epicondylitis: Variables related to recovery. **Brit. J. Sports. Med.,** 19, 224-227.

Goldie, I. (1964) Epicondylitis lateralis humeri: a pathogenical study. **Acta. Chir. Scand.,** 339(Suppl.), 1-119.

Groppel, J. and Nirschl, R.P. (1986) A mechanical and electromyographical analysis of the effects of various joint counterforce braces on the tennis player. **Amer. J. Sports Med.,** 14, 195-200.

Grouchow, H.W. and Pelletier, D. (1979) An epidemiologic study of tennis elbow. **Amer. J. Sports Med.** 7, 234-238.

Haker, E. (1991) **Lateral epicondylalgia (Tennis elbow). A diagnostic and therapeutic challenge.** Department of Physiology II, Karolinska Institute, Stockholm, Sweden, Dissertation.

Hang, Y.S. and Peng, S.M. (1984) An epidemiologic study of upper extremity injury in tennis players with a particular reference to tennis elbow. **J.Formosan Med. Ass.,** 83, 307-315.

Henning, E.M., Rosenbaum, D. and Milani, T.L. (1992) Transfer of tennis racket vibrations onto the human forearm. **Med. Sci. Sports Exerc.,** 24, 1134-1140.

Ilfeld, F. and Field, S. (1966) Treatment of tennis elbow: Use of special brace. **J.A.M.A.,** 195, 111.

Kamien, M. (1988) Tennis elbow in long time tennis players. **Austr. J. Sci. Med. Sports,** 20, 19-27.

Kamien, M. (1989) The incidence of tennis elbow and other injuries in tennis players at the Royal Kings Park Tennis Club of Western Australia from October 1983 to September 1984. **Austr. J. Sci. Med. Sports.,** 21, 18-22.

Kulund, D.N., McCue, F.C and Rockwell, D.A. (1979) Tennis injuries: Prevention and treatment. **Amer. J. Sports Med.,** 7, 244.

LaBelle, H., Guibert, R., Joncas, J., Newman, N., Fallaha, M. and Rivard, C.H. (1992) Lack of scientific evidence for the treatment of lateral epicondylitis of the elbow. **J. Bone Joint Surg.,** 74B, 646-651.

MacKay, W.A. (1983) Resonance properties of the human elbow. **Can. J. Physiol. Pharmacol.,** 62, 802-808.

Morrey, B.F., Askew, L.J. and Chao, E.Y. (1981) Biomechanical study of normal functional elbow motion. **J. Bone Joint Surg.,** 63A, 872.

Morris, H. (1883) Lawn tennis elbow. **Brit. Med. J.,** 2, 557.

Nevelos, A.B. (1980) The treatment of tennis elbow with triamcinolone acetonide. **Curr. Med. Res. Opin.** 6, 507-509.

Nigg, B.M. and Denoth, J. (1980) Sportplatzbelaege (Playing surfaces), **Juris Verlag Publications,** Zurich.

Nirschl, R.P. (1973) Tennis elbow. **Orthop. Clin. North Amer.,** 4, 787.

Nirschl, R.P. (1974) The etiology and treatment of tennis elbow. **Amer. J. Sports Med.,** 2, 308-323.

Nirschl, R.P. (1992) Elbow tendinosis/tennis elbow. **Clin. Sports Med.,** 11, 851-870.

Nirschl, R.P. and Pettroni, F.A. (1979) Tennis elbow: surgical treatment of lateral epicondylitis. **Amer. J. Bone Joint Surg.,** 61A, 832-839.

Peng, S.M. (1978) **Epidemiological study of injury in soft tennis players.** Master's Thesis, Chinese Cultural University, Taipei, Taiwan, ROC.

Priest, J.D., Braden, V. and Gerberich, S.G. (1980) The elbow and tennis, part 2: A study of players with pain. **Physician Sportsmed.,** 8, 77-84.

Priest, J.D., Braden, V. and Gerberich, S.G. (1980) The elbow and tennis, part 1: an analysis of players with and without pain. **Physician Sportsmed.,** 8, 81-91.

Priest, J.D., Jones, H.H. and Nagel, D.A. (1974) Elbow injuries in highly skilled tennis players. **Amer. J. Sports Med.,** 2, 137-149.

Reynolds, D.D., Wasserman, D.E., Basel, R. and Taylor, W. (1982) Energy entering the hands of operators of pneumatic tools used in chipping and grinding operations. in **Vibration Effects on the Hand and Arm In Industry** (eds A.J. Brammer and W. Taylor). John Wiley & Sons, New York.

Roy, S. and Irvin, R. (1983) **Sports Medicine Prevention, Evaluation, Management, and Rehabilitation.** Prentice-Hall, Englewood Cliffs, NJ. pp.220-221.

Runge, F. (1873) Zur genese und behandlung des schreibekrampfes. **Berl. Klin. Wochenschr.,** 10, 245-248.

Sicuranza, M.J. and McCue, F.C. (1992) Compressive neuropathies in the upper extremity of athletes. **Hand Clinics** 8, 263-273.

Snyder-Mackler, L. and Epler, M. (1989) Effect of standard and Aircast tennis elbow bands on integrated electromyography of forearm extensor musculature proximal to the bands. **Amer. J. Sports Med.,** 17, 278-281.

Suggs, C.W., Hanks, J.M. and Robertson, G.T. (1977) Vibration of power tool handles. in **Vibration Effects on the Hand and Arm In Industry** (eds A.J. Brammer and W. Taylor). John Wiley & Sons, New York.

Szabo, R.M. and Gilberman, R.H. (1987) The pathophysiology of nerve entrapment syndromes. **J. Hand Surg.,** 12A, 880.

U.S. News and World Report (1979) January 15.

VonBiehl, G. and Schmitt, J. (1978) Zum problem der epicondylitis als typischen tennissportschaden. **Deut. Z. Sportmed. heft.,** 7, 205-210.

VonKramer, J. and Schmitz-Beuting, J. (1979) Uberlastungsschaden am Bewegungsapparat bei Tennisspielern. **Deut. Z. Sportsmed. heft.,** 11, 44-48.

Weber, K. (1976) Der Tennisellbogen: Prevention and Therapie - auch durch den Tennislehrer? **Leistungssport Berlin,** 6, 299-301.

Werner, C.O. (1979) Lateral elbow pain and posterior interosseous nerve entrapment. **Acta. Orthop. Scan. Suppl.,** 174, 1-62

27 Injuries in junior lawn tennis players

T. Reilly and J. Collyer
School of Human Sciences, Liverpool John Moores University, Liverpool, UK

1 Introduction

Increasing numbers of players in the 9-18 years age bracket are being attracted into lawn tennis participation in England. The greater systematisation of training and demands of practice and competition bring with them a likelihood of increased injuries. This study aimed to:- i) outline the frequency and pattern of injuries in young players and ii) explore causal factors with a view towards identifying preventive measures.

2 Methods

Detailed information on injuries and training patterns were obtained retrospectively for the previous year (1992). Data were collected by means of a questionnaire (32 items) from 100 young players (59 male, 41 female) aged 9-18 years from 5 clubs in Hampshire. The questionnaire was complemented by anthropometric profiles which included measurement of stature and body mass.

3 Results and Discussion

Altogether 51% of the junior players were injured, the difference between male and female being non-significant ($P > 0.05$). Knee (20%), dominant elbow (18%) and dominant shoulder (12%) were the major sites of injury. Tendon (46%) and muscle (29%) were the most commonly injured tissues. Overuse injuries were associated with bone, tendon, ligaments and cartilage ($P < 0.05$) whereas acute injuries were associated with muscle ($P < 0.05$). The age most at risk was at 15 years.

A significant relation was observed between warm-up and injury ($Chi^2 = 17.7$; $P < 0.01$),

Science and Racket Sports Edited by T. Reilly, M. Hughes and A. Lees.
Published in 1994 by E & FN Spon ISBN 0 419 18500 3

lower injury rates occurring in those warming up for 5 min or more (Table 2). This effect was more pronounced when those warming up for 10 min or more were considered. Overuse injury rates increased with the standard of play ($Chi^2 = 6.91$; $P < 0.05$) and with frequency of play, the most vulnerable being the national players. The incidence of injury was 89% at national level, 57% at regional, 51% at county, 45% at club level and 8% in 'fun' players. These figures are in accord with the high incidence reported by Chandler (1989) for senior tennis players for whom overuse injuries comprised 80% of total injuries. Stanistki (1989) also noted overuse to be the dominant cause of injury in children and adolescents in tennis as well as other sports. In the present study the highest injury incidence was in those practising for 16-20 hours a week.

Table 1. Percentage of males and females injured

	Males		Females		Total	
	Number	(%)	Number	(%)	Number	(%)
Uninjured	31	(52.5)	18	(43.9)	49	(49)
Injured	28	(47.5)	23	(56.1)	51	(51)
Total	59	(100)	41	(100)	100	(100)

"Training error" was the most common cause attributed to chronic injuries whereas accidental factors, such as slipping on court (32%) were prominent causes of acute injuries. These data highlight areas where preventive measures can be used to decrease injuries in junior tennis players.

Table 2. Injury and duration of warm-up

	0-5min	5 min +	Total
Uninjured	13	36	49
Injured	35	16	51
Total	48	52	100

The main observations in this study were:

i) There was a significant association between warm-up and injury, the lowest injury figures

being linked with warm-up longer than 10 min. This places emphasis on proper preparation for match-play and practices as preventive measures (Reilly, 1993).
ii) Overall injuries increased with the standard of play and the duration of play. This highlights risk of overuse.
iii) Chronic injuries were linked with training error, an observation corroborated in other sports (Reilly, 1993). This link did not apply to acute injuries which were mostly caused by accidental occurrences.

4 References

Chandler, J. (1990) U.S.P.T.R. **Manual on Sport Science Volume X.** Unites States Professional Tennis Registry, Kentucky.

Reilly, T. (1993) Prevention is easier than cure, in **Intermittent High Intensity Expercise: Preparation, Stresses and Damage Limitation** (eds D.A.D. MacLeod, R.J. Maughan, C. Williams, C.R. Madeley, J.C.M. Sharp and R.W. Nutton), E. and F.N. Spon, London, pp. 583-590.

Stanitski, C. (1989) Common injuries in preadolescent and adolescent athletes: Recommendations for prevention. **Clin. Sports Med.**, 7, 32-41.

28 Badminton injuries

K. Hoy, C.J. Terkelsen, B.E. Lindblad, H.E. Helleland and
C.J. Terkelsen
Orthopedic Department, Randers City Hospital, Denmark

1 Introduction

Participation in all kinds of sports activities has increased considerably during the last decade. In Denmark there is a great tradition of badminton. The game is played at all levels, but there have been only a few good epidemiological studies (Kroner, Schmidt, Nielsen, Yde, Jakobsen, Moller-Madsen and Jensen, 1990).

Most studies have been carried out as case-series or insurance-claim reports. Furthermore, most studies are not population based and do not reveal the socio-economic or other subsequent consequences to the players. No earlier studies have made comparisons between injury definitions.

2 Methods

One hundred badminton players, 5 per cent of all sports injuries, were prospectively registered and treated in the casualty ward of Randers City Hospital during a one year period. Afterwards questionnaires were sent to all participants, three times if necessary. Eighty-nine percent answered the questionnaires. In the same period all active sports participants in the Hospital's uptake area (30 254) were registered according to their sport affiliation (2 620 badminton players).

3 Results and Conclusions

There were an almost equal sex distribution (58 percent men and 42 percent women). The mean age was 30 for male players and 25 for female players. Fifty-five percent of the injuries occurred in club players, the rest of the accidents were found amongst companies' sports and school sports. In the hospital uptake area there were 2 620 active members of badminton clubs (1 650 men and 970 women). The active players were registered in three groups according to age: Group 1: <18 years : 31 percent; Group 2: 18-25 years : 16 percent; Group 3: >25 years: = 63 percent. According to the Abbreviated Injury Scale

Science and Racket Sports Edited by T. Reilly, M. Hughes and A. Lees.
Published in 1994 by E & FN Spon ISBN 0 419 18500 3

(A.I.S.) 17 percent were classified as minor, 56 percent as moderate, and 27 percent as severe, respectively. Fifty-six percent of the severe injuries (A.I.S. = 3) were found in group 3. Nine players reported that earlier injuries had influenced the actual accident. Most of the injuries occurred in the time interval between 12-60 min after onset of the game. The most players (86 percent) trained 1-3 times weekly. Distortions were the most common diagnosis (56 percent), fractures accounted for 5 percent. Tears of ankle ligaments were found in 12 percent, and 14 percent had Achilles tendon tears. One percent had a dislocation of the glenohumeral joint. The hospitalization rate was found to be 21 percent. None of the patients treated as in-patients spent more than 7 days inside hospital. In the age-group 2 and 3, forty-three percent were absent from work due to the injury and 25 percent for more than 3 weeks. The accident caused unemployment to one person. Another player was forced to change work due to the injury. Ten percent of the players stopped their sport after the accident, and only three percent regained their training/sport within one week. As much as 23 percent had to stop from regularly training and matches in 8 weeks.
The conclusion which can be drawn from this study is that a significantly lower injury incidence was found in the group of younger badminton players. The correlation between different injury definitions (A.I.S.) and time absent from sport was significant but was not strong. Moreover severe injuries (A.I.S. = 3) were significantly more common among badminton players compared to other sports.

4 Acknowledgements

This study was supported by the Danish Medial Research Council J. no. 12-4037. Thanks to the Danish Sports Association for providing the data for the number of active sports participants.

5 References

Kroner, K., Schmidt, S.A., Nielsen, A.B., Yde, J., Jakobsen, B.W., Moller-Madsen, B., and Jensen, J. (1990) Badminton injuries. **Brit. J. Sports Med.,** 24, 169-172.

29 Forces in a badminton lunge movement

A. Lees and C. Hurley
Centre for Sport and Exercise Sciences, School of Human Sciences, Liverpool John Moores University, Liverpool, UK

1 Introduction

The lunge movement is common in most racket games. When shots are hit wide the player must move and make a long stretching stride in order to execute a return shot. The unusual position and speed of movement would be expected to place large stresses on the body. These stresses can lead to muscle soreness and muscle damage, and possibly a longer term effect on the joints. Although a successful lunge is a feature of a skilled player, poorer players are often forced into making such a movement due to poor court positioning. Under these circumstances a forced rather than planned lunge may have different kinetic characteristics. The purposes of this study were :-1) to measure the external ground reaction forces generated during a lunge movement in badminton and 2) to estimate the internal muscle forces acting in the major muscles and muscle groups of the support leg.

2 Methods

Thirteen male subjects (age range 18 to 23 years) performed simulated badminton lunges onto a force platform. The subjects selected could be categorised according to ability. Four of the subjects had little badminton playing experience, four were of a medium playing standard and five were University level players. Subjects had to move a short distance and hit a badminton shuttlecock which was dropped from a low height before it hit the ground. This action was felt to be a reasonable simulation of the lunge action in badminton. Vertical and horizontal sagittal plane forces were recorded at 100 Hz. For the five better players cine film was taken of the sagittal plane movement at 100 Hz. Radiographs were taken from these five subjects in order to produce bone models for a bioengineering analysis using the method described by Harrison et al. (1986). Ten successful trials were filmed for each subject and two were selected for detailed analysis at 50 Hz.

Science and Racket Sports Edited by T. Reilly, M. Hughes and A. Lees.
Published in 1994 by E & FN Spon ISBN 0 419 18500 3

3 Results

A characteristic curve (Figure 1) was produced for both the vertical and horizontal ground reaction forces. Heel strike transient (Light et al., 1980), impact loading, amortization (or force reduction) phase, loading and drive-off were clearly identifiable as the main features of the curves marked as A, B, C, D, and E on the graph. Summary data are presented in Table 1.

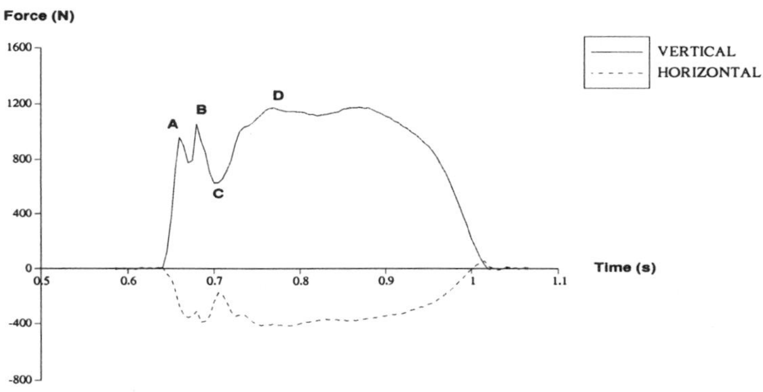

Fig. 1. Vertical and horizontal ground reaction forces in a typical badminton lunge movement.

Table 1. Mean vertical (Fz) and horizontal (Fx) forces in the badminton lunge. Forces are in body weight units.

	Fz			Fx		
	low	medium	high	low	medium	high
A. heel strike transient	0.00	2.03	1.25	0.10	0.74	0.61
B. impact loading peak	3.17	2.67	1.44	2.10	1.75	0.92
C. amortization	0.94	1.20	0.96	0.59	0.69	0.63
D. loading peak	1.72	2.03	1.47	1.13	1.10	0.83
E. drive off peak	-	-	1.10	-	-	0.59

The bioengineering analysis was applied to the more experienced players only, for whom two trials per subject were analysed. Mean data are presented in Figure 2 for each of the major muscle groups analysed. The data are presented from just before impact to just after leg extension had begun in the drive-off. This allowed estimates to be made of the maximum forces in M. Gastrocnemius (4.4 BW), M. Rectus Femoris (3.1 BW), patellar tendon (12.4 BW), hamstring (6.6 BW) and gluteal (17.5 BW) muscle groups.

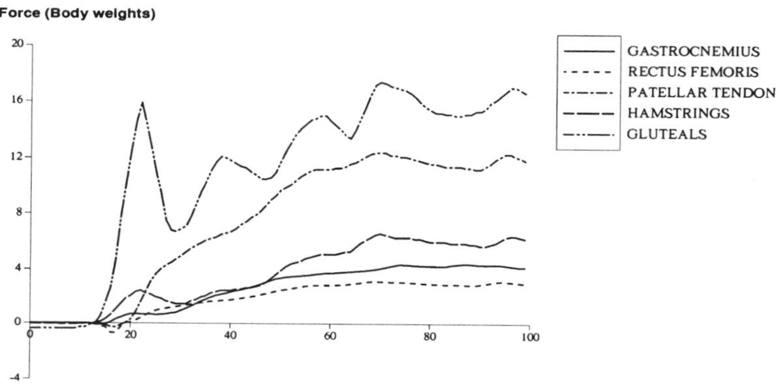

Fig. 2. Muscle forces during the badminton lunge. The end of the action corresponds to the point at which the lunge movement begins to reverse.

4 Discussion

The zero heel strike transient for the low ability group was the result of this group of players making contact with the ground with more of a flat foot rather than heel first. The medium ability players showed higher transients than the high ability group. This suggests that they were lunging more vigorously to make the movement but had not developed the skills or need to reduce this aspect of the force. The magnitude of the vertical force for impact loading was greatest in the novice players and least in the experienced players (significantly different at $P<0.01$). This trend was similar in the horizontal forces. This confirmed that the less experienced players were making a more vigorous movement, probably making contact with the ground with a straighter leg than the experienced players. There were no such trends for the amortization phase and loading peak, although the better players showed lower forces. It is likely demonstrated a more forceful lunge than the low ability players as evidenced by the higher horizontal force, and as a consequence greater vertical forces. The high ability players also demonstrated forceful lunges but had movement skills which reduced the severity of impact. The success of the lunge can also be gauged from the drive-off forces. These could not be measured for the low and medium ability level players as they were very erratic in their form.

The muscle forces showed a trend to gradually increase as the movement progressed until the drive-off had begun. Forces in the anterior muscle groups were lower than found in other activities such as running (Harrison et al., 1986), but larger than these activities in the posterior muscle groups. In particular the hamstrings and the gluteal muscle groups showed a large peak corresponding to the loading phase. This peak may be responsible for a rapid eccentric action of the muscles, and a causative factor in the onset of delayed muscle soreness which is a characteristic consequence of players who are not habituated to this action. A small angle of knee flexion will place a greater compressive force on the knee joint, particularly the patellofemoral joint.

It is likely that the muscle forces in the less experienced players are larger at the beginning of the movement as a result of the higher impact forces, but lower as the movement progresses. The more experienced players were stretching further and attaining a lower position with greater angle of knee flexion. This would put more stress on the posterior muscle groups in the more experienced players who had developed the muscle fitness to cope with the high demands of this action.

5 Conclusion

It is concluded that the forces generated during the lunge action in badminton are highest for inexperienced players and that experienced players modify their action to complete the movement successfully and to reduce their exposure to excessive force. The muscle force estimates identify a possible causative factor for the delayed onset of muscle soreness. On the basis of the force data this would be more troublesome to less experienced players. The lunge movement should therefore be considered an advanced movement skill and novice players should be advised of the physical stresses involved and encouraged to develop the movement skills to reduce their exposure to the forces.

6 References

Harrison, R. N., Lees, A., McCullagh, P. and W.B. Rowe (1986) **A bioengineering analysis of human muscle and joint forces in the lower limb during running**. J. Sports Sci., 4, 207-218.

Light, L. H., McLelland, G. E. and Klenerman, L. (1980) **Skeletal transients on heel strike in normal walking with different footwear**. J. Biomech., 13, 477-480.

30 Incidence of anaemia among the Irish tennis squad

C.P. O'Brien
Blackrock Clinic, Dublin, Eire

1 Introduction

Athletes are constantly trying to improve their physiological capabilities. Many athletes feel that they need to build up their blood to optimise their physiological function. It has been found that 91% of all female elite athletes in the U.S.A. consume nutrient supplements (Clarke, 1990). Iron is a substance which is particularly abused by supplementing athletes. Iron supplements should only be reserved for those who have a documented anaemia caused by iron deficiency. In order observe the incidence of anaemia the 21 subjects who comprised the Irish Tennis Squad were evaluated.

2 Method

There were 21 members of the Irish Tennis Squad who took part in daily squad sessions. There were 11 male subjects with a mean age of 16 years and 10 female subjects with a mean age of 15 years. The age range was from 12 to 21 years. All ate a carnivorous non-vegetarian diet. All the subjects trained six mornings a week for two hours. They practiced tennis for 70% of the time, for 20% of the time they were involved in strength training and for 10% of the time they were involved in endurance training. A venous blood sample was drawn from the ante-cubetal fossa in the seated position on each subject as part of the annual medical screening. Haemoglobin, haematocrit and blood indices were analysed in an auto-analyser (Coulter Stack, Florida).

3 Results

The results of the investigation revealed that all the male subjects were non-anaemic. They had a mean haemoglobin of 14.1 g/dl and a mean haematocrit value of 40.7% (See Table 1.). Of the 10 females 9 were non-anaemic. The tenth subject had a haemoglobin of 10.0 g/dl. Blood indices showed evidence of a microcytic hypochromic anaemia. Full investigations of iron, B12 and folate status as well as evidence for chronic disease and haemolysis were undertaken. The results on this anaemic subject revealed an iron deficiency anaemia. The mean haemoglobin of the female group was 13 g/dl and a mean haematocrit of 41% (See Table 2.).

Science and Racket Sports Edited by T. Reilly, M. Hughes and A. Lees.
Published in 1994 by E & FN Spon ISBN 0 419 18500 3

Table 1. Haemoglobin and haematocrit values of 11 elite Irish male tennis players

Male	Hb (g/dl)	Hct(%)
	15.0	42%
	13.1	38%
	13.9	38%
	14.2	40%
	13.8	39%
	14.0	40%
	13.1	38%
	14.5	40%
	15.5	47%
	15.1	46%
	13.1	40%
Mean	14.1	41%
SD	0.84	3.1%

Male Hb normal range 13 - 18 g/dl

Table 2. Haemoglobin and haematocrit value of 10 elite Irish female tennis players

Female		Hb (g/dl)	Hct(%)
		13.8	41%
		13.5	42%
		13.5	43%
		14.3	47%
		13.2	40%
	*	10.0	32%
		13.4	41%
		12.3	39%
		14.0	44%
		12.9	42%
Mean:		13.1	41%
SD		1.2	3.9%

(* Anaemic) Female Hb normal range: 12 - 16 g/dl

4 Discussion

These athletes are of the age at risk for iron deficiency anaemia (Rubenstein and Wayne, 1985). They are at an age when iron requirements are greatest due to growth. It is also suggested that athletes, particularly female athletes, are more susceptable to anaemia (Clement and Asmundsun, 1982). However, only one of the subjects had evidence of an iron deficiency anaemia. When an anaemia occurs it is essential that all possible causes of anaemia are investigated and the practitioner does not routinely supplement with iron. Iron deficiency is the commonest cause of anaemia. However, folate and B12 deficiencies, anaemia of chronic disease and auto-immune haemolysis can also occur.

The athletic population also has the problem of "athletic anaemia" or pseudo-anaemia. This is a syndrome peculiar to athletes (particularly endurance trained athletes). The patient will have no symptoms of anaemia but will have a lower than normal haemoglobin, typically one to one and a half grammes below the low end of the normal range. There will also be evidence of a low haematocrit. The erythrocytes, however, will be normochromic. This is a dilutional pseudo-anaemia. It is caused by an expanding intra-vascular volume which is generated by aerobic training. High intensity aerobic training causes an increased release of the hormone renin. Renin increases the conversion of angiotensin 1 to angiotensin 2, with subsequent increased production of aldosterone. This hormone causes the increased reabsorption of sodium from the kidney. This results in an expanded intra-vascular volume and a dilutional or pseudo-anaemia (See Fig. 1).

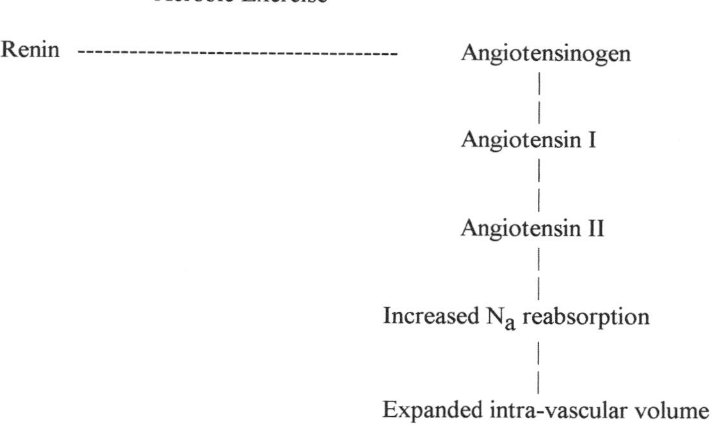

Figure 1. Mechanism of "Pseudo-anaemia".

This haematological adaptation to aerobic exercises follows a dose response curve. Therefore the higher the intensity of aerobic exercise, the greater will be the increase in intra-vascular volume. This syndrome is not pathological, has no symptoms, and requires no treatment.

Iron deficiency, however, is pathological. It frequently presents with dyspnoea, fatigue and weakness. An athlete with an iron deficiency anaemia may also report a reduction in athletic performance. A diagnosis of iron deficiency anaemia requires an abnormally low haemoglobin and haematocrit.

The peripheral blood film will show microcytic and hypochromic red blood cells. Serum iron levels may be reduced below 10 ug/l and total iron binding capacity (level) is elevated. Many factors are known to affect the level of serum iron and changes may be of the order of 100% or more in any individual.

Iron levels are higher in the morning and lower in the evening, it is also subject to monthly variation. Iron may reach very low levels prior to menstruation and there are very great daily variations. Therefore performing an isolated serum iron level analysis is at best unhelpful. Certain sports are at particular risk of iron deficiency anaemia, either from the demands of the sport or from inadequate dietary intake. Gymnastics and weight-lifting are sports which are often associated with reduced iron intake. This is primarily due to the constant need to "make weight" in these sports. Endurance sports, particularly long distance running are at risk of iron deficiency anaemia due to the demands of the sport. Foot strike haemolysis is the 20th century version of the foot soldier's march, haemoglobinurea, and is seen in marathon runners. Gastro-intestinal blood loss (Fisher et al., 1986) and urological blood loss (Selby, 1991) have all been reported in endurance athletes. Tennis, however, is a sport which has a predominant draw on the anaerobic system. The group of athletes under consideration only spent 10% of their training time in endurance training. This may explain the low incidence of anaemia in the group.

Unfortunately, many athletes self-dose with iron. This practice followed a research report in 1976 which showed that non-anaemic rats improved their treadmill time with iron supplements (Finch et al., 1976). However, these findings were never confirmed in humans and present research would suggest that "pumping iron in a non-athletic group will not improve athletic performance". It can be demonstrated that oral iron therapy can enhance haematological status but most studies have failed to demonstrate any measureable improvements in physical performance after iron supplementation, even after haematological status was improved (Dressendorfer et al.,1991).

Iron supplementation therefore should be reserved only for those anaemic athletes whose anaemia has been caused by iron deficiency. This is not only due to its inability to improve physical performance but more importantly due to the great risk of self-dosing with iron. Iron toxicity is a major cause of admission to casualty departments. Iron dosing can be a cause of great morbidity and occasionally, mortality (Table 3.).

Table 3. Side effects of iron supplementation

Routine Low Dose	-	Nausea and vomiting
30 - 60 mg	-	Arthralgia, myalgia and fever
	-	Painful lymphenapothy
	-	Idiopathic haemachromatosis
	-	Possible increased cancer risk
	-	Cardiac arrythmias
> 100 mg	-	Coma
	-	Sudden death
Parenteral	-	1 in 100 chance of anaphalatic reaction

5 Conclusion

Only one of the 21 elite Irish tennis players was anaemic. It was a true iron deficiency anaemia which responded to iron therapy. Athletes who have a high draw on their aerobic energy system are also susceptible to pseudo-anaemia and true iron deficiency anaemia. Tennis has a smaller draw on the aerobic system in both training and play and hence the instance of anaemia is low.

If an anaemia exists all the possible causes should be investigated. Iron dosing in a non-anaemic person should be actively discouraged. It confers no physiological benefit and can be harmful as well as potentially lethal.

6 References

Clarke, N. (1990) **Sports Nutrition Guide Book.** Leisure Press, Champaign, Illinois.

Clement, D.B. and Asmundsun, R.C. (1982) Nutritional intake haematological parameters in endurance runners. **Physician Sportsmed.,** 10, 37-43.

Dressendorfer, R.H., Keen, C.L., Wade, C.E., Claybaugh, J.R. and Timmins, G.C. (1991) Development of runners' anaemia during a 20 day road race: effect of iron supplements.**Int. J. Sports Med.**, 12, 332-336.

Finch, C.A., Miller and L.R., Inamdar, A.R. (1976) Iron deficiency in the rat: physiological and biochemical studies of muscle dysfunction. **J. Clin. Invest.**, 58, 447-453.

Fiser, R.L., McMahon, L.F.Jnr. and Ryan, M.J. (1986) Gastro-intestinal bleeding in competitive runners. **Dig. Dis. Sci.**, 31, 1226-1228.

Rubenstein, D. and Wayne, D. (1985) **Lecture Notes on Clinical Medicine.** Blackwell Scientific Publication, Oxford, England. 3rd Ed., p. 330.

Selby, G.B.(1991) When does an athlete need iron? **Physician Sportsmed.**, 19, (4) 96-102

31 Isokinetic leg strength before and after replacement of Ligamentum Cruciatum Anterior

E. Zinzen and J.P. Clarys
Experimental Anatomy, Free University Brussels, Belgium

1 Introduction

Strength testing has long been of concern to athletes, trainers, supervisors, physiotherapists and sports physicians. For this reason, various methods of testing and training muscle strength are used. The methods of strength training can be split into static (or isometric) and dynamic (or isotonic). The dynamic approach can be further subdivided into dynamic movements with a constant, a variable and/or an accommodating resistance.

In this study, we made use of an isokinetic dynamometer (Kin/Com, Chattex Corp., Chattanooga) which keeps the velocity constant but with an accommodating resistance. It is possible to isolate the muscle groups to be measured; due to the accommodated resistance it is possible to apply maximum loading throughout the entire movement while the moments of strength, work and power can be calculated.

Research indicates that isokinetic measurement using variable resistance is currently a reliable and objective source of information (Cabri and Clarys, 1991; Cabri, 1991; Davies, 1984; Perrin, 1993). To avoid the problem of having to purchase an expensive isokinetic dynamometer, isotonic equipment (with variable resistance) is now available on the market, and according to the literature offers equally good results (Cabri and Clarys, 1991; Clarys and Zinzen, 1991).

However, strength training is specific to the muscle group that is trained. Strength training - at least with an isokinetic dynamometer - is not sport-specific. It is not the case that simply because you have the ideal strength for being a tennis player, you will automatically be a good tennis player. On the other hand, a good tennis player can gain considerable advantage if he or she is able to achieve optimum strength performance.

In general, strength training is used to improve muscle strength. In therapy it helps to recover the lost muscle strength, muscle balance and muscle co-ordination and this as rapidly as possible following injury (Cabri and Clarys, 1991; Cabri, 1991). This is only possible if there is constant quality control of the recovery method employed. This control can be implemented using an isokinetic dynamometer. Such equipment gives

Science and Racket Sports Edited by T. Reilly, M. Hughes and A. Lees.
Published in 1994 by E & FN Spon ISBN 0 419 18500 3

correct information concerning the quality of the strength, provides data concerning left/right balance, and agonist/antagonist balance in the muscle group in question. Ideal strength development is directly related to muscle balance and this balance (or ratios) can differ from sport to sport.

A great deal of research has already been carried out using isokinetic dynamometers with athletes during recovery following injury (Cabri and Clarys, 1991; Davies, 1984; Perrin, 1993). What is lacking is information concerning the muscle characteristics immediately following the injury and prior to surgical operation.

2 Methods

A professional tennis player with a partial rupture of the right Ligamentum Cruciatum Anterior (ACL) was tested prior to his undergoing arthroplasty. The testing on the isokinetic dynamometer consisted of concentric and eccentric actions at different angular velocities of 0.52 and 2.09 rad/s (30°/s and 120°/s) of the quadriceps and hamstring muscles.

A reference group was tested in the same way (Zinzen et al., 1994). The angular velocities of 3.14 and 1.04 rad/s (180°/s and 60°/s) differ from the tennis player because, due to pain in his right knee, he was not able to perform at high velocities. However, a graph of his data provides a good reference curve. A reference group consisted of 15 physical education students (mean age : 21.3 ± 1.8 years; mean body mass : 75.0 ± 7.2 kg and mean height : 181.8 ± 6.5 cm).

On the basis of the information from the first strength test (before surgery) a training programme lasting 7 weeks was developed. The training was initiated 1 week following surgery. During the first two weeks, primarily isometric training was prescribed with the leg in 180° extension, according to which 10 contractions of the quadriceps muscles were carried out, each lasting 10 s. This set of exercises was carried out at least 3 times per day. Subsequently, a careful start was made on individual dynamic exercises carried out on equipment with variable resistance, the weights being determined according to the results of the isokinetic test. In this process, at a slow movement velocity, 10 sets of 10 extensions were carried out with a basic resistance of 35 kg, whilst at a high movement velocity, 10 sets of 25 extensions were carried out with a basic resistance of 10 kg. These dynamic exercises were completed three times per week. In these first two weeks, only the right leg was trained. From the third through the seventh week, general training was carried out on both legs with extra training for the right quadriceps muscles according to the dynamic pattern as described above, and a weekly increase of the resistance of 5 kg per week.

At the end of this seven week training period, a new isokinetic test was carried out to evaluate the gain in strength.

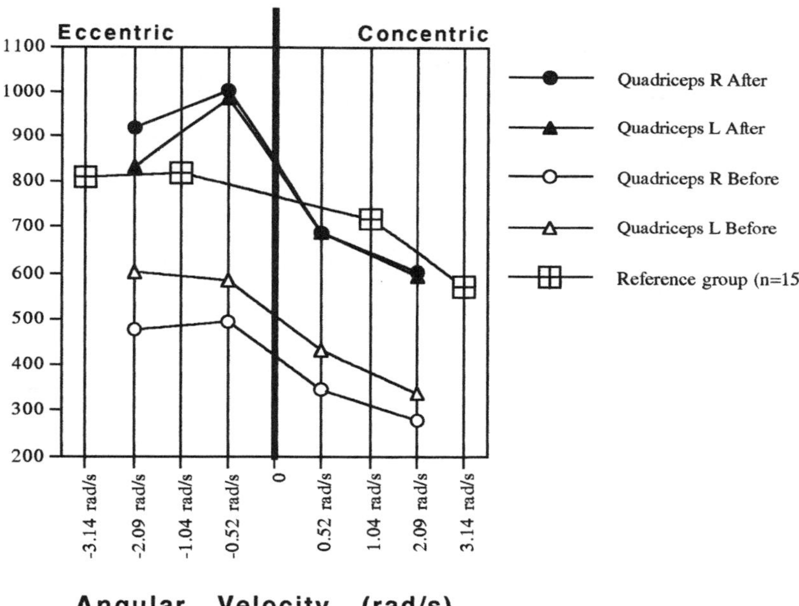

Figure 1. Quadriceps force before and after ACL replacement of a professional tennis player with reference group (physical education students).

Table 1. Left/right comparison of the hamstrings (H) and quadriceps (Q) and H/Q-ratios (left and right) of a professional tennis player before ACL replacement

	Left/Right Hamstrings(%)		Left/Right Quadriceps(%)		H/Q-ratio Left(%)		H/Q-ratio right(%)	
Angular Velocity	Conc.	Ecc.	Conc.	Ecc.	Conc.	Ecc.	Conc.	Ecc.
0.52 rad/s	106	101	125	118	67	63	79	73
2.09 rad/s	117	105	122	125	76	64	79	76
Assumed Normal ratio*	100 ±10	100 ±10	100 ±10	100 ±10	65 ±10	65 ±10	65 ±10	65 ±10

O = no muscular equilibrium

*Davies, 1984

Table 2. Left/right comparison of the hamstrings (H) and quadriceps (Q) and H/Q ratios (left and right) of a professional tennis player after ACL replacement and 7 weeks training

	Left/Right Hamstrings(%)		Left/Right Quadriceps(%)		H/Q-ratio Left (%)		H/Q-ratio right (%)	
Angular Velocity	Conc.	Ecc.	Conc.	Ecc.	Conc.	Ecc.	Conc.	Ecc.
0.52 rad/s	100	107	100	98	75	81	75	74
2.09 rad/s	101	85	98	90	68	68	66	79
Assumed normal ratio*	100 ±10	100 ±10	100 ±10	100 ±10	65 ±10	65 ±10	65 ±10	65 ±10

O = no muscular equilibrium

*Davies, 1984.

3 Results and Discussion

Table 1 gives left/right and agonist/antagonist thigh strength information before the ACL replacement. The right quadriceps was considerably weakened compared to the left leg, and was too weak in relation to its antagonist, the hamstrings. The normal hamstrings/quadriceps ratio is around the 65% mark (Davies, 1984). The circles indicate the muscle imbalances which are considerable.

Figure 1 shows the strength values (N) at the different angular velocities. The strength training programme clearly resulted in an increase of strength of both quadriceps muscles and restored the muscle imbalance between left and right leg. The recovery can be deemed successful, since the strength values reached higher (eccentric) and almost the same (concentric) values as in the reference group.

Table 2 - giving similar information to Table 1, but after surgery and after the training programme - indicates a restoration of the muscle imbalances (left/right - agonist/antagonist). The professional tennis player was capable of returning to competitive matches, only 8 weeks following his arthroplasty, due to this method of rehabilitation.

4 Conclusions

It may be said that this study is far more a case study offering relatively little proof in itself, but it does reinforce the results of investigations already carried out (Cabri 1991; Cabri and Clarys, 1991; Clarys and Zinzen, 1991; Davies, 1984; Perrin, 1993). Again it is suggested that the isokinetic dynamometer is ideal for achieving objective strength evaluation, whilst also proving that strength training is highly effective if carried out on equipment offering variable resistance.

5 References

Cabri, J.M.H. (1991), Isokinetic strength aspects in human joints and muscles. Appl. Ergonomics, 22, 299-302.

Cabri, J.M.H. and Clarys, J.P. (1991) Isokinetic exercise in rehabilitation. Appl. Ergonomics, 22, 295-298.

Clarys, J.P. and Zinzen, E. (1991), Relations EMG-force, Euromedicine 91, S.N. Editel, Edition EMC, Paris, 130-132.

Davies, G.J. (1984) A Compendium of Isokinetics in Clinical Usage and Rehabilitation Techniques. S and S Publisher, La Crosse.

Perrin, D.H. (1993) Isokinetic Exercise and Assessment. Human Kinetics Publishers, Leeds.

Zinzen, E., Clarijs, J.P., Cabri, J., Vanderstappen, D. and Van Den Berg, T.J. (1994) The influence of Triazolam and Flunitrazepam on isokinetic and isometric muscle performance, Ergonomics, 37, 69-77.

Part Six

Psychology of Racket Sports

32 Psychological preparation in racket sports

G. Jones
Department of Physical Education, Sports Science and Recreation Management, Loughborough University, Loughborough, UK

1 Psychological Skills Training

The first important point to consider is that psychological skills can be learned. It is not just a case of discarding performers who under-achieve because they lack confidence, cannot concentrate or fail to handle the pressure of competition. Performers can learn to be more confident, they can learn to concentrate better, and they can learn how to be more composed in pressure situations. Young performers may simply develop these skills over time, perhaps as part of the maturation process; others may need some help and guidance, perhaps from a sport psychologist.

What are the sorts of psychological skills which performers require? Research into psychological skills which distinguish elite from non-elite sports performers provides some strong clues. The research literature generally suggests that elite performers are better than non-elite performers in the areas of anxiety control, self-confidence, attention control and motivation.

In the case of anxiety control, elite performers have been shown to be lower in terms of the intensity of the anxiety response during the crucial moments of competition (Fenz, 1975; Mahoney and Avener, 1977; Mahoney, Gabriel and Perkins, 1987). Elite performers have also been shown to interpret their 'anxiety' symptoms as more facilitative to performance than non-elite performers (Jones, Swain and Hardy, 1993; Mahoney and Avener, 1977). Self-confidence has been found to be higher in elite performers prior to and during performance (Mahoney and Avener, 1977; Mahoney, Gabriel and Perkins, 1987), and elite performers are also more motivated both for competition and training (Mahoney, Gabriel and Perkins, 1987). Finally, elite performers are reported to have better attention control (Mahoney, Gabriel and Perkins, 1987). It is important to note that this research is correlational and not causal in nature, so that such skills can only be seen as being associated with elite performance rather than being the cause of it. Nevertheless, there are psychological factors which clearly distinguish elite and non-elite performers.

Psychological skills are like physical skills. They require a considerable amount of commitment, effort and time to learn them, and once learned they must be practised continually to avoid 'rustiness'. Some of the techniques and strategies which can be used in psychological skills training will be examined in the case study later in this paper, but let us first consider the ultimate aims of such training. The author's view is that psychological skills training has two important objectives, awareness and control. In order to understand what these constitute, we need to consider, at a relatively intuitive

Science and Racket Sports Edited by T. Reilly, M. Hughes and A. Lees.
Published in 1994 by E & FN Spon ISBN 0 419 18500 3

level, how the mind operates. The important factor to consider is that the mind, when considered in the context of controlled as opposed to automatic processing, has a limited capacity in that it can only contain so much information, in the form of thoughts, at any one time. This space is being continually bombarded by a considerable amount of other information which is competing for the space, but this information can only enter when information already in the mind is displaced. The limited capacity of the mind space means, of course, that the content is crucial.

As depicted in Figure 1,' awareness' is about being aware of what are appropriate and inappropriate psychological states prior to and during performance. For example, it is important that a performer is aware of what sort of thought patterns constitute being under-confident, or even over-confident. 'Control' is about having the ability to manipulate psychological states in the form of the mind's thought content. It involves being able to get rid of inappropriate thoughts and replace them with appropriate thoughts. For example, negative thoughts in the form of worry will be inappropriate for most racquet sport players. They will want, instead, to think positively and confidently, since confidence has been shown to be an important predictor of performance (Burton, 1988; Jones, Swain and Hardy, in press). A sports performer who is both psychologically aware and in control one who is psychologically very strong.

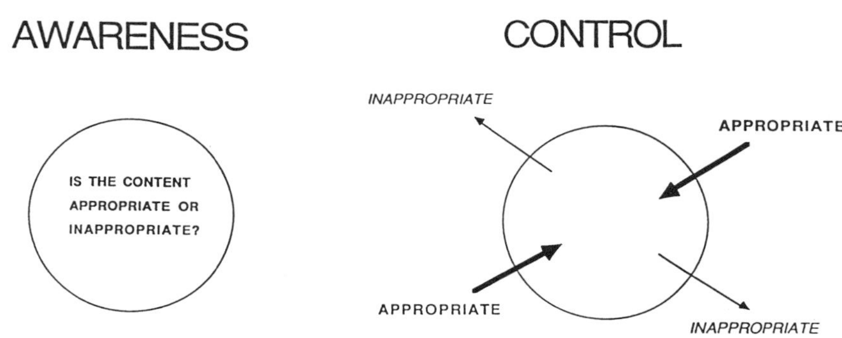

Fig. 1. Psychological awareness and control.

How can this psychological strength be achieved? Performance profiling has been shown to be a powerful tool in developing the awareness of the performer and also in helping to identify techniques and strategies for enhancing control.

2 Performance Profiling

Psychological skills training typically involves the performer being prescribed a set menu of psychological strategies and techniques to learn. In this way, the performer has a relatively passive role to play in the decision-making process, in terms of which techniques to learn, for example. This has important implications for the motivation of the performer since according to the locus of causality principle of Deci and Ryan's (1985) Cognitive Evaluation Theory, such externally controlled situations will probably weaken the performer's intrinsic motivation to implement and adhere to psychological skills training (Bull, 1991; Butler and Hardy, 1992). Performance profiling has been proposed as a technique which can overcome such a problem.

Performance profiling was devised by Butler (1989) as an application of Kelly's Personal Construct Theory (1955) to sport psychology. In employing this strategy, the performer is encouraged to:

> "...explore and communicate that which he or she is already taking for granted. Exploring the performer's perspective thus enhances his or her own awareness, as well as enabling the coach and sport psychologist to discern something of the performer's perspective. The repertory grid (Fransella & Bannister, 1977; Beail, 1985) prevails as the principle method of facilitating a person's construct system...... The attraction lies in eliciting that which is important to the performer, in contrast to tests or questionnaires which plot the performer against axes chosen by the psychologist. It frees the performer to construct a picture of himself or herself in terms which readily make sense, rather than forcing the performer to respond on pre-determined measures." (Butler & Hardy, 1992; pp. 254-255)

Butler (1989) adapted the repertory grid by mapping the performer's personal construct system on to a performance profile. According to Butler and Hardy (1992), performance profiling generally involves two basic procedures: firstly, identification by the athlete of constructs which he or she perceives to constitute the fundamental qualities of elite performance; and secondly, the athlete's own assessment of his/her present status along each of these constructs, followed by presentation of his/her scores in a visual profile. Butler and Hardy advocated that when performance profiles are in the process of being constructed with individual sports performers, the use of prompts from the sport psychologist sometimes helps them to bring all their personal constructs into consciousness. Furthermore, it is important that the labels used to describe the constructs are those generated by the athlete concerned.

Whilst performance profiling has several uses (see Butler and Hardy, 1992; Jones, 1993), the primary aim is to increase the intrinsic motivation of the performer so that he/she will implement and adhere to psychological skills training. The constructs identified through the performance profiling process as areas of desired change are generated by the performer, who is thereby provided with a degree of self-determinism not always evident to the same extent in other approaches to psychological skills training.

2.1 Constructing the performance profile

Butler's (1989) original approach to performance has been modified by Jones (1993). The performance profiling sheet as devised by Jones is shown in Figure 2, together with an example of how a partially completed profile might look. The performer is first of all asked to identify and write down on the left of the profile those constructs or attributes which he/she perceives the "ideal (sport) player" to possess. The performer is then asked to rate the importance (I) of each of the constructs to the ideal performer in that sport on a scale from 1 ("not important at all") to 10 ("of crucial importance"). The performer is then asked to rate his/her current level of skill (Subject Self-Assessment; SSA) on each construct on a scale from 1 ("couldn't be any worse") to 10 ("couldn't be any better"). The profile also includes the level of skill on each construct (i.e. Ideal Self-Assessment ; ISA) expected of the ideal performer, assumed to be a '10' on all constructs.

The next stage is to substract SSA from ISA for each construct and then to multiply that value by the importance score in order to arrive at a 'discrepancy' (D) score; the bigger the discrepancy score, the more the room for improvement. In this way the performer essentially maps out those areas on which there is room for improvement.

CONSTRUCT	I	ISA	SSA	(ISA-SSA)	D (ISA-SSA) x I
speed	10	10	9	1	10
concentration	10	10	7	3	30
agility	9	10	6	4	36
motivation	10	10	10	0	0
handling media	6	10	6	4	24
		10			
etc.		10			

Key: I = Importance; ISA = Ideal Self-Assessment; SSA = Subject Self-Assessment; D= Discrepancy

Fig. 2. Constructing the performance profile: an example.

3 Putting It Into Practice: A Case Study

This section describes a case study in which performance profiling formed the basis for the author's successful delivery of a sport psychology service, based on a cognitive behavioural approach, to an elite performer ranked among the top ten in the world in her sport. Performance profiling was used in this case study for three major purposes:

1) to aid the sport psychologist in the identification of an appropriate psychological intervention;

2) to maximize the performer's self-motivation to partake in and adhere to the psychological intervention;

3) as a means of monitoring any changes during the psychological intervention.

3.1 The performer

The performer was a female racket sport player who was ranked in the top ten in the world in her sport. On several occasions during her career she had encountered problems with the governing body of her sport over her behaviour on court, resulting on one occasion in her being fined and suspended.The performer presented herself as having a problem with her concentration on court. This problem generally manifested itself in two types of situation. Firstly, she often let what she perceived to be "poor shots" and/or "bad decisions" by the officials distract her and detract from her play. Secondly, she described the way in which she tended to "panic under pressure" (e.g. when the scores were close towards the end of a match). It was clear that she was relatively weak on the awareness and control factors identified earlier.

3.2 Measures

Several initial detailed discussions occurred between the sport psychologist and performer, during which she was asked to construct a performance profile and also to complete the Sport-Related Psychological Skills Questionnaire (Nelson and Hardy, 1990).

3.2.1 Player's performance profile

The player's performance profile was constructed in the same manner as described in Section 2 (see Jones (1993) for the player's full performance profile). She identified 25 constructs, with discrepancies ranging from 0 to 50.

The performer was then requested to think back to the original reason for consulting the sport psychologist and asked "of the constructs you have identified a discrepancy on, if you could improve upon any of them, which would be the major ones which could help you to resolve the original problem?" She identified four constructs; 'concentration' (D=50), 'preventing frustration' (D=40), 'composure' (D=36) and' relaxed attitude' (D=30).

3.2.2 Sport-Related Psychological Skills Questionnaire (SPSQ)

Nelson and Hardy's (1990) SPSQ is a 56-item measure of seven psychological skills: imaginal skill; mental preparation; self-efficacy; cognitive anxiety (i.e. the ability to control cognitive anxiety); concentration skill; relaxation skill; and motivation.

3.3 Cognitive behavioural intervention

The next stage was to decide upon an appropriate cognitive behavioural intervention for the performer which would develop both awareness and control. The principles involved in a cognitive behavioural approach are based upon a mediational model in which cognitions play a vital role in behavioural responses (Mace, 1990). On the basis of the four constructs (i.e. concentration, preventing frustration, composure and relaxed attitude) identified by the performer as requiring improvement, the sport psychologist proposed the adoption of a multimodal stress management approach. This involved the use of a combination of a number of different component parts (i.e. cognitive restructuring, imagery, relaxation and simulation training) from the various packages available (e.g. Meichenbaum, 1985; Smith, 1980; Suinn, 1972) as viewed appropriate for this individual's circumstances (see Burton, 1990). A central focus of the intervention was a modified version of applied relaxation (Ost, 1988). The sport psychologist provided an extensive and detailed rationale regarding the use of this particular form of relaxation and why it could be effective in the performer's case. The performer was first of all asked to think of her mind as a three-dimensional space, the shape of a sphere, and of limited capacity. Various exercises were then undertaken to demonstrate the limited capacity of the 'space'. The sport psychologist then related this to situations during a match when the subject became frustrated by 'incorrect' decisions or by her own perceived poor play, or became cognitively anxious at crucial points in the match. It was explained that the negative thoughts which characterized the frustration and anxiety were filling her space and that there was no room left for thoughts about the next rally.

At this stage, a cognitive restructuring technique based upon Ellis' (1962, 1970) rational emotive therapy was employed in an attempt to rationalize the ineffectiveness and futility of arguing with officials' decisions. Via a process of deduction, the subject calculated that she had argued with officials' decisions several hundred times during her career. The subject was then asked to relate how many times the officials had changed their decisions in her favour on these occasions; the response was "three or four". Via this form of reasoning, the performer quickly became aware of the futility of such an action, and that to fill her 'space' with thoughts of anger and frustration was not only pointless, but also counterproductive in terms of her concentration. The subject was in full agreement with these proposals, but admitted that she had not considered such responses in these terms previously.

Having enhanced the performer's awareness of the effects of her negative thought patterns in certain situations, the next stage was to explain to the performer how the use of applied relaxation could help her control the thoughts which filled her space under such times of potential frustration, anxiety,and consequent loss of concentration.

By means of a meditation-based relaxation technique, the performer could fill her mind space with thoughts of her breathing and in this way prevent negative thoughts from entering. At this point, the subject was in full agreement and eager to commence the training.

3.3.1 Relaxation training

It was explained to the performer that the aim was to learn the 'skill' of relaxation which could be applied very rapidly and in any situation both on and off court. The term 'skill' was employed in order to emphasize that, like any physical skill, it requires time and practice to learn (Ost, 1988). The relaxation training adopted was a modified version of applied relaxation with the major difference being that instead of employing progressive relaxation as the starting point, a meditation-based relaxation technique, similar to Benson's (1975) relaxation response, was used. This technique basically comprises concentration on breathing and using a mantra or key word spoken silently on each exhalation. When learned, this technique allows total focus on breathing and the mantra, and thus acts as a means of controlling the content of the mind space referred to in Section 1.

The initial phase of learning involved a general twenty minute version which was aimed at deep relaxation. This included counting procedures and relaxation-enhancing music. Once proficient at this form of relaxation, the performer then moved on to a shorter version lasting five minutes which was aimed at helping her to remain composed during the period before important matches. The performer then moved on to a 'quick' form of relaxation in which she used only a few breaths within an approximately twenty second period. This was to be used on court in between rallies and games and was aimed at helping her to regain composure and control her attentional focus. The performer was provided with a cue which was designed to trigger her quick relaxation in between rallies; this was simply to visually focus on the trademark on her racquet and to relax as she walked across court to either serve or receive serve. As this training progressed, the performer preferred to use this strategy only when she had played a poor shot or had a 'bad' call against her, or just before she played a crucial point.

3.3.2 Transfer of training to the competitive environment

Two forms of training were adopted as a means of enhancing the efficacy of the relaxation skill of the performer in competitive situations. These were imagery and physical practice in the presence of simulated competition stressors.

In the case of the imagery technique, the performer was requested to identify and describe two occasions which typified the problems of temperament she encountered on court, one of which should be the result of a poor decision by the official and the other one emanating from her own poor play. The occasions resulting from this exercise were characterized by the pressure of playing crucial points during which she had experienced considerable frustration, anxiety and loss of concentration and felt that she had lost the matches concerned as a result. Following detailed description of each of these occasions, the performer, under the guidance of the sport psychologist, then used imagery to reconstruct the precise circumstances and replay the precise sequence of events, including her behaviour, feelings, and thoughts at the time. Once she could successfully achieve this, she was then asked to repeat the imagery but this time to restructure it and to see and feel herself performing the relaxation skill, as described in the previous section, at the crucial point of the poor call or poor play. After several attempts, the performer was able to achieve this to an acceptable degree of proficiency and was recommended to practise it as often as possible.

On numerous occasions during this phase of the training, the performer engaged in simulation training in the form of practice matches which were refereed by an individual who had been primed to call some 'debatable rulings' against her. At all times, these practice matches were played against nationally-ranked male players and were highly competitive. With the additional use of video recordings of these matches, in which the camera focused exclusively on the performer in question, her behaviour was monitored and gradually restructured to perfect the relaxation skill for use on court. The emphasis throughout was on remaining calm and in control in such situations by employing the skill she had learned.

3.4 Intervention evaluation

The primary form of intervention evaluation was via administration of the performance profiling procedure at three and six months as a means of monitoring the performer's progress and, simultaneously, evaluating the effectiveness of the intervention. This version of the profiling used the constructs that the performer had previously identified, but on each occasion the subject was asked for her SSA on each of the constructs. As shown in Table 1, the discrepancies for all four constructs decreased over the intervention period, and in the cases of relaxed attitude and composure the discrepancies actually disappeared. On questioning, the performer confirmed that she did feel much more relaxed, composed and in control during matches than at the pre-intervention stage. While there was still some 'room for improvement' in terms of being able to concentrate and preventing frustration, she felt that she had improved enormously as a result of the intervention.

Table 1. Changes in discrepancy scores during the intervention

CONSTRUCT	PRE	3 MONTHS	6 MONTHS
Concentration	50	30	20
Preventing Frustration	40	30	10
Composure	36	18	0
Relaxed Attitude	30	20	0

These findings are supported by the data from the SPSQ which was also administered after three and six months of the intervention. The scores for cognitive anxiety, concentration skill and relaxation skill showed a dramatic improvement during the intervention. Her self-efficacy scores also showed a major improvement, which was almost certainly due to the fact that she now had an effective coping strategy available for use in pressure situations.

These changes were also borne out in her performance in the major championship in the world in her sport which took place shortly after the six month assessment. She actually won this championship for the first time in her career, this was a considerable achievement since no other player of the same nationality had won this event for several decades. She attributed this success, both privately and in the communication media, to her training in relaxation.

4 Conclusion

The case study reported here illustrates how the performance profiling procedure can serve to enhance the delivery of sport psychology services. A major strength of the performance profiling technique is clearly in facilitating the sport psychologist's efforts to implement and structure mental training programmes which meet the very specific needs of individual performers Another factor is that by effectively involving the performer in the decision-making process, his/her self-motivation to implement and adhere to mental training is likely to be high. Furthermore, performance profiling, when administered during the psychological intervention, provides a valuable source of feedback regarding progress both to the sport psychologist and to the performer. Indeed, performance profiling has many potential uses in the field of sport and is likely to prove a very valuable tool at the disposal of individuals providing a sport psychology service.

Whilst a large part of the success of this particular programme was undoubtedly due to the performance profiling process adopted in the initial stages, the contribution of the cognitive behavioural intervention employed was also clearly crucial. The study demonstrates, in particular, the importance of tailoring the intervention to meet the specific demands of the athlete in order to optimize its efficacy (cf. Vealey, 1988). Furthermore, the benefits of being able to employ a relaxation skill during performance have also been illustrated. In particular, 'quick relaxation', when practised to a high level of proficiency, can be particularly effective in allowing athletes to regain composure and attentional control in high pressure situations. A crucial component of using applied relaxation in this way is, of course, the application of the relaxation skill itself to the sport environment. This case study demonstrates that the transfer of training of the general technique to the competitive environment can be facilitated by the use of imagery and placing the performer in the presence of simulated competition stressors (cf. Jones & Hardy, 1990).

5 References

Beail,N. (Ed.) (1985) **Repertory Grid Technique and Personal Constructs.** Croom Helm, London.

Benson, H. (1975) **The Relaxation Response**. Avon Books, New York.

Bull, S.J. (1991) Personal and situational influences on adherence to mental skills training. **J. Sport Exerc. Psychol**., 13, 121-132.

Burton,D. (1988) Do anxious swimmers swim slower? Re-examining the elusive anxiety-performance relationship. **J. Sport Exerc. Psychol**., 10, 45-61.

Burton,D. (1990) Multimodal stress management in sport: current status and future directions, in **Stress and Performance in Sport** (eds J.G.Jones & L.Hardy) Wiley, Chichester, pp. 171-201.

Butler,R.J. (1989) Psychological preparation of Olympic boxers, in **The Psychology of Sport: Theory and Practice** (eds J.Kremer & W.Crawford) BPS Northern Ireland Branch, occasional paper, pp. 74-84.

Butler,R.J., & Hardy,L. (1992) The performance profile: theory and application. **Sport Psychol.**, 6, 253-264.

Deci,E.L., & Ryan,R.M. (1985) **Intrinsic Motivation and Self Determination in Human Behavior.** Plenum Press, New York.

Ellis,A. (1962) **Reason and Emotion in Psychotherapy.** Lye Stuart, New York.

Ellis,A. (1970) **The Essence of Rational Psychotherapy: A Comprehensive Approach to Treatment.** Institute for Rational Living, New York.

Fenz,W.D. (1975) Coping mechanisms and performance under stress, in **Psychology of Sport and Motor Behavior** (eds D.M.Landers, D.V.Harris & R.W.Christina)

Penn State HPER Series, University Park, Pennsylvania. pp. 3-24.

Fransella,F., & Bannister,D. (1977) **A Manual for Repertory Grid Technique.** Academic Press, London.

Jones, G. (1993) The role of performance profiling in cognitive behavioural interventons in sport. **Sport Psychol.**, 7, 160-272.

Jones, G., & Hardy, L. (1990) Stress in sport: experiences of some elite performers, in **Stress and Performance in Sport** (eds J.G.Jones & L.Hardy), Wiley, Chichester pp. 247-277.

Jones,G., Swain,A. & Hardy,L. (1993) Intensity and direction dimensions of competitve state anxiety and relationships with performance. **J. Sports Sci.,** 11, 525-532.

Kelly,G.A. (1955) **The Psychology of Personal Constructs.** Norton,New York.

Mace,R. (1990) Cognitive behavioural interventions in sport, in **Stress and Performance in Sport** (eds J.G.Jones & L.Hardy) Wiley, Chichester, pp. 203-230.

Mahoney, M. & Avener, M. (1977) Psychology of the elite athlete: an exploratory study. **Cog. Therapy Res.**, 1, 135-141.

Mahoney, M.J. , Gabriel, T.J. & Perkins,T.S. (1987) Psychological skills and exceptional athletic performance. **Sport Psychol.**, 1, 181-199.

Meichenbaum, D. (1985) **Stress Inoculation Training.** Pergamon, New York.

Nelson, D., & Hardy, L. (1990) The development of an empirically validated tool for measuring psychological skill in sport. **J. Sports Sci.**, 8, 71.

Ost, L.G. (1988) Applied relaxation: description of an effective coping technique. Scand. **J. Behavior Therapy,** 17, 83-96.

Smith, R.E. (1980) A cognitive-affective approach to stress management training for athletes, in **Psychology of Motor Behavior and Sport** (eds C.Nadeau, W.Halliwell, K.Newell, & G.Roberts), Human Kinetics, Champaign, Illinois, pp.54-73.

Suinn, R. (1972) Removing emotional obstacles to learning and performance by visuomotor behavior rehearsal. **Behavior Therapy,** 3,308-310.

Vealey, R.S. (1988) Future directions in psychological skills training. **Sport Psychol**., 2, 318-336.

33 Mental training for junior tennis players resident at the Rover L.T.A. school, Bisham Abbey 1987–1993: Issues of delivery and evaluation

P.C. Terry
Lawn Tennis Association & West London Institute, UK

1 Introduction

The 1980's witnessed almost linear growth in the use of sport psychology consultants by National Governing Bodies of sport in Great Britain (Terry & Harrold, 1990)(see Figure 1) while expansion in the United States appears to have followed a similar upward trend (Gould et al., 1991). The expanding literature on mental training has generally supported its use, although judgments about its efficacy have too often originated from the sport psychologists themselves without the benefit of empirical support, or have been based upon anecdotal evidence from athletes and coaches. It is apparent that conceptual models for the delivery and especially the evaluation of mental training programmes have received scant attention. Where objective evaluations of mental training have occurred, it has been shown that mental training can lower anxiety (Hellstadt,1987; Elko & Ostrow, 1991), enhance visual imagery ability (Rodgers, Hall & Buckolz, 1991), and improve performance (Li-Wei et al., 1992). An ongoing weekly programme of mental training for elite, junior tennis players (n=27) resident at the Rover LTA School, Bisham Abbey has been taught since 1987. The present purpose is to outline the structure of the programme and to evaluate its success.

2 Structure of the programme

The mental training programme has utilised a model involving five phases: assessment, education, implementation, problem solving and evaluation (see Figure 2). Inherent in this model is a general tendency away from group strategies and towards individualisation as the programme progresses. Similarly, the programme tends to focus on implementation and problem solving during competition periods whereas assessment and education tend to take place during periods of little competitive activity. It could be said therefore that the model proposes a periodised structure whereby mental

Science and Racket Sports Edited by T. Reilly, M. Hughes and A. Lees.
Published in 1994 by E & FN Spon ISBN 0 419 18500 3

training parallels and becomes integrated with a player's physical and technical preparation schedule.

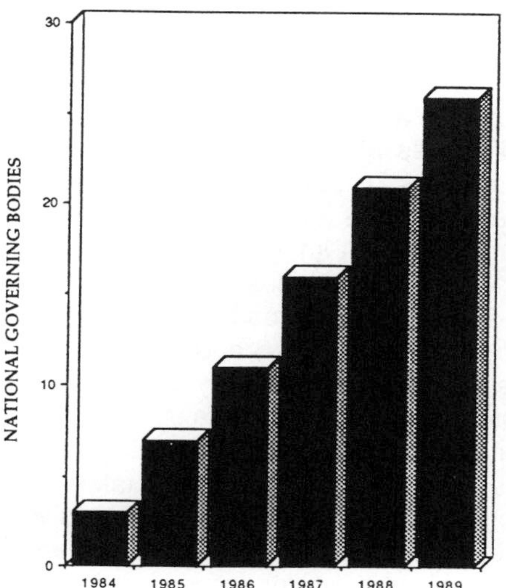

Fig.1. Growth of National Governing Bodies utilising psychological support 1984-1989.

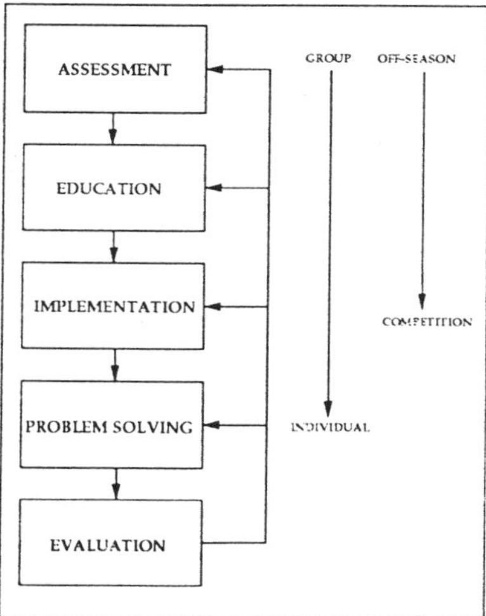

Fig. 2. General strategy for mental training programmes.

2.1 The assessment phase

The assessment phase includes psychometric testing, semi-structured interviews, self-assessment and performance observation. Psychometric testing, the justification for which is an enduring point of contention among applied sport psychologists, is employed primarily to individualise the programme towards specific needs rather than to make predictions. It has been argued that the lack of reliable relationships between trait measures and athletic performance effectively negates their use in applied settings. However, tests which provide a simple but often revealing "snapshot" of the individual help to identify areas where education may have greatest impact. Hence tests such as the Tennis Test of Attentional and Interpersonal Style (Van Schoyck & Grasha, 1981), the Eysenck Personality Inventory (Eysenck & Eysenck, 1963), and the Movement Imagery Questionnaire (Hall & Pongrac, 1983) may form an early part of the process by which the psychological characteristics of individuals are understood.

This process is supported by interviews and self-assessment exercises which further reveal the mindset of players. By far and away the most revealing component of the assessment phase is observation and video analysis of players during competition. By identifying behavioural responses to match-play situations, especially reactions to mistakes, disputes and "big points" where psychological momentum often turns decisively, key pointers for subsequent phases of the programme are provided. When players sit through video replays of their own unproductive responses during critical moments in competition there is often enhanced commitment to change.

2.2 The education phase

The education phase has been built around psychological skills development such as relaxation training, stress management, attentional control training, body language training, motivation strategies, self-efficacy training and the use of imagery. These are taught in groups during regular weekly sessions, usually involving 6 - 12 players and one or two sports psychologists. Players monitor their own progress and establish objectives for the development of psychological skills. These are reviewed every four weeks.

Players are exposed to a range of mental training exercises drawn from the literature (e.g. Loehr, 1987; Terry, 1989: Weinberg, 1990) and are encouraged to utilise those which they feel comfortable with and which prove effective for them as individuals. The programme is based on a principle of planned redundancy, whereby players develop skills and knowledge which facilitate independence from the sport psychologist. Although the education phase equips players with practical techniques, for instance, to maintain calm or energise or mentally rehearse, it is not seen as the central thrust of the programme. In isolation, knowledge of psychological skills may serve to confuse rather than clarify, and experience suggests that the key phase involves teaching players how to implement this knowledge effectively in practice or match situations.

2.3 The implementation phase

The implementation phase revolves around the integration of learned mental skills into competition routines for pre-match preparation, service, service return, between points, changeover, and other situations deemed critical by individual players. It is very common for the robustness of these routines to be put to the test in various simulation exercises. For example, biofeedback techniques are utilised to assess relaxation ability when time stressors are imposed, such as "You have 20 seconds to lower your arousal level (galvanic skin response) by 50 points (scale 0 - 1000)." This exercise simulates the task of regaining composure between points or at changeover after a frustrating period of play. It also develops greater self-awareness of emotional arousal.

Many of the simulation exercises occur on court. "Mr.Concentration" contests are conducted regularly in which players receive grades according to their ability to maintain focus during serving whilst other players try to distract them. Similarly, match-play situations are set up, often involving tie breaks, in which the sport psychologist manipulates events, giving bad calls or switching rackets, to engender maximum frustration for one or both of the players on court. This especially challenges the self-discipline of players between points, during which time they are encouraged to follow the four stage routine of 1) positive physical response; 2) relaxation response; 3) preparation response; 4) ritual response, devised by Loehr (1990). Such aspects of implementation are often integrated into coaching sessions with the involvement of the coaching staff which tends to reinforce the impact. Essentially these simulation exercises follow the overload principle, in that a player's capacity to produce an effective response is developed by being exposed to progressively more demanding situations.

2.4 The problem solving phase

The problem solving phase has been based around individual counselling sessions. Players are taught to be proactive in dealing with performance-related issues and to request one-to-one sessions with the sport psychologist to prevent rather than to cure problems. Each player has a monthly individual session but can request additional meetings. When a problem is identified, a player is guided towards a solution which is implemented during practice or tournament play and its effectiveness evaluated at the next meeting. The sport psychologist will regularly provide support at important tournaments to contribute to last minute "fine tuning" and occasionally to intervene during crises of confidence.

Motivation strategies, notably personal goal setting and token reward structures, are employed during each phase. For example, a weekly feature of the programme is the presentation of the Yellow Jersey, awarded for attitude, effort, self-discipline and performance.The dynamics of player-athlete relationships has also been a focus of attention, involving weekly meetings with coaching staff and monitoring perceived coaching behaviour, using the Leadership Scale for Sports (Chelladurai & Saleh, 1980). If significant discrepancies are revealed between a player's perceptions of the coach and the coach's self-perceptions, these are discussed between coach and sport psychologist. Throughout the programme, players are responsible for keeping a record of their mental training activities, but a clinical model of recording all player-sport psychologist interaction is also employed as a safeguard.

3 Evaluation of the programme

In addition to the ongoing evaluative process built into the programme, mental training effectiveness is evaluated annually based on information from four sources (Figure 3).

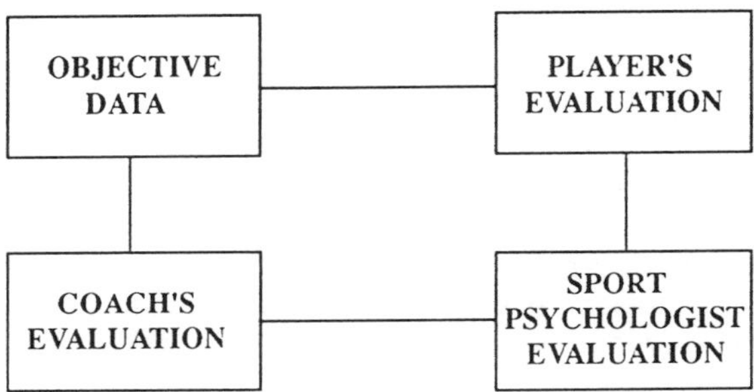

Fig. 3. Model for evaluating mental training.

3.1 Objective data

During the assessment and education phases, players complete psychological skills tests to quantify relaxation ability, visual and kinesthetic imagery ability and attentional control. Relaxation ability is assessed using a galvanic skin response (GSR) measure on Biogram (Synergy Software, Letchworth), a computerised biofeedback system. The task is to lower GSR whilst seated in a quiet environment. The dependent measure is the minimum recorded reading during a three minute period on a scale of 0-1000. Visual and kinesthetic imagery are assessed using the Movement Imagery Questionnaire (Hall & Pongrac, 1983), an 18-task self-report inventory, in which players rate the ease or difficulty with which they complete visual and kinesthetic imagery tasks. Each modality is scored on a scale of 9-63. Attentional control is assessed by performance in "Holding an image" (Terry, 1989) a self-report task in which players time their ability to focus exclusively on a task-related image to the exclusion of all other stimuli. Performance is expressed in seconds, totalled for five self-paced attempts.

Tests are repeated at the end of a six week training period, during which time players complete three, 15-minute sessions per week listening to a cassette tape containing exercises for controlled breathing, guided imagery and centering. The results in Table 1, which summarise data gathered from resident players for 1991-92, indicate significant improvements in all four psychological skills. The process by which improvements in psychological skills are demonstrated to players is seen as an important precursor to improved on-court performance. Previous authors have commented on the motivational impact of such a process (Cohn, Rotella & Lloyd, 1990; Rodgers et al., 1991). Recipients of the programme have collectively won more than 30 National Junior titles, the 1993 Australian Open Junior title, and the 1993 European Junior team title, although it is impossible to determine the contribution of mental training to these achievements.

Table 1. Test-retest comparisons for four psychological skills tests before and after a six-week period of mental training

Test	n	Pre- Mean	Pre- S.D.	Post- Mean	Post- S.D.	t	df	P<
Relaxation	15	298.5	172	259.7	185	3.00	14	0.01
Visual imagery	14	32.6	11.0	25.1	7.9	3.83	13	0.005
Kinesthetic imagery	14	36.3	11.6	27.9	8.1	5.76	13	0.0001
Attentional control	12	82.8	33.0	132.8	67.9	3.43	11	0.01

3.2 Player evaluation

The mental training programme is evaluated by players using the Consultant Evaluation Form (Partington & Orlick, 1987). The results for 1991-92 are contained in Table 2. These ratings compare favourably with evaluations reported for sport psychology consultants working with U.S. Olympic squads, and suggest that the programme is perceived by players to have contributed to their development. In addition, players are asked to rate the programme on a seven point scale from "Of no value" to "Extremely valuable". Responses for 1991-92 indicate that 78% found the programme "Extremely valuable".

3.3 Coach evaluation

Coach evaluation of the mental training programme is ongoing and semi-formal. Coach perceptions of individual needs, and feedback on the effectiveness of interventions, are discussed at National Training staff meetings held weekly at the school. Coaches have the option of withdrawing their players from the programme at any time but to date none has chosen this option.

3.4 Sport psychologist evaluation

A yearly summative report of the programme is produced which incorporates feedback from players and coaches, as well as summary data from objective tests. Such reports naturally tend towards a favourable evaluation as they influence decisions about the continuation of the programme. Considering the financial implications of such decisions, this source of evaluation carries the least impartiality and, for that reason, perhaps the least weight. The prime function of the summative report is to make recommendations about the development of the programme for the following year.

Table 2. Descriptive statistics for player (n=15) perceptions of the mental training programme using the Consultant Evaluation Form (Partington & Orlick, 1987)

Item	Mean	S.D.
Useful knowledge about mental training to apply directly to my sport	8.6	1.6
Individualised mental training programme based on my input and needs	9.0	1.4
Open, flexible and ready to collaborate with me	8.9	1.6
Positive, constructive attitude	9.4	1.2
Trustworthy	9.1	1.5
Easy to relate to	8.6	1.8
Fitted in with the group	9.1	1.1
Helped me draw on my strengths	8.8	1.6
Helped me overcome possible problems	8.9	2.0
Provided clear, practical, concrete strategies	8.9	1.8

Note. All items scored on a 0-10 scale

4 Summary

This paper has outlined models for structuring and evaluating mental training programmes. An attempt has been made to provide insight into some of the practical issues experienced by sports psychologists working with young athletes at residential sports schools. The models are based on the principle of regular contact and close liaison between sport psychologist, player and coach, whereby the sport psychologist becomes "one of the team". The use of objective data when evaluating mental training effectiveness is proposed. Experience and evaluation of the present programme suggests that mental training contributes to the development of elite junior tennis players.

5 References

Chelladurai, P. & Saleh, S.D. (1980) Dimensions of leader behaviour in sports: Development of a leadership scale. J. Sport Psychol., 2, 34-45.

Cohn, P.J., Rotella, R.J. & Lloyd, J.W. (1990) Effects of a cognitive-behavioural intervention on the pre-shot routine and performance in golf. Sport Psychol., 4, 33-47.

Elko, P.K. & Ostrow, A.C. (1991) Effects of a rational-emotive education program on heightened anxiety levels of female collegiate gymnasts. Sport Psychol., 5, 235-255.

Eysenck, H.J. & Eysenck, S.B.G. (1963) Eysenck Personality Inventory. Hodder & Stoughton, Sevenoaks, Kent.

Gould, D., Murphy, S., Tammen, V. & May, J. (1991) An evaluation of U.S. Olympic sport psychology consultant effectiveness. Sport Psychol., 5, 111-127.

Hall, C.R. & Pongrac, J. (1983) Movement imagery questionnaire. University of Western Ontario Press, London, ONT., Canada.

Hellstedt, J.C. (1987) Sport psychology at a ski academy: Teaching mental skills to young athletes. Sport Psychol., 1, 56-68.

Li-Wei, Z., Qi-Wei, M. Orlick, T. & Zitzelsberger, L. (1992) The effect of mental-imagery training on performance enhancement with 7 to 10 year old children. Sport Psychol., 6, 230-241.

Loehr, J. (1987) Mental Toughness Training for Sports. Leisure Press, Champaign, IL.

Loehr, J. (1990) Providing sport psychology services to professional tennis players. Sport Psychol., 4, 400-408.

Partington, J. & Orlick, T. (1987) The sport psychology consultant evaluation form. Sport Psychol., 1, 309-317.

Rodgers, W., Hall, C. and Buckolz, E. (1991) The effect of an imagery training program on imagery ability, imagery use, and figure skating performance. J. Appl. Sport Psychol., 3, 109-125.

Terry, P.C. (1989) The Winning Mind. Thorsons, Wellingborough, UK.

Terry, P.C. & Harrold, F. (1990) Development of sport psychology in Britain. Presented at Centre of Excellence seminar "Sport Science in Action". West London Institute, July 1990.

Van Schoyck, S.R. & Grasha, A.F. (1981) Attentional style variations and athletic ability: The advantages of a sports-specific test. J. Sport Psychol., 3, 149-165.

Weinberg, R. (1990) The Mental Advantage. Human Kinetics, Champaign, IL.

34 How effective are psychological techniques used to enhance performance in tennis? The views of some international tennis coaches

A. Moran
Department of Psychology, University College, Dublin, Eire

1 Introduction

Competitive tennis is a mentally demanding sport (Loehr, 1990). For example, the untimed and "stop-start" nature of its play may cause performers' attention to wander during a match. While undesirable in any sport, lapses of attention are especially costly in tennis because its scoring system is such that the loser of a match could have won *more* games than the winner (e.g. 0-6, 7-6, 7-6). Not surprisingly, tennis psychologists have responded to its mental challenge by advocating a variety of psychological techniques which purport to improve the consistency and "mental toughness" of players on-court (e.g. see Loehr, 1990; Mackenzie, 1991; Weinberg, 1988; Winter & Martin, 1991). Indeed, some of these techniques have been marketed commercially as instructional videotapes (e.g. Loehr, 1989; Yandell, 1990) and audiotapes (Porter, 1990). But how effective are these performance-enhancement strategies? Unfortunately, apart from a few notable exceptions (e.g. Weinberg, Grove & Jackson, 1992), few studies have been conducted on the practical efficacy of psychological techniques to improve tennis performance. Accordingly, the purpose of this paper is to rectify this evaluative neglect by exploring one aspect of this field, namely, the issue of what expert tennis coaches think about mental skills training in tennis. This topic is important because sport psychology cannot make progress unless it receives regular feedback from its consumers, such as players and coaches, about the validity and utility of its theories. However, somewhat surprisingly, coaches have received relatively little research attention from sport pychologists (but see Chelladurai, 1993).

In passing, it is worth noting that, over 60 years ago, the pioneer of sport psychology, Coleman Griffith (1926), warned of the dangers of passing instructional principles "from college generation to generation *without examination* and oftentimes without any real factual bases" (p. 3, *italics mine).*

2 Method

The subjects consisted of 30 full-time professional tennis coaches who attended the seventh International Tennis Federation's World Coaches' Workshop in the Riverview Club, Dublin, Ireland, between 6-10 October 1991. They represented the national tennis associations of the following 13 countries / regions: Australia (n=2), Canada (n=2), East Africa (n=1), El Salvador (n=1), France (n=1), Great Britain (n=4), Holland (n=3), Indonesia (n=1), Ireland (n=4), Italy (n=1), Mexico (n=2), South Africa (n=1) and the USA (n=7). The average age of this sample was 37.63 years (range of 25 and *SD* of 8.05 years). The mean number of hours which this group spent in coaching tennis per week was 22.58 (*SD* = 14.20).

Science and Racket Sports Edited by T. Reilly, M. Hughes and A. Lees.
Published in 1994 by E & FN Spon ISBN 0 419 18500 3

The average number of years of professional coaching experience which this group had was 12.72 (*SD* = 7.05). Three-quarters of the coaches (23 out of 30, or 76.7%) had coached touring professional players on the international "circuit".

A specially-devised, 27-item Likert-scaled questionnaire called *The Survey of Mental Skills in Tennis* was used to probe such topics as the importance of mental skills in determining success in competitive tennis; the "trainability" of these skills; their relative importance in tennis and the main difficulties encountered in coaching these skills. This questionnaire was administered to coaches who attended a sport science seminar the World Tennis Coaches' Workshop in the Riverview Club, Dublin. The response rate (about 60%) was determined largely by linguistic factors: coaches who did not speak English fluently did not complete their questionnaires. A copy of this questionnaire is avalable from the author.

3 Results

3.1 Importance and trainability mental skills in tennis

To begin with, 90% of the coaches believed strongly that mental skills were *very important* in determining success in competitive tennis (Q. 7). Further, all but one of them believed that mental skills could be trained in players (Q. 13). Not surprisingly, 90% of them reported that they devoted a period of time each week to *"analysis and discussion"* of mental skills (Q. 8). Apparently, the main barriers to this activity were a lack of time (reported by 26.7% of the sample) and difficulties in translating theoretical knowledge of sport psychology into practical drills (20%).

Table 1. Coaches' ratings of importance of certain mental skills in tennis

Skill	Mean importance score*	SD	Rank
1. Motivation	6.6	0.73	1
2. Concentration	6.5	0.86	2
3. Self-confidence	6.4	0.81	3
4. Mental prep.	6.0	0.85	4
5. Anxiety-control	5.9	1.04	5
6. Anger-control	5.9	1.07	5
7. Visualization	5.3	1.17	7

*Higher scores indicate greater importance (as 1=not at all important and 7= extremely important)

3.2 Importance of specific mental skills

Using a series of 7-point scales (from 1= *"not at all important"* to 7= *"extremely important"*), the coaches were asked to rate the importance of seven mental skills (adapted from Weinberg, 1988) in determining success in competitive tennis (Q. 22). These skills were concentration, self-confidence, motivation, visualization, anxiety control, anger control and pre-game mental preparation. The coaches' ratings, presented in Table 1, show that although all the skills were regarded as important, the three which attracted the highest ratings were motivation (X=6.6, *SD* $\pm$0.73), concentration (6.5, *SD* $\pm$ 0.86) and self-confidence (6.4, *SD* $\pm$ 0.81).

This finding is confirmed by significance testing. Thus a series of t-tests was conducted between all pairs of importance ratings in Table 1. Results showed that 14 out of the 21 t-tests were significant ($P < 0.05$). In particular, the comparisons involving the mental skills of **motivation, concentration** and **self-confidence** with all the others yielded the greatest number of significant differences.

Table 2. Coaches' views of utility of certain psychological techniques used by tennis players

Rank-order / technique (1="most"; 13="least" useful)		Mean rated utility	SD
1.	Positive self-talk	6.28	0.65
2.	Imagery of next shot	6.17	0.81
3.	Imagery of tactics	6.10	0.72
4.	Setting performance goals	6.03	0.82
5.	Taking deep breaths	5.93	1.08
6.	Slowing down behaviour	5.76	0.87
7.	Pre-shot routines	5.30	1.09
8.	Using "trigger" words	5.18	1.57
9.	Breathing out audibly	4.97	1.59
10.	Closing eyes	4.66	1.23
11.	Looking at strings	4.70	1.54
12.	Muscular relaxation	4.62	1.18
13.	Blowing on hands	3.76	1.38

One rather puzzling finding concerns the fact that of the seven mental skills listed in Table 1, visualization was rated relatively less important than the others Yet, as Table 2 reveals, two techniques based on imagery (e.g. "forming a clear mental picture of where you would like to place your serve") were rated very highly. Perhaps the coaches did not clearly understand the term "visualization".

3.3 Efficacy of specific psychological techniques

Next, we explored the perceived utility of a variety (n=13) of behavioural techniques alleged to enhance the mental skills of tennis players. Details are presented of the average utility ratings and rank-order of these techniques in Table 2 . From this table, it seems that coaches believe that constructive self-talk, visualization and setting "performance" goals are among the most useful psychological performance-enhancement strategies for players.

3.4 Mental skills training: What next?

We concluded by asking the coaches to indicate their most urgent needs in the field of mental skills training. They gave top priority to the need for a practical checklist on how to design and implement programmes in this field.

4 Discussion

Before discussing our findings, three weaknesses in our research should be acknowledged. First, as our data constitute opinions, rather than performance measures, the evidence which we have gathered bears only <u>indirectly</u> on the topic of interest. Thus we are dealing with the perceived efficacy of certain techniques, not with their actual consequences for performance "on-court". Second, reservations must be expressed about the generality of our findings in view of the relatively small sample size (*n*=30).

A final source of bias concerns the possibility of response bias. This is raised by the fact that the sample comprised a self-selected group of delegates at a sport science seminar, rather than a random group of coaches "in the field". Bearing these limitations in mind, however, at least three conclusions emerged. First, motivation, concentration and self-confidence were deemed to be the most important mental assets of successful tennis players. Second, it was felt that these qualities were "trainable". Next, most of the psychological techniques advocated in the popular literature on performance enhancement were perceived as being practically valuable. Techniques which attracted especially favourable evaluation were self-talk, visualization and the establishment of "performance goals". Conversely, strategies like "looking at the strings" and "blowing on the hands" were viewed more sceptically. Interestingly, in a recent review of Loehr's (1989) *16 second cure"* video, Moore (1990) echoed this scepticism of these latter two strategies

In conclusion, our results show that expert tennis coaches are keenly aware of the role that mental factors play in determining successful performance in tennis. They also welcome psychological efforts to improve the mental preparation and competitive performance of players. But their views about the practical utility of psychological performance enhancement strategies need to be augmented by additional evidence. For example, what do the players themselves think of these mental techniques? What specific effects do they have on players' performances? Do players have problems in remembering *when* to use them (see Moran, 1993)? Another potentially fruitful avenue for research in this field concerns expert-novice differences in meta-cognitive skills. From cognitive theory (e.g. Bedard & Chi, 1992), it seems likely that expert tennis players should have greater awareness of their own decision-making and attentional processes than novices.

5 Acknowledgements

I wish to acknowledge gratefully the assistance in data collection received from Denis Collete, Leif Dahlgren, Matt Doyle, Frank van Fraayenhoven, Marcel Ferralli, Pauline Harrison, Peter Lowther, Kevin Smit, Stan Smith and Dr. Ronald B. Woods. I also wish to thank Barbara Dooley for statistical advice.

6 References

Bedard, J., & Chi, M. T. (1992) Expertise. **Curr. Directions in Psychol. Sci.,** 1, 135-139.

Chelladurai, P (1993) Leadership, in **Handbook of Research in Sport Psychology** (eds R. N. Singer, M. Murphey and L. K. Tennant). Macmillan, New York. pp. 647 - 671.

Griffith, C. R. (1926) **Psychology of Coaching**. Scribners, New York

Loehr, J. (1989) **Mental Toughness Training for Tennis: Vol. 1: The16 Second Cure**. Grand Slam Communications, Delray Beach, Florida.

Loehr, J. (1990) **The Mental Game: Winning at Pressure Tennis**. Plume/ Penguin, New York..

Mackenzie, M. (1991) **Tennis: The Mind Game**. Dell Books, New York.

Moore, B. (1990) Review of J. Loehr's, Mental Toughness Training for Tennis: The 16 Second Cure (Miami, Fla: FTM Sports).**Sport Psychol., 4,** 431 -432.

Moran, A. (1993) **Attentional skills training: Integrating cognitive theory and sport psychology**, in Sport Psychology: An Integrated Approach (eds S. Serpa, J. Alves, V. Fereira and A. Paula-Bruto). International Society of Sport Psychology, Lisbon. pp. 371-373.

Porter, K. (1990) **Guided visualization for tennis (audiotape)**. Porter Performance Systems, Eugene, Oregon.

Smith, R. E. (1989) Applied sport psychology in an age of accountability. **J. Appl. Sport Psychol.,** 1, 166-180.

Weinberg, R. S. (1988) **The Mental Advantage: Developing your Psychological Skills in Tennis**. Leisure Press, Champaign, Illinois.

Weinberg, R., Grove, R., & Jackson, A. (1992) Strategies for building self-efficacy in tennis players: A comparative analysis of Australian and American coaches. **Sport Psychol.**, 6, 3-13.

Winter, G., & Martin, C. (1991) **Sport "Psych" for Tennis.** South Australian Sports Institute, Adelaide, South Australia.

Yandell, J. (1990) **Visual Tennis: Mental Imagery and the Quest for the Winning Edge.** Doubleday, New York.

35 Anxiety state of tennis players: a comparative study

A.N.I. El Gammal
College of Education Sport Department, Tanta University, Cairo, Egypt

1 Introduction

There is a strong relationship between psychological states and sports performance. Anxiety is one psychological factor which has a great effect on human behaviour, especially through competition. The effect of anxiety may be dependent on the degree of anxiety experienced. If anxiety motivates the learning of adaptive behaviour, it serves a useful purpose. Because anxiety is so pervasive in human life, particularly in social situations, we can hardly hope to abolish it. It is important, at least, to harness this powerful motive for constructive rather than destructive purposes. Spielberger (1972) described two kinds of anxiety: anxiety as a trait and anxiety as a state. Anxiety state is related to stress situations like sport competitions.

In the present study there was an attempt to examine the anxiety state of tennis players before matches and the effect of anxiety level on losing set points. The purpose of this study was to investigate the differences between Egyptian and non-Egyptian tennis players with respect to anxiety state. Two specific questions were addressed:

(i) Are there any differences between Egyptian and non- Egyptian tennis players in anxiety state?

(ii) Do players with a high anxiety state perform less well than those with a low level?

2 Methods

This study was carried out on professional tennis players in Cairo. The sample consisted of thirty-five Egyptian players, and thirty-five non-Egyptian players from different countries. It was concluded in January 1993.

Science and Racket Sports Edited by T. Reilly, M. Hughes and A. Lees.
Published in 1994 by E & FN Spon ISBN 0 419 18500 3

The Arabic form of the state anxiety questionnaire (Abd El-Khalek, 1990) was used for the Egyptian subjects. The English state anxiety questionnaire (Spielberger, 1972) was used for the non-Egyptian subjects. Anxiety state was measured before five matches. Scores at set point through five matches were measured retrospectively.

3 Results and Discussion

Results indicated that the mean scores of the Egyptian players (64 ± 10) were higher than for non-Egyptian (38 ±8) in anxiety state ($P<0.01$). It was also shown that high anxiety state players were more vulnerable in losing set points. The level of anxiety was significantly related to losing set points, the correlations being 0.43 for Egyptians and 0.39 for the non-Egyptians ($P<0.01$).

The non-Egyptian tennis players scored lower than the Egyptian group on anxiety state. This might have been due to:-

(i) poor psychological knowledge among Egyptian players;
(ii) ways of mentally preparing and training.

Results also indicated that the level of anxiety state was related to losing set points through matches. Players of low anxiety won set points more than players with high anxiety. It is known that when a person is faced by task demands, two types of response are expressed: those that are related to performance and task completion, and those that are not. The first type of response is assumed to be motivated by task-specific drives, such as achievement motivation. The second type of response is motivated by learned anxiety. Among these latter responses are feelings of inadequacy and helplessness.

Players low in anxiety react to such situations with increased attention and effort. The highly anxious individual may be more likely to form self-deprecating concepts of himself under stress.

4 References

Abd El-Khalek, A.M. (1990) **The development and validation of the Arabic form of STAF.** Cairo University.

Spielberger, C.D. (1972) **Anxiety: Current Trends in Theory and Research**, Academic Press, New York.

36 Athletic identity of national level badminton players: a cross-cultural analysis

H. Matheson, B.W. Brewer*, J.L. Van Raalte* and B. Andersen**
University of Wolverhampton, Walsall, UK
**Springfield College, Springfield, USA*
***University of Wyoming, Laramie, USA*

1 Introduction

Athletic identity is the degree to which an individual identifies with the role of the sportsperson (Brewer, Van Raalte, & Linder, in press). Although high levels of athletic identity may signify a commitment to excellence in sport, there may be risks associated with a strong and exclusive identification of the self with the role of sportsperson (Brewer et al., in press). Research has shown that athletic identity is negatively correlated with adjustment to sport injury (Brewer, in press) and sport career termination (Hinitz, 1988).

In previous research, athletic identity has been found to increase with level of sport involvement. As would be expected, competitive sportspersons have greater athletic identity than recreational sportspersons and people who do not participate in sport (Brewer et al., in press; Good et al., 1993). In general, males have been found to identify more strongly with the role of sportsperson than females (Brewer, Van Raalte, & Linder, 1991; Brewer et al., in press), although this gender difference tends to diminish as the level of sport involvement increases (Good et al., 1993; Van Raalte & Cook, 1991).

To date, no research has examined athletic identity cross-culturally or with racket sport participants. Therefore, the purpose of this study was to assess the athletic identity of national level badminton players in two different cultures (British and Malaysian). Based on research suggesting that Western cultures tend to view the self as independent of others and that Eastern cultures tend to view the self as interdependent with others (Markus & Kitayama, 1991), we hypothesized that members of the British national badminton team would have higher athletic identity scores than members of the Malaysian national badminton team.

2 Method

2.1 Subjects

Subjects were members of the British national women's ($\underline{n}$ = 7) and men's ($\underline{n}$ = 7)

Science and Racket Sports Edited by T. Reilly, M. Hughes and A. Lees.
Published in 1994 by E & FN Spon ISBN 0 419 18500 3

badminton teams and the Malaysian national women's (n = 9) and men's (n = 8) badminton teams.

2.2 Procedure

Subjects completed a demographics sheet and the Athletic Identity Measurement Scale (AIMS) (Brewer et al., in press), which assesses the degree to which an individual identifies with the role of sportsperson. The reliability and validity of the AIMS have been demonstrated in a number of studies. The AIMS has test-retest reliability coefficients of 0.89 over a two-week period (Brewer et al., in press), 0.60 over a ten-week period (Brewer & Linder, 1992), and 0.59 over a three-month period (Brewer, Denson, & Jordan, 1992) have been obtained. Alpha reliability coefficients ranged from 0.80 to 0.93 in administrations of the AIMS to eight independent samples (Brewer, 1991; Brewer et al., 1992; Brewer et al., 1991; Brewer et al., in press; Good et al., 1993). There is also substantial support for the convergent (Brewer et al., in press; Good et al., 1993) and divergent (Brewer et al., 1991, in press) validity of the AIMS.

3 Results

One subject did not complete the AIMS correctly and was therefore not included in analyses involving the AIMS. British subjects had a mean age of 25.92 (SD = 3.27) years and had an average of 15.14 (SD = 3.78) years of badminton experience. Malaysian subjects had a mean age of 19.47 (SD = 2.21) years and had an average of 7.59 (SD = 3.30) years of badminton experience. Results of a t-test indicated that the British subjects were significantly older, $t(29) = 6.54$, $P < 0.005$, and more experienced, $t(29) = 5.94$, $P < 0.005$, than the Malaysian subjects.

Table 1. Means and standard deviations of AIMS scores

	Gender	
Country	Male	Female
United Kingdom		
X	55.43	50.00
SD	6.95	6.61
Malaysia		
X	56.75	39.88
SD	6.18	23.46

The internal consistency of the AIMS with these subjects was acceptable (alpha = 0.87). Results of a 2 X 2 (culture X gender) analysis of variance (ANOVA) indicated that males (X = 56.13, SD = 6.35) scored significantly higher on the AIMS than females (X = 44.60, SD = 17.92), $F_{1,26} = 5.55$, $P < 0.05$. The culture main effect and the culture X gender interaction were not statistically significant. Means and standard deviations of AIMS scores are presented in Table 1.

4 Discussion

In this investigation, it was found that national level male badminton players had significantly greater athletic identity than national level female badminton players and that British national level badminton players did not differ from Malaysian national level badminton players in terms of athletic identity. The gender difference in athletic identity replicates previous research (Brewer et al., 1991; Brewer et al., in press) and is noteworthy in that comparisons of male and female elite sport participants have failed to produce significant differences in several studies (Good et al., 1993; Van Raalte & Cook, 1991). The acceptable internal consistency reliability coefficient for the AIMS demonstrates the cross-cultural utility of the AIMS as a measure of athletic identity in elite racket sport participants.

There are several potential explanations for the non-significant difference between the British and Malaysian players on athletic identity. First, the small sample size (and the resultant lack of statistical power) may have prevented the occurrence of a significant difference. Second, it may be that the AIMS is not sensitive to cultural differences in the construal of the self. Third, it is possible that a significant cross-cultural difference in athletic identity would have emerged had the Malaysian players been equivalent in age to the British players. An interdependent view of the self may develop with age and maturity. Fourth, it may be that there actually is no difference between British national level badminton players and Malaysian national level badminton players on athletic identity. Although cross-cultural differences in motivation for sport participation have been documented (Curry & Weiss, 1989), perhaps the demands of being a member of a national badminton team inspire similar levels of identification with the role of sportsperson independent of culture. Further, it is possible that the Malaysian players may have adopted a more independent view of the self as a result of their international travels. The fact that Malaysia was British territory until 1957 and therefore has shared cultural heritage with the United Kingdom may also account for the nonsignificant difference in athletic identity between the British players and Malaysian players. Clearly, further research with larger, comparably aged samples is needed to verify which, if any, of these is a viable explanation of the current results.

5 References

Brewer, B.W. (in press) Self-identity and specific vulnerability to depressed mood. **J Personality**.

Brewer, B.W., Denson, E.L., and Jordan, J.M. (1992) **Temporal stability of major planning, career planning, and athletic identity in freshman student athletes**. Paper presented at the Ninth Annual Conference on Counseling Athletes, May, Springfield, MA, USA.

Brewer, B.W., and Linder, D.E. (1992) **Distancing oneself from a poor season: Divestment of athletic identity**. Paper presented at the annual meeting of the Association for the Advancement of Applied Sport Psychology, October, Colorado Springs, CO, USA.

Brewer, B.W., Van Raalte, J.L., and Linder, D.E. (1991) **Construct validity of the Athletic Identity Measurement Scale**. Paper presented at the annual meeting of the North American Society for the Psychology of Sport and Physical Activity, June, Monterey, CA, USA.

Brewer, B.W., Van Raalte, J.L., and Linder, D.E. (in press) Athletic identity: Hercules' muscles or Achilles' heel? **Int J Sport Psychol**.

Curry, T.J., & Weiss, O. (1989) Sport identity and motivation for sport participation: A comparison betweeen American college athletes and Austrian student sport club members. **Sociol. Sport J.**, 6, 257-268.

Good, A.J., Brewer, B.W., Petitpas, A.J., Van Raalte, J.L., and Mahar, M.T. (1993) Identity foreclosure, athletic identity, and college sport participation. **Academic Athletic J.**, Spring, 1-12.

Hinitz, D.R. (1988) **Role theory and the retirement of collegiate gymnasts**. Unpublished doctoral dissertation, University of Nevada, Reno, USA.

Markus, H.R., and Kitayama, S. (1991) Culture and the self: Implications for cognition, emotion, and motivation. **Psychol Rev**, 98, 224-253.

Van Raalte, N.S., and Cook, R.G. (1991) **Gender specific situational influences on athletic identity**. Paper presented at the annual meeting of the North American Society for the Psychology of Sport and Physical Activity, June, Monterey, CA, USA.

37 The effectiveness of quantitative and qualitative feedback on performance in squash

D. Brown and M. Hughes*
School of Human Sciences, Liverpool John Moores University, Liverpool, UK
**The Centre for Notational Analysis, Cardiff Institute, Cardiff, UK*

1 Introduction

Analysis of sports performance is the focal point of the coaching process. Coaching is a deliberate act of intervention in sport with the intention of improving performance. Any review of the literature highlights the importance of feedback in this process. It is likely that the most accurate means by which this can be achieved is through the use of a specific notational analysis system. Since the first tentative stages of notational analysis in the mid-1970's, considerable effort has been made to refine its procedures and develop a methodology that is consistent, reliable and valid. Many procedures have been developed, ranging from simple, fast and accurate hand notation systems, to very complex interactive systems using computers, video and a different interfaces. Research has mainly focused on descriptive studies concerning patterns of play (Sanderson 1983; Franks et al., 1983; Hughes, 1985; Hughes, 1986) but little effort has been made to assess the feasibility of applying notation systems into a real sporting environment on a long term basis. The role of qualitative feedback in the learning process has been well researched and documented (Schmidt, 1982; Salmoni et al., 1984; Wood et al., 1992).

The aim of this study is therefore to study the effectiveness of one such notation system. It is intended to compare the effects of quantitative feedback (computerised analysis) with qualitative feedback (video analysis).

2 Method

2.1 Experimental design

Eight subjects of similar playing ability (based on relative positions on an order of merit ladder system) were selected, so as to obtain realistic results (when competing against each other) for analysis purposes. Further to this, the arrangement of the pre- and post-test database of games was designed so that individuals did not compete against players more than two places above or below them on the ladder. It was felt that a gulf in ability between players would lead to unrealistic results. All subjects played at the same club and attended the same coaching sessions on a weekly basis. Also, all matches throughout the study were video-taped on the same court, and at the same time and day of the week, thus controlling for environmental variables.

The subjects were split into two groups of four, and for the purposes of the study they were defined as the experimental group and the control group. Within the groups, each

Science and Racket Sports Edited by T. Reilly, M. Hughes and A. Lees.
Published in 1994 by E & FN Spon ISBN 0 41^ 3500 3

player was treated as a single-subject design.

2.2 Subjects

Eight junior male players with an age range of 10 to 15 yesrs were selected for this study. All were members of the same squash club, and represented their county in their respective age groups. Allocation of the subjects into the experimental and control groups was performed so that a range of the eight ladder positions was present in each group.

2.3 Apparatus

The computerised squash notation and analysis system enabled comprehensive and accurate recording and analysis of squash matches. The system was written in Visual Basic which enabled a Graphical User Interface (using Microsoft Windows). Information could be entered into the computer using the `Mouse', via representations on the screen of the court, for position, and specially designed screen functions for player, time and action. The notation and analysis programs were run on a 386 Amstrad (IBM compatible) computer. The matches were notated post-event from the video tape and the edited results presented to the subjects within a week.

2.4 Validation of the system

For validation purposes a squash match was notated by hand using a video recorder and monitor in the laboratory. The hand notated data were then processed and output produced for the game. The same match was then notated using the computerised notation system, and output data were produced by the analysis program. The computerised output data were compared with the hand notated data for any discrepancies in the match information. This procedure was performed on two separate occasions by different individuals, but notating the same match. No discrepancies were found between the hand notated match data and the computerised match data, and the match information data produced by the separate individuals showed no discrepancies.

2.5 Procedure

The study took place over a six month period. The eight junior male subjects were separated into two groups of four. An experimental group received quantitative feedback based on specific computerised notational analysis whilst a control group received qualitative feedback in the form of video feedback. The first two months were used to obtain a database of three matches per subject for both groups. Each match was recorded on video using a portable video set-up behind the court. The matches were then notated and analyzed on the computerised system in the laboratory, and the relevant data for each subject were compiled. For the purpose of the study all the matches were pre-arranged, taking place at coaching sessions when and as required. Subjects played the matches against other players involved in the study.

For subjects in the experimental group, each individual database was analyzed and areas of high error distribution were established. This was achieved through the analysis program which provided summary details of each match and 3-D histogram presentation of specific shot parameters shown during the match. Printouts were then obtained so as to provide the subjects with a visual picture of their areas of high error distribution. Subjects in the experimental group were each given 15 minutes feedback based upon the results of the initial database analysis. During each feedback session subjects were verbally informed of their specific weak areas as determined by the computerised system. Verbal information was substantiated visually by the 3-D histogram printouts. Also areas of weakness were recorded into log-books which were given to each subject so that he had a written reminder of the feedback that he had received.

The control group was given the same amount of feedback, 15 minutes on an individual basis. This feedback was provided in the form of video analysis. Verbal cues were provided to the subjects to highlight important aspects of their game. Logbooks were also provided for this group. In addition both groups were requested to keep note in their logbook of how often they played and/or trained. At the end of the study all the log books were analysed. Following the initial data-base analysis and feedback, three further sessions were given, at intervals of four weeks. Similar feedback procedures were adopted for the two groups.

It was decided to use unforced errors as an inverse index of performance. These were normalised by calculating them as a percentage of the total number of shots played. Both t-tests and paired t-tests were used to compare the sets of data.

3 Results

Table 1 shows the percentage changes observed in unforced error distributions comparing post-test database analysis values to pre-test database values, for each subject in the experimental group. Based on the subject values observed, the mean overall group improvement was only 6.7%. From the pre- and post-test data, statistical tests were performed on each subject of the experimental group to test for any significant improvements in unforced error distributions observed when comparing post-test data to pre-test data.

Table 1. The percentage of errors as a fraction of the total shots played by each of the subjects, in the experimental group, at each of the five sessions

Subjects	Trial 1	Trial 2	Trial 3	Trial 4	Trial 5
Subject A	10.6	9.6	4.4	5.1	4.9
Subject B	7.6	6.9	11.4	5.7	11.5
Subject C	10.2	11.1	13.9	7.4	7.4
Subject D	8.4	10.3	8.7	11.8	10.5

The results of this analysis are summarised in Table 2. It is evident that, of the four subjects analysed, subject A was the only subject successful in making a significant improvement in error distribution during the period of the study. Subject C showed a visual improvement in the unforced error percentage, but the improvement was not substantial enough to prove significant ($P>0.05$). Analysis of the log book for each

Table 2. A summary of the results of the statistical tests applied to the individual subject data of the experimental group.

Experimental Group	T - Test Value	Significance
SUBJECT A	-3.157	$P<0.01$
SUBJECT B	1.722	$P>0.05$
SUBJECT C	-1.276	$P>0.05$
SUBJECT D	0.990	$P>0.05$

member of the experimental group indicated that on average: subject A played / practised 4.5 times a week; subject B played / practised 1.6 times a week; subject C played / practised 1.8 times a week; and subject D played / practised 1.7 times a week; throughout the duration of the study period.

Table 3 shows the percentage improvement in unforced error distributions made by members of the control group. This group was analysed only at the initial database level and at the fifth trial. Two of the group showed slight improvements (not significant, $P>0.05$), but the other two had markedly higher unforced error figures. The overall mean group change was shown by the mean value of -15.22%.

Table 3. The change in performance of the control group and the results of the t-tests

Subjects	% error change	T-test value	Significance
Subject E	-63.2	2.209	P>0.05
Subject F	14.0	-0.360	P>0.05
Subject G	6.4	-0.130	P>0.05
Subject H	-15.2	1.321	P>0.05

Analysis of the log book for each member of the control group indicated that on average: subject E played / practised 4 times a week; subject F played / practised 3.25 times a week; subject G played / practised 1.66 times a week; and subject H played / practised 2.4 times a week; throughout the duration of the study period.

As well as tests on individual members of each group, tests were performed on each group as a whole. Independent T-tests were firstly performed on each group separately to determine whether an overall improvement in unforced error distribution was present within each group over the period of the study. Finally, the data were examined to establish whether the improvements by the experimental group were higher than those of the control group. All these tests produced non-significant results.

4 Discussion and Conclusions

For analysis purposes each subject was treated as a single subject design case study. Advantages of this design were such that observed changes in data obtained could be more confidently attributed to specific interventions for each individual. This design is deemed beneficial where a limited number of subjects is available and a lot of time is required for training subjects, or, as in this study, time is needed for the feedback process to take place and have effect. Both qualitative and quantitative data (as in this study) are regarded as legitimate sources of information in case study designs (Smith, 1988).

For each member of the experimental group the pre-test base analysis revealed different aspects of weak play. These particular aspects of weak play then formed the basis of the quantitative feedback sessions that each individual received. This enabled each case study to focus on different areas of the game; in an attempt to reduce subjects overall unforced error percentages as the study progressed.

In this study the following observations were made:

(1) No significant differences in levels of improvement were found between the experimental and control group.

(2) No significant improvements in unforced error distributions were shown by either the experimental or control group.

(3) Individually, no members of the control group showed significant levels of improvement. Only one member of the experimental group showed a significant improvement in unforced error distributions over the period of the study.

Factors that limited the study included the minimal number of feedback sessions provided due to time restraints and the conduct of the majority of coaching sessions around a group structure. The age and ability of the subjects may have had a bearing on the results produced. In some cases, the precision of the feedback provided may have exceeded a subject's individual information-processing capacity, leading to an inadequate comprehension of the information provided. A wide range in levels of improvement was shown within both the experimental and control group, despite all members receiving the same duration and form of feedback. These differences may be attributed to levels of motivation, and an individual's cognitive strategies and abilities.

The results of this study highlight points that need to be considered in future research of this nature:

(1) Further research should incorporate a study group which receives no feedback. A control group of this nature would then account for possible improvements that were not as a result of the feedback. Although research does seem to suggest that feedback leads to an improvement in performance (Schmidt, 1982), an individual may have improved as a result of increased training/practice sessions, or a change in attitude, i.e. increased levels of motivation and desire to win.

(2) Post-test interviews with each subject would have been a useful addition to the study. The subjects' own thoughts and opinions as to the effectiveness of the feedback could then be considered: Was it beneficial? Did they feel it improved their performance?, Did it motivate them?, Was it easy to understand?. An individual may have felt than an improvement in his ability had resulted from the feedback, but this improvement may not have been visible to the observer as a reduction in unforced errors. Subjects may have changed the way they played, or thought about the game in a different manner.

(3) Future research could compare the effects of feedback on a group of senior players with the corresponding effects of feedback on a group of junior players. Also in future research it is important that the feedback is applied through an individual coach-to-player basis, not on a group coaching basis.

(4) The concept of individual differences is an extremely important area to consider in studies of feedback. Research should centre round possible relationships between individually dependant psychological variables and the relative improvements in performance observed as a result of feedback. The areas of particular interest are those of motivation, and individual cognitive styles and abilities.

(5) Frequency of performance/training and its effect on the response to feedback would seem to be an important variable that requires detailed investigation. There would seem to be a minimum frequency of performance/training for the response to be beneficial.

5 References

Franks, I.M., Goodman, D. and Miller, G. (1983) Analysis of performance: qualitative or quantitative. **Science Periodical on Research and Technology in Sport**. March.

Hughes, M.D. (1985) A comparison of the patterns of play in squash. in **International Ergonomics** (eds I.D. Brown, R. Goldsmith, K. Coombes and M.A. Sinclair).Taylor and Francis, London, pp.139-141.

Hughes, M.D. (1986). A review of patterns of play in squash. in **Sport Science.** (eds J. Watkins, T. Reilly and L. Burwitz). E. and F. Spon, London, pp. 363-368

Salmoni, A.W., Schmidt, R.A. and Walter, C.B. (1984) Knowledge of results: and motor learning: a review and critical appraisal. **Psych. Bull.**. 3, 355-386

Sanderson, F.H. (1983) A notation system for analysing squash matches. **Phys. Ed Rev.** 6, 19-23

Schmidt, R.A. (1982) **Motor Control and Learning: A Behavioural Emphasis.** Human Kinetics Press, Champaign, Ill.

Smith, R.E. (1988) The logic and design of case study research. **Sports Psychol.** 2, 1-12.

Wood, C.A., Gallagher, J.D., Martino, P.V. and Ross, M. (1992) Alternate forms of knowledge of results: interaction of augmented feedback modality on learning. **J. Human Mov't. Stud.,** 22, 213-230.

38 A computerised analysis of female coaching behaviour with male and female athletes

E. Harries-Jenkins and M. Hughes*
School of Human Sciences, Liverpool John Moores University, Liverpool, UK
**Centre for Notational Analysis, Cardiff Institute, Cardiff, UK*

1 Introduction

Psychologists have accepted for many years that certain behaviours are conducive to effective learning (Bandura, 1969). Whilst much of the research in this area has concentrated on the educational implications of teaching behaviour, little work has examined the implications of coaching behaviour on the athlete. Early observation systems primarily used hand notation (Lacy and Darst, 1984) which allowed for the quantitative recording of a coach's verbal comments. Recent advances in computer technology have enabled the development of a Computerised Coaching Analysis System (CCAS) - (Franks et al., 1988).

Previous research using the CCAS has concentrated mainly on analysing the behaviour of male coaches. Hence one aim of this project was to expand the subject area by examining the behaviour of female coaches.

Claxton and Lacy (1986) identified the gender of athletes and coaches as one variable which could affect behaviour patterns. Previous studies focused on the effect of a coach's gender on athletes' perception of coaching ability (Weinberg and Ragan, 1984; Lacy and Goldston, 1989). Little research (Eitzen and Pratt, 1989) has examined the effect that the athlete's gender has on coaching behaviour. Accordingly, a second aim of the project was to examine the behaviour of female coaches towards male and female athletes.

Since the computerised analysis of behaviour was still relatively untried, the final aim of the research was to evaluate the CCAS as a behaviour observation system. The criteria of Martin and Bateson (1986) were adopted for this evaluation.

2 Methods

2.1 Subjects and procedures

Three female Lawn Tennis Association grade three coaches (age 27 ± 3.2 years; number of years with grade three experience 7 ±1.7 years) currently teaching at one tennis centre, were observed over three practice sessions. Session one was used to familiarise the coaches with the presence of the video camera. Sessions two and three acted as the observation/testing sessions;

Science and Racket Sports Edited by T. Reilly, M. Hughes and A. Lees.
Published in 1994 by E & FN Spon ISBN 0 419 18500 3

here the coaches undertook 21 drills with a group of intermediate tennis players (ten males and eight females) age 11 (±2.2) years.

Prior to each session coach input forms were sent to each subject in order to collate details of age and years of experience, obtain the names and details of each drill to be coached, the skill(s) to be coached and the criteria for a successful performance of the skill(s).

Each drill was systematically analysed using the Coach Analysis Programme from the CCAS. After the preliminary details of coach, observer, date, drill, skill, criteria for a successful skill performance, and file name had been entered into the computer via the QWERTY key board, each comment made by the coach was coded using the Coach Analysis Programme overlay and power pad (Johnson, 1987). Each of the 21 drills underwent the same notation process taking approximately 30 hours to do so.

Table 1. Mean frequency of behavioural categories per drill

Category	Coach 1 (%)	Coach 2 (%)	Coach 3 (%)	
Individual	55	57	63	
Team	30	36	29	**
Group	15	7	8	
Verbal Commentary	61	68	59	
Demonstration	34	28	35	
Reconstruction	5	4	6	
Skill related	51	48	56	*
Non-skill related	49	52	43	
Behaviour	0	10	0	
Effort	23	22	14	
Organisational	60	52	77	**
Other	14	14	4	
Appropriate	97	99	100	**
Inappropriate	3	1	0	
Positive	50	61	52	
Neutral	46	31	45	*
Negative	3	6	2	

Key: * - No significant difference, P> 0.05 ;** - Significant difference; P< 0.05

2.2 Statistical analysis

In order to compare the type of behaviours exhibited by each coach, Chi-square analysis for one sample (nominal) data was used on each category of the coach analysis programme. Significance was deemed to have resulted when $P<0.05$.

In comparing the behaviour exhibited by the coaches towards the male and female athletes the data from the gender identification form were combined with the coach analysis output and placed on a spreadsheet. Here the frequency of each coding category for males and females was calculated. These data were subsequently analysed using Chi-square, significance level: P<0.05.

3 Results

Table 2. Mean frequency of behavioural categories made to each gender per drill.

Category & Gender	Coach 1	Coach 2	Coach 3	
Comments to Females	20	28	29	
Comments to Males	26	36	35	*
Mixed	54	36	36	
Public (male)	26	17	16	
Public (female)	24	14	13	
Private (male)	30	37	33	*
Private (female)	30	31	31	
Correct (male)	11	11	13	
Correct (female)	11	6	13	*
Reinstruct (male)	17	15	15	
Reinstruct (female)	13	18	18	
Incorrect (male)	4	2	4	
Incorrect (female)	5	1	3	
Interrogative (male)	6	21	7	
Interrogative (female)	3	19	8	
Evaluative (male)	12	11	13	
Evaluative (female)	11	10	13	
Descriptive(male)	26	12	27	*
Descriptive (female)	19	8	14	
Prescriptive (male)	10	15	11	
Prescriptive(female)	11	8	13	
Affective (male)	13	15	18	
Affective (female)	15	17	16	
Positive(male)	22	29	27	
Positive (female)	28	26	22	
Neutral (male)	32	23	29	*
Neutral (female)	21	16	22	
Negative(male)	2	3	0	
Negative (female)	1	3	0	

Key: * - No significant difference, P> 0.05 ; ** - Significant difference; P< 0.05

The data were analysed with respect to the pattern of behaviour between the three coaches and the general pattern of behaviour for all the coaches. Table 1 highlights the degree of significance when the groups of categories (denoted by the double line) were analysed for each coach.

There was no significant difference in the behaviour patterns between the coaches. All showed a similar and consistent profile of behaviour.

The behaviour of the subjects towards male and female athletes in a number of behaviour categories was examined. These included the number of comments, direction of comment, focus of comment, intent and tone of comments. These data are presenred in Table 2.

4 Discussion and Conclusions

4.1 General coaching behaviour

There was no significant difference in the pattern of behaviour presented by each subject. This result is in agreement with the work of Rushhall and Siedentop (1972) who suggested that behaviour becomes more consistent with experience. All three coaches interacted primarily with individual athletes. This individual interaction may be due to the very nature of tennis as an individual sport, or, as highlighted during informal discussions, to the fact that the coaches felt such interaction with the athletes was more conducive to the acquisition of new skills. This agrees with previous research (Martens et al., 1981).

There was no significant difference in the number of skill and non-skill related comments, a result which contradicted previous research by Tharpe and Gallimore (1976) and Dubois (1981). This may be due to the small sample size and/or the age of the athletes. Younger children often need more non-skill instruction than do older children.

Previous research (Smith et al, 1979, Smith and Smoll, 1983) has indicated that in terms of non-skill commentary coaches give more organisational instructions than any other type. Lacy and Goldston, (1989) took this further by stating that female coaches issue significantly more organisational comments than male coaches. In both instances the results derived from the Coaching Analysis Programme correspond with this research. All three coaches made significantly more organisational comments to the athletes.

Each coach exhibited more positive than negative tone in her comments. This finding corresponded to previous research which has continually found that coaches are more likely to exhibit positive rather than negative behaviour towards athletes (Tharpe and Gallimore, 1976; Smith et al., 1979).

4.2 Coaching behaviour towards male and female athletes

There was no significant difference in the number of comments spoken to the male and female athletes. The coaches adopted an *a-gender* approach to coaching as recommended by Eitzen and Pratt (1989).

In comparing the setting of the comments towards the different genders, it was expected that the coach would present more private comments to the female athletes than to the males. No such difference was observed. During informal discussions with the subjects after the observation period, all stressed the importance of using a setting which was appropriate to the situation rather than the gender of the recipient.

It was expected that female coaches would be more lenient towards the female athletes than the males. It was anticipated that they would make a higher percentage of comments related to an incorrect performance to males than females, make more affective comments and use a more positive tone to the female athletes as compared to the males. However, none of these predictions were upheld.

In accordance with the research of Eitzen and Pratt (1989), the female coaches showed little leniency towards female athletes, rather they demanded optimal performance from both genders. Appropriate comments were made to individuals and situations independent of gender.

An additional explanation of the equality in praise used by the coaches has been suggested by Weinberg and Jackson (1979). They stated that coaches recognise that male athletes, particularly children, are deemed to be more affected by losing and/or poor performance than females, and hence more likely to become emotional. Therefore praise was given regularly.

4.3 The Computerised Coaching Analysis System

A final aim of the project was to evaluate the CCAS as a behaviour observation tool. The criteria for success were based on those suggested by Martin and Bateson (1986).

The CCAS fulfilled four of the six criteria by providing: 1) a keyboard (power pad) with sufficient number of keys to record all the categories without using multiple key presses; 2) a reliable and secure method of data storage; 3) visual feedback as to the keys pressed; 4) the quick rectification of errors via the back-up key.

However, the CCAS failed to reach the two remaining criteria: 5) the CCAS did not have sufficient memory to store all the data - only 21 files could be accessed at any one time; 6) The system must be dependable, in terms of both hard and soft-ware. For a significant proportion of the project the hardware (power pad) was not operable due to problems with its power supply. Once this was rectified the hard and soft-ware proved reliable.

5 References

Bandura, A. (1969) **Principle of Behaviour Modification**. Holt, Rhinehart & Winston, New York.

Claxton , D.B. and Lacy, A.C. (1986) A comparison of practice field behaviours between winning high school football and tennis coaches. **J. Appl. Res. Coaching and Athletics,** 1, 188-200

Dubois, P.E. (1982) The behaviour of youth football coaches. in **Studies in the Sociology of Sport** (eds A.O. Dunleavy, A.W. Miracle and C.R.Rees) Texas Christian University Press, Fort Worth, pp349-360.

Eitzen, D.S. and Pratt, S.R. (1989) Gender differences in coaching philosophy: the case of female basketball teams. **Res. Quart. Exerc. Sport**., 60, 152-158

Franks, I.M.; Johnson, R.B.; and Sinclair, G.D. (1988) The development of a computerised coaching analysis system for recording behaviour in sporting environments. **J. Teaching Phy. Ed.,** 8, 23-32

Johnson, R.B. (1987) **Measuring the Reliability of Computer Aided Systematic Observation Instrument**. Unpublished Masters Thesis. University of British Columbia.

Lacy, A.C. and Darst, P.W. (1984) Evolution of a systematic observation system: The ASU coaching observation instruments. **J. Teaching Phys. Ed.,** 3, 59-66

Lacy, A.C. and Goldston, P.D. (1989) Behaviour analysis of male and female coaches in high school girls basketball. **J. Sport Behaviour**., 13, 29-38

Martens, R., Christina, R.W., Harvey, J.S. and Sharkey, B.J. (1981) **Coaching Young Athletes**. Human Kinetics Publishers, Champaign, Ill.

Martin, P, and Bateson, P. (1986) **Measuring Behaviour: An introductory Guide.** Cambridge University Press, Cambridge.

Rushall, B.S. and Siedentop, D. (1972) **The Development and Control of Behaviour in Sport and Physical Education**. Lea & Febiger, Philadelphia.

Smith, R.E. and Smoll, F.L. (1983) **Psychological Stress in Youth Sports Sources, Effects and Intervention Strategy**. American academy of Paediatrics, Evanston Ill.

Smith, R.E., Smoll, F.L. and Curtis, B. (1979) Coaching behaviours in little league baseball. in **Psychological Stress in Youth Sports.** (eds F.L. Smoll and R.E. Smith)Hemisphere, Washington D.C., pp173-201.

Tharpe, R.G. and Gallimore, R. (1976) What a coach can teach a teacher. **Psychol. Today**, 9, 75-78

Weinberg, R.S. and Jackson, A. (1979) Competition and extrinsic rewards: effects on intrinsic motivation and attribution. **Res. Quart. Exerc. Sport**, 50, 494-502

Weinberg, R.S. and Ragan, J. (1984) Effects of competition success/failure, and sex on intrinsic motivation. **Res. Quart. Exerc. Sport**, 50, 503-510

39 Expert knowledge structures for racket play

J.A. Shelton and P. Brooks
The Centre for Psychology, Liverpool John Moores University, Liverpool, UK

1 Introduction

In recent years, following the introduction of hypermedia authoring software such as GUIDE, HYPERCARD and TOOLBOOK, the creation of hypermedia training packages is now a practical possibility. Such systems allow users to interact not only with simple text and graphics but also with computer-controlled sound, video and with sophisticated animation. Conventional hypertext systems have allowed users to explore text in individualised, non-sequential ways. In hypermedia systems, the addition of both sound and visual images significantly enhances the richness of the instructional material. This should facilitate the quality of interaction.

It is suggested that the application of hypermedia techniques to computer-based instructional systems now offers the real possibility of developing teaching systems to support and improve playing and coaching skills for tennis and other racket sports. Expert coaching skills are a scarce resource where demand far exceeds supply. The encapsulation of coaching and playing expertise in a dynamic format should help to alleviate the heavy demands on coaches.

2 Knowledge structures

As a first stage in the development process of hypermedia systems, details of the sports and/or coaching skills need to be identified, modelled and represented. Suitable theoretical frameworks for the representation of sport and physical education knowledge have been proposed by Vickers (1983) who suggested that such knowledge is hierarchically organized into three levels: subordinate; basic and superordinate. Within each level certain skills may be prerequisite to other skills. From this basis, an initial knowledge structure for tennis play has been constructed . Part of the knowledge structure is shown schematically in Figure 1.

At the basic level are some of the knowledge elements which will match the 'basic skills' commonly referred to in tennis coaching manuals (e.g. Applewhaite and Moss, 1987). At the lowest or

Science and Racket Sports Edited by T. Reilly, M. Hughes and A. Lees.
Published in 1994 by E & FN Spon ISBN 0 419 18500 3

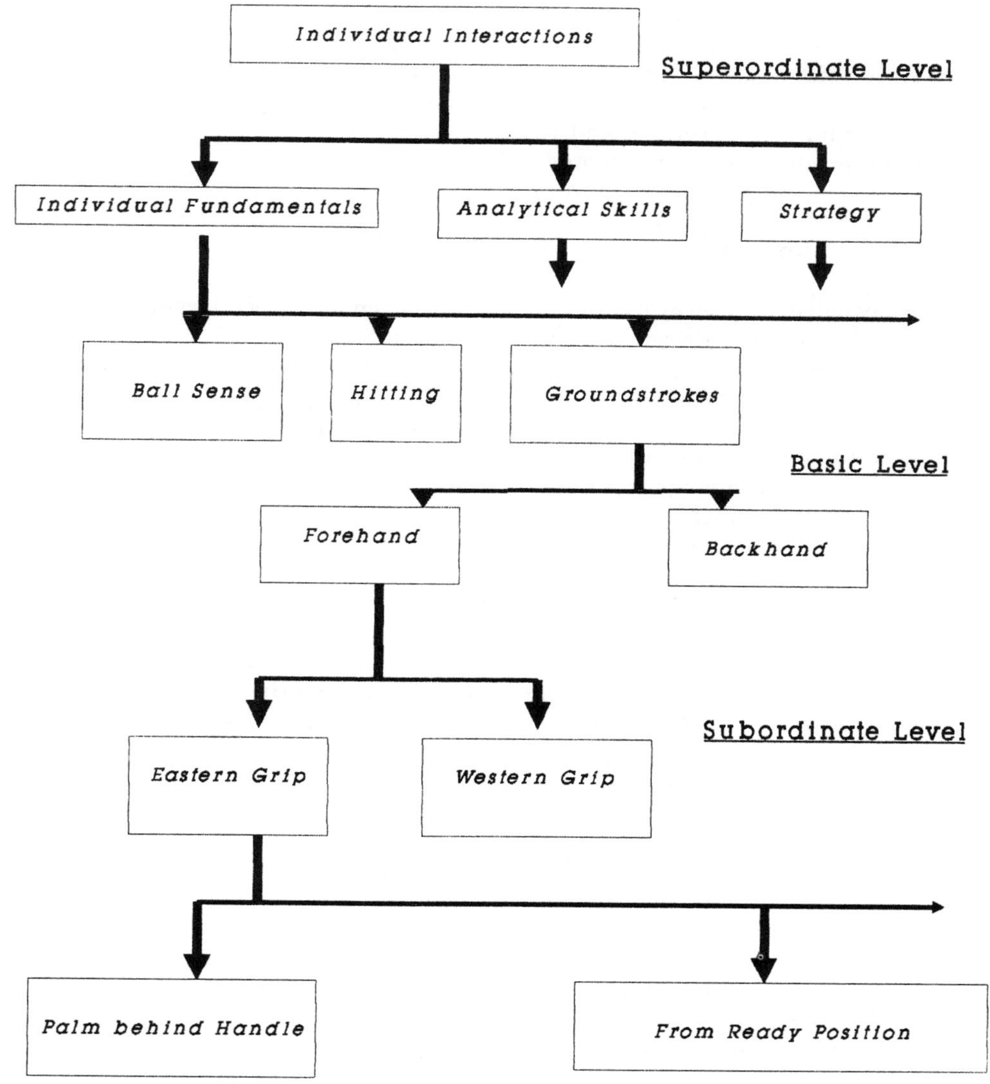

Figure 1 Schematic model for the analysis of tennis play

subordinate level, each basic skill is further subdivided into those elements of mechanical skills required for the basic skill's performance. At the highest or superordinate level, these fundamentals (e.g. serving) are combined with analytical skills (e.g. my opponent has a poor backhand service return) and strategies (e.g. serve to the backhand) appropriate to the psychomotor skill.

3 Development and Discussion

Knowledge structures for tennis play have been developed largely based upon Vicker's representations. To test the completeness of the tennis knowledge representations, these have been incorporated into the development of an 'Intelligent Job-Aid' (IJA) expert support system (see Rush et al, 1990) to support tennis coaches. The IJA is a small prototype expert support system which was designed to offer information and diagnoses and to explain its decisions by the use of the explanation facilities of the expert system. This system incorporated interactive video technology to illustrate playing faults and their remediation.

The expert support system and the advice which it offers has been tested by novice coaches and its knowledge structures have been validated by officials of the British Lawn Tennis Association Coaching department. Experience with the system has shown that the IJA does offer accurate information and diagnoses to novice coaches and its decisions are suitably explained. In 2-3 years, it is anticipated that knowledge structures based on the principles outlined above could form the basis for hypermedia tutoring systems in a wide variety of racket and other sporting areas.

4 References

Applewhaite, C. and Moss B. (1987) **Tennis: The Skills of the Game.** Crowood Press, London.

Rush, D.G., Edwards, P.A.M, Pountney, D.C., Shelton, J.A. and Williams, D. (1990) The design and development of an AI-assisted interactive video system for the teaching of psychomotor skills. in Lovesey, E.J. (ed.), **Contemporary Ergonomics 1990**, Taylor and Francis, London, pp 150 -156.

Vickers, J.N. (1983) The role of expert knowledge structures in an instructional design model for Physical Education. **Journal of Teaching Physical Education.**, 8, 17-32.

Part Seven
Match Analysis

40 Computerised notation of racket sports

M. Hughes
Centre for Notational Analysis, Cardiff Institute of Higher Education, Cardiff, UK

1 Introduction

General, rudimentary and unsophisticated forms of notation have existed for centuries. Hutchinson (1970) cited evidence that, for at least five centuries, attempts had been made to devise and develop a system of movement notation. Further, the Egyptians, thousands of years ago, made use of heiroglyphs to read dance, and the Romans employed a primitive method of notation for recording salutatory gestures. Historical texts give substantial evidence of a crude form of dance notation much later, in about the fifteenth century. Thornton (1971) stated that the early attempts at movement notation may well have `kept step' with the development of dance in society, and as a consequence the early systems were designed to record particular movement patterns as opposed to movement in general.

It becomes apparent that dance notation constituted the `starting base' for the development of a general movement notation system. Arguably the greatest development in dance notation was the system referred to as `Labanotation' or `Kinetography-Laban' (Laban, 1975), so-called after its creator, Rudolph Laban in 1948. The first publication of a comprehensive racket sport notation was not until 1973, when Downey developed a detailed system which allowed the comprehensive notation of lawn tennis matches. Detail in this particular system was so intricate that not only did it permit notation of such variables as shots used, positions, and so on, it also catered for type of spin used in a particular shot. Downey's (1973) notation system has served as a useful base for the development of systems for other racket sports, specifically badminton and squash, but few coaches or researchers have ever used it.

Several systems have been developed for the notation of squash, the most prominent being that by Sanderson and Way (1977). These authors made use of illustrative symbols to notate 17 different strokes, as well as incorporating court plans for recording accurate positional information. The major emphasis of this system was on the gathering of information concerning `play patterns' as well as the comprehensive collection of descriptive match data. Sanderson (1983) felt that `suggestive' symbols were better than codes, being easier for the operator to learn and remember, and devised a code system. These were used on a series of court representations, one court per activity, so that the player, action and position of the action were all notated. In addition, outcomes of rallies were recorded, together with the score and the initials of the server. The position was

Science and Racket Sports Edited by T. Reilly, M. Hughes and A. Lees.
Published in 1994 by E & FN Spon ISBN 0 419 18500 3

specified using an acetate overlay with the courts divided into 28 cells.

The system took an estimated 5-8 hours of use and practise before an operator was sufficiently skilful to record a full match during the game itself. Processing the data could take as long as 40 hours of further work. Sanderson (1983) used this system to gather a database and show that squash competitors play in the same patterns, winning or losing, despite the supposed coaching standard of `....if you are losing change your tactics'. It would seem that the majority of players are unable to change the patterns in which they play.

Most of the data that Sanderson and Way (1977) presented were in the form of frequency distributions of shots with respect to position on the court. This posed a problem of presenting data in three dimensions - two for the court position definition, and one for the value of the frequency of the shots. Three-dimensional graphics at that time were very difficult to present in such a way that no data were lost, or, that were easily visualised by those viewing the data. Sanderson (1983) overcame this problem by using longitudinal and lateral summations. Not only were the patterns of rally-ending shots examined in detail, but also those shots, (N-1), that preceded the end shot, and the shots that preceded those, (N-2). In this way the rally ending patterns of play were analysed. The major pitfall inherent in this system, as with all long-hand systems, was the time taken to learn the system and the sheer amount of raw data generated, requiring so much time to process.

Hand notation systems are in general very accurate but they do have some disadvantages. The more sophisticated systems involve considerable learning time. In addition, the amount of data that these systems produce can involve many hours of work in processing them into forms of output that are meaningful to the coach, athlete or sports scientist. Even in a game like squash, the amount of data produced by using the system developed by Sanderson and Way required 40 hours of work to process one match.

The introduction of computerised notation systems has enabled these two problems, in particular the data-processing, to be tackled in a positive way. Used in real-time analysis or in post-event analysis in conjunction with video recordings, they permit immediate, easy access to data. They also enable the sports scientist to present the data in graphical forms which are more easily understood by the coach and athlete. The increasing sophistication and reducing cost of video systems have greatly enhanced post-event feedback, ranging from playback with subjective analysis by a coach to detailed objective analysis by means of notation systems.

2 Computerised Notation of Racket Sports

Using computers does introduce extra problems of which the system-users and programmers must be aware. Possibilities of operator errors, or hardware and software errors are increased. Four major purposes of notation can be outlined:-

1. analysis of movement;
2. tactical evaluation;
3. technical evaluation;

4. statistical compilation.

The information derived from this type of computerised system can be used for several purposes as suggested by Franks et al. (1983):-

(i) immediate feedback;

(ii) development of a database;

(iii) indication of areas requiring improvement;

(iv) evaluation;

(v) as a mechanism for selective searching through a video recording of the game.

All of the above functions are of paramount importance to the coaching process, the initial purpose of notational analysis. The development of a database is a crucial element, since it is sometimes possible, if the database is large enough, to formulate predictive models as an aid to the analysis of different sports, subsequently enhancing training and performance.

2.1 Systems development

The initial difficulty in using a computer is entering information, and one can trace the development of notation systems in general, and also of racket sports in particular, through the struggle to overcome this problem. The traditional method is use of the QWERTY keyboard. Unless the operator possesses considerable skills, this can be a lengthy and boring task. Assigning codes to the different actions, positions or players that have some meaning to the operator, can make key entry easier. The next step is to assign areas of the keyboard to represent areas of the pitch, numbers for the players, and another section of the keyboard for the actions.

Hughes (1985) modified the manual method so that a match could be notated live at courtside using a microcomputer. Because of difficulties with the speed of the game and the storage capacity, only one player was notated at a time. A considerable database on different standards of squash players was established (Hughes, 1986). The differences in patterns of play between recreational players, country players and nationally ranked players were examined. The method involved the digitization of all the shots and court positions, using numer codes for both position and shots, and any subsequent rally end-conditions. A detailed analysis of the frequency distribution of shots showed that the recreational players were not accurate enough to sustain a tactical plan, being erratic with both their straight drives and their cross-court drives. They played more short shots, and although they hit more winners they also hit more errors.

The county players played a simple tactical game generally, keeping the ball deep and predominantly on the backhand, the weaker side of most players. They hit significantly more winners with straight drives. Their short game, consisting of boasts, drops and rally-drops, although significantly less accurate than the nationally ranked players, rendered them significantly more accurate than the recreational players.

The nationally ranked players, because of their far greater fitness, covering ability and better technique, employed the more complex tactics, using an 'all-court' game. Finally, the serves of the county players and the recreational players, because of shorter rallies, assumed greater importance than the serves of the ranked players.

An alternative to using the poroblems of using the QWERTY keyboard to enter data is to use a secifically designed keyboard (Franks et al., 1983; Alderson and McKinnon, 1985). Each of these research teams had keyboards made to meet the ergonomic demands of the problems specific to the sport under analysis.

The next step forward in this area, and it considerably eased the problems of data entry both in terms of skill requirements and learning time, was the introduction of the digitization pad. In Britain most workers have utilised the `Concept keyboard' (Hughes and Feery, 1986; Sharp, 1986; Treadwell, 1988) whilst in Canada, at the Notational Analysis Centre at UBC, Vancouver, another similar pad, the 'Power Pad', has been utilised (Franks et al., 1986). Both of these instruments are programmable, touch sensitive, pads, over which one can place an overlay with a graphic represention of the pitch and aptly labelled keypad areas for the actions and the players. This considerably reduces the skill required for fast data entry, and the learning time required to gain this level of skill. Hughes and McGarry (1989) used a concept keyboard based system to analyse elite players and top nationally ranked players; their findings confirmed that the elite players use an all-court game dependent upon speed and forced movement of their opponents.

A voice interactive system of entering data into the computer was introduced by Taylor and Hughes (1988). Although the research was severely limited by the amounts of funding, and therefore the level of technology that could be used, the authors were still able to demonstrate that this type of system can be used by the computer `non-expert'.

An unusual application of computerised notation that used a concept keyboard connected to an IBM computer, was that by Tillin (unpublished dissertation, Liverpool Polytechnic, 1990), who notated the levels of aggression by female players at Wimbledon. Each shot was given a score from a scale of aggression, determined by pace, placement and from where the ball was taken. The scale was from '1' to '7', '1' being for a totally defensive soft shot, '7' being for an all-out, attacking shot for the line from an attacking position. Aggression was then correlated with the game and match scores to examine whether the successful players were more or less aggressive on the critical points in a game, or in the critical games of a set. She found that generally players were less aggressive on the critical stages of the match, but that on critical points the player who was losing would be more attacking. Play was found to be progressively more aggressive as each set continued.

A recent innovation in attempting to solve the problems of data entry was the utilisation of a new language, visual basic, which enables a graphical user interface, that is, the operator enters data by moving an arrow round the screen using the 'mouse' and clicking to enter a selected item. All IBM-compatible systems can run these software packages. This language was used to write a system for squash, which was used by Brown and Hughes (this volume) to examine the effectiveness of quantitative feedback to squash players. Whilst this system of data entry will not be as quick as the concept keyboard, when used by a fully trained and experienced operator, it is again very easy to use, attractive to the eye and the extra hardware requirements are nil. A similar system was used Hughes and Clarke (this volume) to analyse the differences in the playing patterns of players at Wimbledon, on grass, to those of players at the Australian Open, on a synthetic surface

In an attempt to circumvent the problems posed by presenting frequency distributions on two-dimensional representations of the playing area, Hughes and McGarry (1989) developed a system that updated Hughes' (1985) system, using a concept keyboard for input and using an Acorn BBC microcomputer. They specifically tackled the problem of three-dimensional graphical output of the data from a squash match. The longitudinal and lateral presentations that Sanderson (1983) had used to try to make data more visual and therefore more easily understood, have never succeeded with most coaches and athletes. Their system has been well received by squash coaches. The data were displayed in multi-coloured three-dimensional histograms, that could be rotated to enable viewing from different angles. Recent systems which utilise the Windows environment for the programming language, visual basic, are readily interactive with graphics packages, so that visual interpretation of the data is very much simpler. This area of data presentation and analysis has untold potential in conveying to the coaches and athletes the importance of feedback.

2.2 Movement analysis

Hughes, Franks and Nagelkerke (1989) were interested in analysing the motions of athletes of any sport, without having to resort to the long and arduous job of cinemategraphic analysis, nor the semi-qualitative methods associated with notational methods, used live or from video. They attempted to combine the best of both systems without the faults of either, in creating a system to analyse movement in squash. They designed a tracking system that enabled the use of the immediacy of video, and, by using mixed images on the same VDU screen, accurate measurements of the velocities and accelerations of the players, usually associated with film analysis. A `Power Pad ' was used to gather positional data along with the time base. A video camera was positioned so that the image of the playing area representation on the Power Pad coincided with the video image of the real court - the two images were superimposed using a video-mixer. Careful alignment of the images of the two `playing areas', enabled the subject, and the tracking stylus on the bit pad, to be both viewed at the same time, and an accurate tracing of the movements of the player onto the simulated playing area in real time. A validation of the system showed its accuracy and the short learning time required by operators.

Hughes and Franks (1994) applied this system to squash, comparing the motions of players of differing standards. They presented comparative profiles for four different standard of players, spanning from club players to the world elite. The profiles consisted of analyses of distance travelled, velocities and accelerations during rallies The work provides reference data against which physiological studies of squash play can be guaged. The average distance travelled during rallies by both recreational and regular club players was short, the mean distance being approximately 12 m for both top club players and recreational players. Hughes and Franks presented suggestions about specific training drills for the sport. Their system could also compare the individual profiles of players to those of their peer group so giving a direct expression of relative fitness and mobility. An analysis of the 1989 World Champion, Jehangir Khan, compared to the top six in the world (whose data included his own profile) clearly showed the vast advantage that he had over the other top squash players.

3 The Future of Notation Analysis

The idea of the development of 'all-purpose', generic software has some attractions to it, especially if it is easy to use and flexible enough for coaches/sports scientists to define the specific sport system and its output form for themselves. Work in some centres has almost reached this point now. Another technological advance that will make computerised notation more easily handled by the non-specialist will be the introduction of "voice-over" methods of data entry. Taylor and Hughes (1988) have demonstrated that this is possible, but relatively expensive at present day prices. These are expected to drop rapidly over the next couple of years and voice-interaction should therefore be a natural extension of any computing hardware system.

The integration of both these technological developments with computerised-video feedback will enable both detailed objective analysis of competition and the immediate presentation of the most important elements of play. Franks and Nagelkerke (1988) developed such a system for use with soccer and field hockey, although the technology could as easily be applied to the racket sports. Computerised systems on sale now enable the analysis, selection, compilation and representation of any game on video to be processed in a matter of seconds. The coach can then use this facility as a visual aid to support the detailed analysis.

As these systems are used more and more, and larger databases are created, a clearer understanding of each sport will follow. The mathematical approach, typified by Eom (unpublished Master's thesis, UBC Vancouver, 1989), will make these systems more accurate in their predictions. At the moment the main functions of the systems are analysis, diagnosis and feedback - few sports have gathered enough data to allow prediction of optimum tactics in set situations. Where large databases have been collected (e.g. soccer and squash) models of the games have been created and this has led to predictive assertions of winning tactics (Partridge and Franks, Parts I and II, 1989; McGarry and Franks, 1993). This has led to some controversy, particularly in soccer, due to the lack of understanding of the statistics involved and their range of application. Nevertheless, the function of the systems could well change, particularly as the financial rewards in certain sports are providing such large incentives for success.

4 Conclusion

Notation analysis of racket sports has developed from the first notation systems published in the early seventies, which were complex and difficult to use. They produced so much data that to process them would take a great amount of time. As the discipline has matured, so has the realisation that making systems complicated does not make them more scientific. The significant advances in the use of both hand and computerised notation systems have been in both the simplification of data gathering and data analysis, and the growing sophistication in the validation of these systems.

The real future of notation analysis lies in the awareness of coaches, athletes and sports scientists of its applications to all sports, and its potential in integrating all the elements of science supporting that sport. Irrespective of whether the most sophisticated and expensive of systems is being used, or a simple pen and paper analysis, as long as either system produces accurate results that are valid and easy to understand, then coaches, athletes and sports scientists will increase their insights into sport performance.

4 References

Alderson, J. and McKinnon, G. (1985) A computerised system for analysing squash. Presentation at the BANC/NCF Workshop on Notational Analysis, Sheffield, July.

Downey, J.C. (1973) **The Singles Game.** E.P.Publications, London.

Franks, I.M. & Nagelkerke, P. (1988) The use of computer interactive video technology in sport analysis. **Ergonomics,** 31, 1593-1603.

Franks, I.M., Goodman, D., & Miller, G. (1983a). Analysis of performance: qualitative or quantitative. **Sci. Periodical Res. Tech. Sport**, March.

Franks, I.M., Johnson, R & Sinclair, G.D. (1988) The development of a computerised coaching analysis system for recording behaviour in sporting environments. **J. Teaching Phys. Ed.,** 8, 23-32.

Franks, I.M., Nagelkerke, P. & Goodman, D. (1989) Computer controlled video: an inexpensive IBM based system. **Computers Educ.,** 13, No.1, 33-44.

Franks, I.M., Sinclair, G.D., Thomson, W., & Goodman, D. (1986). Analysis of the coaching process. **Sci. Periodical Res. Tech. Sport**, January.

Hughes, M.D. (1985) A comparison of the patterns of play in squash. in **International Ergonomics** (eds I.D. Brown, R. Goldsmith, K. Coombes and M.A. Sinclair).Taylor and Francis, London, pp.139-141.

Hughes, M.D. (1986). A review of patterns of play in squash. in **Sport Science.** (eds J. Watkins, T. Reilly and L. Burwitz). E. and F. Spon, London, pp. 363-368

Hughes, M.D. & Feery, M. (1986) Notational Analysis of Basketball. Communication to BASS Conference, September, Birmingham University.

Hughes, M. & Franks, I.M. (1994) A time-motion analysis of squash players using a mixed-image video tracking system. Ergonomics (in press)

Hughes, M.D. & McGarry, T. (1989) Computerised notational analysis of squash. Communication to Science in Squash Conference. Liverpool Polytechnic, November.

Hughes, M., Franks, I.M. & Nagelkerke, P. (1989) A video-system fo the quantitative motion analysis of athletes in competitive sport. **J. Human Mov't Stud.**, 17, 212-227.

Hutchinson, A. (1970) **Labanotation - The System of Analysing and Recording Movement.** Oxford University Press, London.

Laban, R. (1975) **Laban's Principles of Dance and Music Notation.** McDonald & Evans Ltd., London.

Partridge, D. & Franks, I.M. (1989) A detailed analysis of crossing opportunities from the 1986 World Cup. (Part I) Soccer Journal. May-June, pp. 47-50.

Partridge, D. & Franks, I.M. (1989) A detailed analysis of crossing opportunities from the 1986 World Cup. (Part II) Soccer Journal. June-July, pp. 45-48.

Sanderson, F.H. (1983) A notation system for analysing squash. **Phys. Ed. Review,** 6, 19-23.

Sanderson, F.H. & Way K.I.M. (1977) The development of an objective method of game analysis in squash rackets. **Brit. J. Sports Med.**, 11, 188

Sharp, R. (1986) Presentation: Notation Workshop. VIII Commonwealth and International Conference on Sport, Physical Education, Dance, Recreation and Health (Glasgow).

Taylor, S. & Hughes, M.D. (1988) Computerised notational analysis: a voice interactive system. **J. Sports Sci.** 6, 255.

Thornton, S. (1971) **A Movement Perspective of Rudolph Laban.** MacDonald and Evans, London.

Treadwell, P.J. (1988) Computer aided match analysis of selected ball-games (soccer and rugby union). in **Science and Football** (eds T.Reilly, A.Lees, K.Davids & W.Murphy). E. & F. Spon., London, pp. 282-287.

41 A comparison of playing patterns of elite squash players, using English scoring to point-per-rally scoring

M. Hughes and I. Knight*
Centre for Notational Analysis, Cardiff Institute, Cardiff, UK
**School of Human Sciences, Liverpool John Moores University, Liverpool, UK*

1 Introduction

In May 1988 a new scoring system was introduced to the game of squash rackets by the Squash Rackets Association in an attempt to make the game more attractive to television viewing audiences. This system, initially known as "American scoring", was renamed "point-per-rally scoring", and differed from the traditional scoring system in that a point is scored at the end of every rally regardless of whether the winner held serve or not. The purpose of this study is to establish whether or not the introduction of this new scoring system produced any difference in the patterns of play exhibited in competition by elite male squash players when compared to the traditional "English" scoring, and whether or not any reduction in both the average rally length and the number of let and stroke appeals occurred.

2 Method

The study was conducted in two parts. Firstly, 500 rallies played under each scoring system, taken from a number of matches involving players in the top 30 in the world, were notated using a computerised notation system. Analysis was then conducted upon this notated information in the form of selected chi-square and t-tests, percentage and ratio calculations, and through a selection of three-dimensional presentations of the frequency distributions of each of the shots across the playing surface and the rally end variables. A specific number of rallies was used rather than an exact number of games or matches, in order that the information obtained for analysis would be exactly comparable and quantifiable, i.e. the exact same number of rally end conditions would occur.

3 Results

The average data for the rallies under the two different scoring systems are compared in Figures 1 and 2. Chi-square analysis of the distribution of all the shots revealed that a difference in the patterns of play under the two scoring systems ($P<0.01$) with t-tests indicating that point-per-rally scoring produces significantly more winners ($P<0.05$). No significant difference was found in the respective length of rallies played under the

Science and Racket Sports Edited by T. Reilly, M. Hughes and A. Lees.
Published in 1994 by E & FN Spon ISBN 0 419 18500 3

Comparison of English scoring
to point-per-rally scoring.

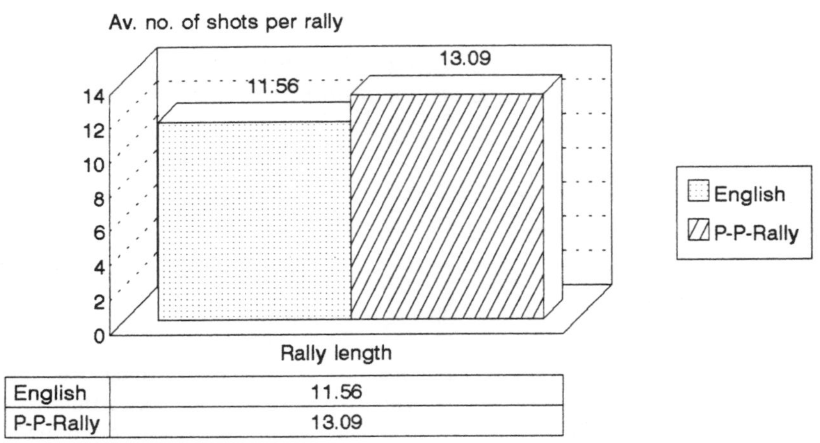

English	11.56
P-P-Rally	13.09

Fig 1. A comparison of the average length of rallies under the two scoring systems.

Comparison of English scoring
to point-per-rally scoring.

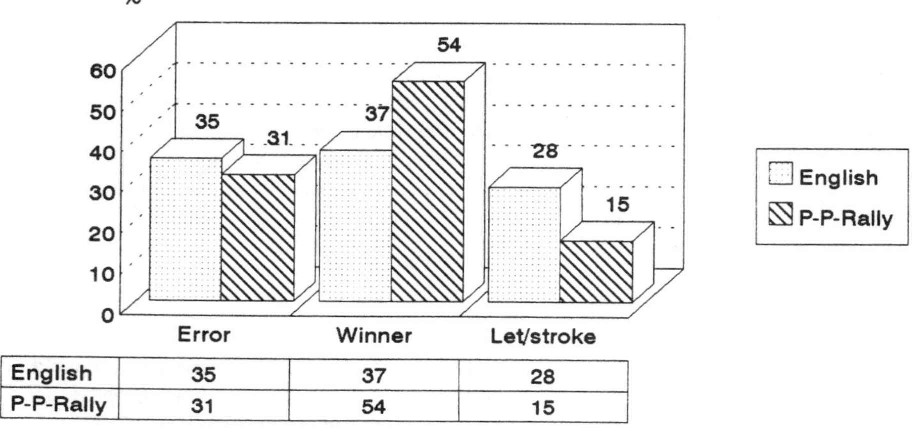

	Error	Winner	Let/stroke
English	35	37	28
P-P-Rally	31	54	15

Fig 2. Comparison of rally-end conditions between the two systems of scoring.

two systems. Point-per-rally scoring was also found to produce significantly fewer let/stroke appeals than English scoring ($P<0.01$).

More detailed analysis, comparing the rally end conditions associated with short (attacking) and long (defensive) shots and their distribution of frequencies across the court, showed that point-per-rally scoring produced a more attacking pattern of play than did English scoring, with significantly more volleys, drop shots and attacking mid-court drives being played.

4 Discussion and Conclusions

It was found that point-per-rally scoring, in comparison to English scoring, produces no significant difference in the average length of the rallies. This was surprising, as the original belief was that the rallies in the new system would be shorter and therefore more interesting to the general public. The reasons for this may be the extremely high levels of fitness of the elite players, enabling retrievals when under great pressure, and developed strategies by the players to minimise errors.

Significantly more winners were observed with point-per-rally scoring. It was hoped that this would be a product of the new system, that players would attack more irrespective of who was serving, thus removing the defensive, "boring" play that players adopt under the old rules when receiving serve. No significant difference between the two systems of scoring were observed in the number of errors. It was thought that the number of errors would increase if players were playing more attacking shots. It would seem that players have developed strategies and tactics that minimse the errors while enabling more winners.

Significantly less let/stroke appealswere found with point-per-rally scoring. This factor should help to make the game more entertaining to the general public, often confused both by the appeals and the ensuing decisions.

Further analysis of the different shots and the positions from which they were played showed that point-per-rally scoring produces a more attacking style of play amongst elite male players than does English scoring.

42 Winning squash: predicting championship performance from a priori observation

T. McGarry and I.M. Franks
School of Human Kinetics, University of British Columbia, Vancouver, Canada

1 Introduction

Notation analysis of sport is used to reinforce desired athletic behaviour and, where necessary, prescribe appropriate remedial action. Its utility for preparing for forthcoming competition, however, is often restricted. The reporting of summary match statistics, for instance, fails to depict the dependencies of discrete observations to other behavioural events, even though these sequential relationships may be of primary importance in determining subsequent outcome. Computer analytic procedures for the notation of sport performance now afford the easy collection, storage and analysis of large amounts of sequential data from various sport competitions (Franks et al., 1987), while the recent advance of statistical techniques such as log-linear analysis further enable the sport scientist to more fully explore these time dependent data (Eom and Schutz, 1992).

Sport notation analysis typically allows the association of a particular event to earlier occurrence(s), or, alternatively, the retrospective prediction of such events from their antecedent(s). A stochastic analysis is an appropriate mathematical technique for modelling sport performance and forecasting such results from empirical data. Primary applications of stochastic processes lie in the evaluation of sport scoring systems (Schutz, 1970; Clarke and Norman, 1979; Pollard, 1987) and in the identification of optimal decision making strategies (Hannan, 1976; Clarke, 1979, Pollard, 1985).

While many models have been developed for the analysis of sport, none has attempted to predict sport performance from previous athletic behaviour. This can be achieved by establishing playing profiles from observational analysis and contesting these profiles through a stochastic simulation. McGarry and Franks (1992) showed some success at forecasting match outcome in competitive squash using this technique. A recommendation of their study was to further qualify the winners and errors to allow for the subsequent modelling of the interaction which exists between players.

This study reports the use of a model for the forecasting of competitive squash behaviour. The model interleaves the playing profiles through classifying winners as either unconditional or conditional and errors as either unforced or forced. (An unconditional winner is awarded irrespective of the opposing player while a conditional winner is considered contingent on the opponent. Likewise, an unforced error occurs

Science and Racket Sports Edited by T. Reilly, M. Hughes and A. Lees.
Published in 1994 by E & FN Spon ISBN 0 419 18500 3

without due cause whereas a forced error is credited as a direct result of the opponent's play.) This study attempts to determine whether these modifications improve the utility of the model as a reliable indicator of future squash performance.

2 Method

2.1 Description of squash

Squash is a competitive game contested between two players. A match is played to the best of three or five games to either International or American scoring. A game under American scoring attributes victory to the first player to reach fifteen points where a point is awarded independent of service (although service is awarded to the non-serving player should he/she win the rally). Various tie scoring options exist but are not accounted for in the stochastic model.

2.2 Software development

The software was written in the programming language Turbo-Pascal using an IBM compatible personal computer. The software comprises a hierarchical menu structure and is considered to be "user friendly", thereby supporting general use by coaches and athletes alike. Data collection, analysis, presentation and the simulation model are accessed through a "parent program" and interfaced to provide a comprehensive, stand-alone analytic system for the game of squash.

2.3 Data collection

Sixteen position cells, fifteen shot types and five outcome conditions were identified for recording competitive squash behaviour (see Fig.1). These entities and their corresponding definitions were agreed upon with an expert and a preliminary study undertaken to assess intra- and inter-reliability coefficients of the observer and instrument.

2.4 Stochastic model

A Markov process decrees that the transition of a process from one state to the next is dependent upon its present state only and independent of past states. In the stochastic model (see Fig.2) the process initially resides in the state Shot=0 since the first shot of a contest must be a serve. The process then advances to either a Ball-In or Ball-Out condition which determines whether the ball is in or out of play respectively. (The transition between states within the model is based on a simulated random call and empirical data.) If in play, the process continues to the next state and the receiver's shot response is assigned from 1 (drive) through 14 (cross-court lob). The process repeats recursively until a shot is assigned out of play whereupon the process transits to either the Ball-In/Out or Ball-Out state. The Ball-Out state is terminal and awards the outcome of unconditional winner, unforced error or let. In the Ball-In/Out state the outcome is contingent, in part, upon the opponent's profile. Thus, the process either confirms the outcome (conditional winner or forced error) or returns to the Ball-In state for continuation of the rally. The outcome of a rally denotes the start of the next until the contest ends when a winning score is reached.

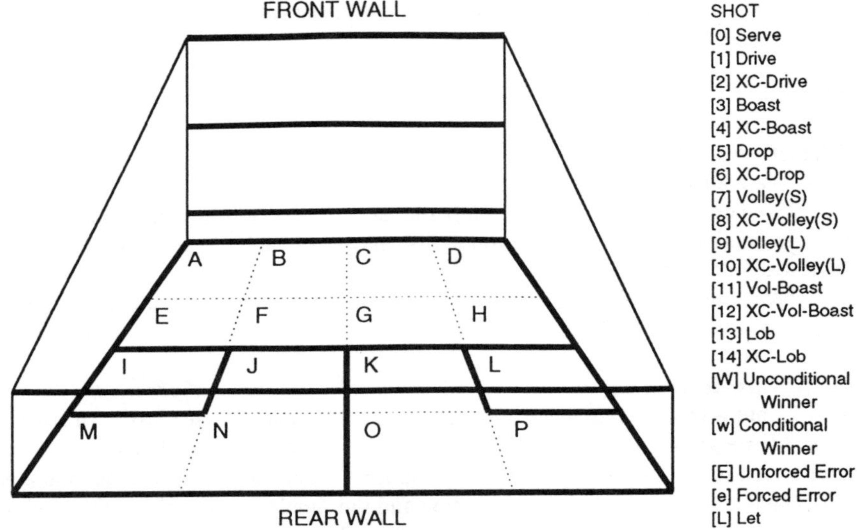

Fig. 1. Diagram of the squash court and discrete behaviours.

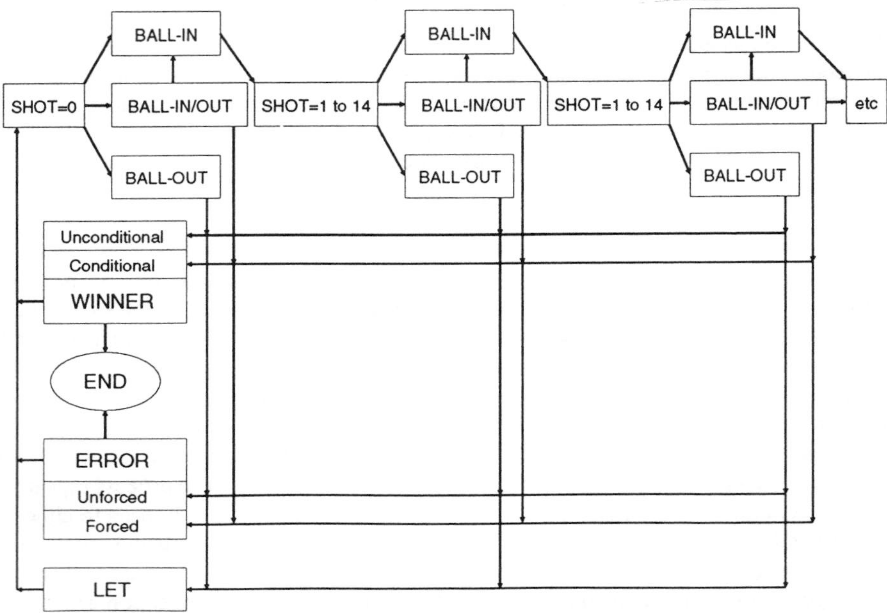

Fig.2. Stochastic model for the prediction of competitive squash match play.

2.5 Procedure

Video tournament data from the quarter-finals through final of the men's Canadian Open Championship, 1988, contested to the American scoring system were analysed in this study. Intra- and inter-reliability checks of the observer and instrument indicated the data to be reliable.

The data were analysed and a playing profile established for each player. A playing profile comprises a probability matrix depicting likely shot response to each preceding condition (the shot by the opponent). The playing profiles were contested through computer simulation and the projected results contrasted to the empirical data.

3 Results and Discussion

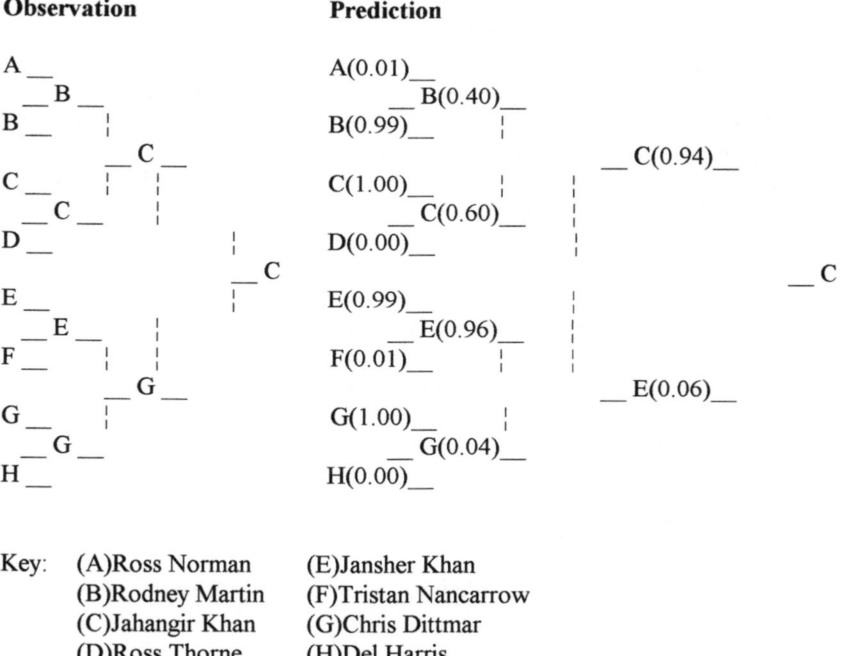

Fig.3. Observed and predicted tournament progression from the quarter-finals.

The model successfully forecasts the actual tournament victor from the quarter-final round data, but fails to correctly predict the second semi-finalist (see Fig.3). It is not clear if this indicates a weakness of the model, or if the observation itself is unexpected. (Jansher Khan is second only to Jahangir Khan in the 1988 World rankings).

Table 1. Table of predicted results from the quarter-final, semi-final and quarter-final and semi-final data

Data	Prediction	3-0	3-1	3-2	2-3	1-3	0-3	Score	Win
QF	SF1(B v C)	.102	.136	.163	.194	.223	.182	0-3	.599
QF	SF2(E v G)	.570	.281	.112	.016	.016	.005	1-3	.963
QF	F (C v G)	.784	.185	.029	.001	.001	.000	3-0	.998
SF	F (C v G)	.243	.300	.211	.110	.077	.059	3-0	.754
QF and SF	F (C v G)	.648	.258	.073	.011	.009	.001	3-0	.979

The model suggests that enough information exists in the quarter-final matches to successfully forecast the eventual tournament winner. The model achieves this through identifying the strongest player in each half of the draw and proceeding through the tournament structure. The results (see Table 1) imply the existence of an underlying order which influences match outcome. Further evidence exists in the prediction from the semi-final data which forecast the same victor from different data. The results imply that the playing profiles capture a behavioural characteristic from systematic observational analysis which is a determinant of future success in competitive squash. The discriminating features which effect match outcome, however, are not yet isolated and warrant further investigation.

The interaction between the profiles is of interest since a strong player may force his/her opponent to adopt a weaker profile than is merited. Conversely, a weak player may exaggerate a moderate player's profile to the detriment of the simulation model. The interdependency of the profiles in both the previous model and the revised model can be tested through rank ordering the players according to their assessed playing strength. (Contesting all players to each other in Round Robin fashion determines their rank order from the data.) If the above dependency exists, then the quarter-final pairs will associate strongest rank to weakest rank, next strongest to next weakest and so on. The results (see Table 2) show that the stronger profiles are not accompanied by the associated weaker profile of the opponent for either model.

Table 2. Tournament seeding and rank ordering of the contestants from the quarter-final data for both models*

Player	Seed	$Rank_i$	$Rank_{ii}$	Player	Seed	$Rank_i$	$Rank_{ii}$
Ross Norman	-	6	6	Jansher Khan	2	3	3
Rodney Martin	5	2	2	Tristan Nancarrow	-	7	7
Jahangir Khan	1	1	1	Chris Dittmar	3	4	4
Ross Thorne	-	5	5	Del Harris	-	8	8

*i=Previous model (McGarry and Franks, 1992); ii=Revised model

The results demonstrate that the tournament winner can be predicted from successively earlier athletic performances and support the earlier unpublished findings of McGarry and Franks (1992). A judgement of the improvement of model utility, however, is inconclusive due to a lack of difference in behaviour between the two models. This may be due to the large margins of success observed in each contest (see Table 1) which negated any subtle effects of the conditional assignments, or to the limited data available from a single contest. The second place ranking of Rodney Martin by both models contradicts the fifth place tournament seeding and supports the expectation that more matches over a relatively short period of time are preferred for the reliable prediction of future sport performance.

If an underlying process for successful squash can be identified which not only describes past observation but successfully predicts behaviour, then the model can be used to guide coaching practice to fit a winning profile more fully. An appealing application of the model is the identification of optimal tactical strategies for adoption against particular opponents.

4 References

Clarke, S.R. (1979). Tie point strategy in American and International squash and badminton. **Res. Quart., 50**, 729-734.

Clarke, S.R., and Norman, J.M. (1979). Comparison of North American and International squash scoring system - analytic results. **Res. Quart., 50**, 723-728.

Eom, H.J. and Schutz, R.W. (1992). Transition play in team performance of volleyball: a log-linear analysis. **Res. Quart., 63**, 261-269.

Franks, I.M., Wilson. G.E. and Goodman, D. (1987). Analysing a team sport with the aid of computers. **Canad J. Sport Sci., 12**, 120-125.

Hannan, E.L. (1976). An analysis of different serving strategies in tennis, in **Management Science in Sports 4** (eds R.E. Machol, S.P. Ladany and D.G. Morrison), North Holland, New York, pp. 125-135.

McGarry, T. and Franks, I.M. (1992). The use of a computer-assisted stochastic simulation system for the prediction of squash match play. Communication to the First World Congress of Notational Analysis in Sport. Wirral, UK.

Pollard, G.H. (1985). A statistical investigation of squash. **Res. Quart., 56**, 144-150.

Pollard, G.H. (1987). A new tennis scoring system. **Res. Quart., 58**, 229-233.

Schutz, R.W. (1970). A mathematical model for evaluating scoring systems with specific reference to tennis. **Res. Quart., 41**, 552-561.

43 The service in lawn tennis: how important is it?

J.D.G. Furlong
John Furlong School of Tennis, Doncaster, UK

1 Introduction

The tie break was introduced into major tennis championships in 1979 as a means of limiting the length of matches. If service is all-important, then a low percentage of service breaks is to be expected and a corresponding high percentage of tie breaks, thus making the latter a measure of service effectiveness. The data used were drawn from the Men's and Ladies' singles and doubles events at the Wimbledon and French championships, thus standardising for the highest level of play on the fastest and slowest surfaces.

The first part of the study (Study A) used only the 1992 results. The second part (Study B) used results ranging over the period 1979 to 1992.

Considerable interest has been expressed in the relative importance of service to men and women tennis players and the effect of fast and slow surfaces with respect to service effectiveness. Thus the purpose of Study A was to determine differences, if any, between men and women and the effect of the very fast and very slow surface, with respect to service effectiveness.

2 Method

The comparison of the eight events, Men's and Ladies' singles and doubles on Wimbledon grass and French clay on the basis of percentage of tie breaks was tested for significanct diffeences using chi-square tests. The chi-square test was highly significant, so in order to locate the one or more differences the test involving the normal distribution for comparing two proportions or percentages was used to examine the twenty-eight possible comparisons.

Science and Racket Sports Edited by T. Reilly, M. Hughes and A. Lees.
Published in 1994 by E & FN Spon ISBN 0 419 18500 3

3 Results and Discussion

3.1 Study A

For the comparison of the eight events, $Chi^2 = 76.47$, $P<0.001$. This is very strong evidence that there was one or more differences between events.

Table 1. Tie break percentages from the largest down to the smallest

Event	Percentage of tie breaks
Men's doubles Wimbledon	26.8
Men's doubles French	23.8
Men's singles Wimbledon	17.3
Ladies' doubles Wimbledon	14.5
Men's singles French	11.9
Ladies' doubles French	9.7
Ladies' singles French	6.7
Ladies' singles Wimbledon	5.1

The size of the percentage gap as depicted in Table 1 can be misleading. For example, to achieve a significant difference between the two men's singles requires a smaller gap than for the two ladies' doubles, because the sample sizes (number of sets played) was 440 for Wimbledon Men's singles and 444 for French Men's singles. In contrast, for the Wimbledon and French Ladies' doubles, the sample sizes were both 124. However, all sample sizes can be classed as large, this simplifying the statistical calculations and giving confidence to the results.

Table 2. Comparison of events

No.	Comparison	Z Score	Result
1	Men's single Wimbledon Ladies' singles Wimbledon	4.62	Men better than women; P<0.001
2	Men's single Wimbledon Men's doubles Wimbledon	2.86	Doubles better than singles; P<0.01
3	Ladies' singles Wimbledon Ladies' doubles Wimbledon	3.08	Doubles better than singles; P<0.01
4	Men's singles French Men's doubles French	3.35	Doubles better than singles; P<0.001
5	Men's singles Wimbledon Men's singles French	1.85	NS
6	Men's doubles Wimbledon Men's double French	0.61	NS

Table 2. (Continued) Comparison of events

No.	Comparison	Z Score	Result
7	Ladies' doubles Wimbledon Ladies' doubles French	1.12	NS
8	Ladies' singles Wimbledon Ladies' singles French	0.89	NS
9	Ladies' singles Wimbledon Ladies' doubles French	1.68	NS
10	Men's doubles Wimbledon Ladies' doubles Wimbledon	3.37	Men better than women; $P<0.001$
11	Men's doubles French Ladies' doubles French	2.99	Men better than women; $P<0.01$
12	Men's singles French Ladies' singles French	2.33	Men better than women; $P<0.05$
13	Ladies' singles French Men's doubles Wimbledon	6.10	Men better than women; $P<0.001$
14	Ladies' singles Wimbledon Men's doubles Wimbledon	8.98	Men better than women; $P<0.001$
15	Men's singles French Ladies' singles Wimbledon	2.95	Men better than women; $P<0.01$
16	Men's doubles French Ladies' doubles Wimbledon	1.92	NS
17	Ladies' singles French Men's doubles French	4.89	Men better than women; $P<0.001$
18	Men's singles Wimbledon Ladies' singles French	3.93	Men better than women; $P<0.001$
19	Men's singles French Men's doubles Wimbledon	4.84	Doubles better than singles; $P<0.001$
20	Ladies' singles Wimbledon Men's doubles French	5.41	Men better than women; $P<0.001$
21	Ladies' singles French Ladies' doubles Wimbledon	2.52	Doubles better than singles; $P<0.05$
22	Men's doubles Wimbledon Ladies' doubles French	3.77	Men better than women; $P<0.001$
23	Men's singles Wimbledon Men's doubles French	1.65	NS
24	Men's singles French Ladies' doubles Wimbledon	0.72	NS
25	Ladies' singles French Ladies' doubles French	1.03	NS

Table 2. (Continued) Comparison of events

No.	Comparison	Z Score	Results
24	Men's singles French Ladies' doubles Wimbledon	0.72	NS
25	Ladies' singles French Ladies' doubles French	1.03	NS
26	Men's singles Wimbledon Ladies' doubles Wimbledon	0.68	NS
27	Men's singles French Ladies' doubles French	0.69	NS
28	Men's singles Wimbledon Ladies' doubles French	2.06	Men better than women; $P<0.05$.

Note

$> 1.96 = P<0.05$
$> 2.58 = P<0.01$
$> 3.29 = P<0.01$

Table 1 which ranks tie break percentages in order of magnitude shows a percentage of nearly 27% for Wimbledon Men's doubles down to the Ladies' singles in France, and at Wimbledon where the percentage is between 5% and 7%. This suggests that service is much more effective in Wimbledon Men's doubles than either of the Ladies' singles. It is also apparent that service is a more effective weapon for Men than it is for Women, except maybe, when the women are playing doubles. The sixteen comparisons in Table 2 numbered 1, 10-18, 20, 22, 24, 26-28 are the events that compare men with women. The smallest gaps are between Men's singles and Ladies' doubles; in fact there is no significant difference, except in the case of number 28 (Men's singles Wimbledon x Ladies' doubles France), and this is significant in favour of men ($P<0.05$).

What is now apparent is that service has most success in doubles, due to the fact that in this event serve and volley is a very significant factor, even for the women. Maybe, Men's singles at Wimbledon was marginally better than Ladies' doubles in France, because the faster grass surface encourages men to serve and volley all the time, even on second service. Serve and volley then, would seem to be important, because only at Wimbledon is there slight evidence that Men's service in singles is better than Women's service in doubles.

Comparisons 10, 11, 16, 22, compare Men and Ladies playing doubles. Men are significantly better except in comparison 16, Men's doubles France x Ladies' doubles Wimbledon, where there is no significant difference. Perhaps this is because the women would serve and volley virtually 100% of the time on grass and maybe the men less so on clay.

Comparison of surfaces is done by 5-8, the gender factor being eliminated. There is no significant difference between the two surfaces. The remaining comparisons are listed in Table 3.

Table 3. Remaining comparisons

No.	Comparison	Z Score	Results
2	Men's singles Wimbledon Men's doubles Wimbledon	2.86	Doubles better than singles; P<0.01
3	Ladies' singles Wimbledon Ladies' doubles Wimbledon	3.08	Doubles better than singles; P<0.01
4	Men's singles French Men's doubles French	3.35	Doubles better than singles; P<0.001
9	Ladies' singles Wimbledon Ladies' doubles French	1.68	NS
19	Men's singles French Men's doubles Wimbledon	4.84	Doubles better than singles; P<0.001
23	Men's singles Wimbledon Men's doubles French	1.65	NS

There is a bigger difference in comparison 3 compared with 2. This may be because, in 2, serve and volley predominates in singles as well as the doubles, whereas in 3, most ladies would not serve and volley in singles even at Wimbledon but would do so in doubles. Number 4 reveals a large difference, and the argument rationalising this is the same. The doubles players would serve and volley virtually all the time, whereas the singles players on clay, would most of the time stay back, particularly on second service. This again endorses the view that serve without volley is relatively ineffective.

Comparison 9 is not significant, suggesting that Women singles players at Wimbledon are doing some serving and volleying and the Women on the French clay are not doing enough.

In comparison 19 the difference is enormous. The argument is the same as before:- relatively little serve and volley on the clay in Men's singles, practically none on second serve. By contrast in Wimbledon Men's doubles serve and volley would be virtually 100%.

Comparison 23 is interesting. The lack of significant difference may be due to the very high serve and volley factor in Men's singles at Wimbledon.

It seems that service is most effective in doubles particularly for Men, chiefly because serve and volley is operative on both first and second services. The Male service is still a big weapon in singles on clay, but less effective because there is much less serve and volley particularly on the second service.

The service in the Ladies' singles game is little more than a means of putting the ball into play. There is very little serve and volley in Ladies' singles even at Wimbledon. Serve and volley is the exception rather than the rule. The most notable exception is Martina Navratilova. This study showed no significant difference between the two surfaces, although a glance at Table 1 suggests that serve and volley is more effective on grass.

This could be due to several reasons. Spin services are more vicious on the grass and therefore, ideal to follow to the net. The bounce on grass is not always true, thus putting the receiver at a disadvantage and favouring the volleyer.

Also it may be that a volleyer is able to keep a better footing on grass. Finally, there is the greater commitment that players have to volleying on grass, believing that this is the correct thing to do.

3.2 Study B

Table 4. Wimbledon 1979 - 1992

Year	Men's singles tie break percentage	Ladies' singles tie break percentage
1992	17.3%	5.1%
1991	18.9%	8.3%
1990	15.0%	7.1%
1989	18.8%	9.5%
1988	14.1%	9.5%
1987	17.2	5.1%
1986	17.5%	9.1%
1985	16.8%	9.4%
1984	17.5%	10.6%
1983	17.4%	12.6%
1982	18.0%	9.5%
1981	16.0%	7.1%
1980	16.5%	6.3%
1979	16.4%	7.1%

For the comparison of percentage tie breaks over the fourteen years 1979 to 1992 the Chi-square statistic was used. The result for Men was $Chi^2 = 7.32$; well short of the tabulated significance value, $P < 0.05$. It is therefore confidently concluded that there is no significant change in tie break percentage over the period 1979 to 1992.

The result for the Ladies was $Chi^2 = 21.34$, $(P>0.05)$. However, 21.34 is not far short of the tabulated significance value of 22.36 indicating the unevenness of the Ladies results.

Another approach was to examine what is effectively a time series, for a trend, linear or otherwise over the period 1979 to 1992. There was no evidence for this $(P>0.05)$.

In view of the widespread belief that improved racket technology has over the years produced faster serving, we might have expected to see a trend over the years showing an increase in tie break percentage and therefore in the effectiveness of the serve. That this is not so, is maybe due to increase in the effectiveness of return of service, also due to improved racket technology. It may also be due to there being no significant change in serve and volley skills over this period.

44 Surface effect on elite tennis strategy

M. Hughes and S. Clarke*
The Centre for Notational Analysis, Cardiff Institute, Cardiff, UK
**School of Human Sciences, Liverpool John Moores University, Liverpool, UK*

1 Introduction

The four major events in the tennis calendar, the Grand Slams, are now played on four different surfaces, since the Australian Open moved from Perth to Melbourne, and changed from grass to a synthetic surface. There is a lack of knowledge concerning the strategy of elite tennis players on the different types of surfaces. The more knowledge that is available to the coaches and athletes of the sport the more effective can the coaches be, as this knowledge acts as feedback within the coaching process. The importance of feedback has been clearly stressed by Franks et al. (1983) and Hughes (1985). Although a number of studies have concentrated on statistical and chance relationships in tennis (King and Baker, 1979; Ladany and Machol, 1977; Croucher, 1986), few have analysed the patterns of play so that an objective database can be compiled for the development of informed coaching and tactical planning. The aim of this study is to provide a quantitative comparison of elite players on two vastly different surfaces, at Wimbledon (grass) and and at the Australian championship (synthetic).

2 Method

2.1 The notation system

An Amstrad PC/7386/SX80 computer was used, along with a monitor, keyboard and mouse. A VHS video recorder, was used for post-event analysis. It had a jog/shuttle function so that it was possible to move through the action frame by frame where needed, and to play the action more slowly than real time.

The notation input and analysis software was specifically written for the purpose of this project. This system used a mouse-driven Windows environment to record the information, that is a graphical user-interface (G.U.I.). The player making a shot was

Science and Racket Sports Edited by T. Reilly, M. Hughes and A. Lees.
Published in 1994 by E & FN Spon ISBN 0 419 18500 3

recorded, the position on the representation of the court, the time at which the shot was made and finally the shot itself were all recorded using this G.U.I. The shot description was split into sections, each designated from on-screen pull down menus and sub-menus. One item from each category was chosen to define the shot played. The groupings were as listed in Table 1.

Table 1. The grouping, into menus and sub-menus, of variables that define a specific shot type

Menu 1	**Sub-menu 1**	**Sub-menu 2**	**Sub-menu 3**
Forehand	Serve	Topspin	Ground-shot
Backhand	Smash	Norm(flat)	Volley
	Drive	Backspin	Half-volley
	Lob	Slice	
	Drop	Block	

Table 2. The rally end options for a shot in tennis

Menu 2
Winner
Wide - right
Wide - left
Long
In net
Service ace
Service let
Winner off net
Miss-hit

2.2 Data collection

The 1992 Wimbledon Championships was recorded from the B.B.C. and the Australian Open tournament from satellite TV. Selected rallies from each tournament were analysed. Care was taken to include all the stages of matches and that there was a balancing of rallies, in terms of wins and losses, between the two sets of data. The study was limited to male players only. The data consisted of 11 different players involved in 7 matches for Wimbledon, and 9 different players involved in 5 matches at the Australian Open. All these matches were from between the third round and the quarter-final stage. By the third round it was thought that a player had proved that his pattern of play was successful for the surface, in beating at least two other professionals.

3 Results and Discussion

3.1 Time factors

Table 3. shows the data collected on different factors during and between rallies. The average number of shots in a rally was 52% greater at the Australian Open than at Wimbledon; however the average time of each rally was 93% greater. This indicates that not only was the number of shots on grass less but that the shots occurred in more rapid succession to each other. The time factors between when the ball is in play, were found to be similar for both surfaces. This was not expected, as it was thought that if the rallies were longer, the players would take longer to recover between points. Considering the quicker sequence of shots, it may be that a shorter rally of more intense action may be as tiring as a longer but less intense one, both requiring a similar length of recovery. The time between serve of the same point was longer on grass probably because the server was trying to get to the net after serving and if the serve was faulty it would take longer to get back into position.

Table 3. A summary analysis of the activities on different factors during and between rallies at the two tournaments

Factors	**Wimbledon`**	**Australian Open**
Mean no. of shots in a rally	3.09	4.72
Mean rally length(s)	2.50	4.82
Mean time between rallies(s)	22.33	23.24
Mean time between games with no change of ends(s)	32.20	32.23
Mean time between games with a change of ends (s)	112.40	116.50
Mean time between serves (s)	11.06	9.61

With this type of general match data it is possible to generate an overview of matches on the respective surfaces - an example of this being the prediction of the length of an average match on each surface. In predicting the length of matches, the data in Table 3, together with data on the numbers of first and second serves, were utilised. The calculations for a match with a score of 6-4, 6-4, 6-4 are shown in Table 4.

Table 4. A comparison of playing time of two similar matches, one played at Wimbledon, one played at the Australian Open. The data are extrapolated from the means of the data from the analyses presented above.

Actions in match	**For Wimbledon**		**For Australia**	
	Mean time	Total time	Mean time	Total time
15 change ends	112.40	1686.00	116.50	1747.50
14 new games	32.20	450.80	32.23	451.22
150 between rallies	22.33	3349.50	3.14	3450.00
174 rallies	2.52	438.48	4.87	857.12
81 between serves	11.06	895.86	9.61	778.41
		-------		-------
		6820.64		7284.25
	Total time = 1 h 54 min		**Total time=2 h 1 min**	

3.2 Positional analysis

The frequency distribution of all shots and respective rally ending conditions were compared with respect to position on court for the two surfaces and Chi-square applied to test for significant differences. These data are summarised in Table 5.

Table 5. Chi-squared analysis of different specified variables with respect to frequency distributions across the court (Grass v Synthetic surface)

	CRITICAL VALUE (1%)	TEST STATISTIC	SIGNIFICANCE
1st SERVES	18.5	6.14	NS
2nd SERVES	11.3	0.51	NS
ALL SERVES	18.5	7.85	NS
SERVE WINNERS	11.3	0.39	NS
BALL -errors	13.3	3.58	NS
BALL-winners(w)	9.2	4.95	NS
BALL-all shots (d)	9.2	26.02	P<0.01
BALL-all shots (w)	9.2	0.43	NS
PLAYER-all shots (d)	9.2	129.86	P<0.01
PLAYER-all shots (w)	9.2	24.90	P<0.01
PLAYER- winners	9.2	1.35	NS
PLAYER-errors	9.2	9.27	P<0.01

3.2.1 The serve

The effectiveness of the serve, as indicated by the number of aces and service winners, was found to be variable. The number of aces from the first serve were 7.88% and 6.70% for grass and the synthetic surface, indicating that a similar number of aces resulted. The number of aces served was insufficient to provide enough data to analyze statistically. The percentages of service winners (when the server does not have to play another shot) gave greater variation, with the higher values resulting from grass. This indicates that although the receiver could hit the ball and so stop it from becoming an ace, it was harder to return the ball in court, making the serve more effective on grass.

3.2.2 The return of serve

The greater proportion of the returns of serve was found on the synthetic surface. Eleven percent more serves could be returned; this also emphasized the greater service effectiveness on grass. The distribution of the returns of serve was found to be generally down the centre of the court as the aim of the receiver was to keep the ball in play.

3.2.3 Error and winner distribution

The percentages of winners (not including the serve) hit on grass and the synthetic surface were 32% and 23% respectively, indicating that it is likely more winners result from playing on grass. The percentages of errors (not including the serve) hit on grass and the synthetic surface were 59% and 70% respectively, indicating that it is likely more errors result from playing on the synthetic surface. The winner and error data together were found to be independent of surface; errors were the main cause of the end of a rally.

3.2.4 Ball and player position

There was enough evidence to indicate that there is a surface effect on the depth, not the width, of shots. However, the player-position variable demonstrated a surface effect on the depth, and the width of the position at which a player makes a shot. The Australian Open data suggest a skewing of the position towards the left of the court. This would seem to be due to players running round their backhand, due to the slower speed of the ball on this surface. The position from which winners were hit in terms of depth, was found to be independent of surface but the position of errors was dependent on surface. More errors were hit from the back of the synthetic court; this would be due to the greater proportion of shots played from near the baseline. From this argument it may seem logical to predict there would be more winners hit from near the net on grass, but this was not found to be the case.

4 Conclusions

This research has shown that the play on grass produced shorter rallies, both in terms of number and duration. The time between serves was slightly greater but overall a match with a score of 6-4, 6-4, 6-4, would last 7 minutes longer on the synthetic surface. The serve was more effective on grass, although placement was found to be independent of surface. The overall patterns of play differed; on grass, play was skewed towards the net whereas on the synthetic surface it was towards the baseline, in terms of player position and ball bounce. More winners resulted at Wimbledon, more errors at the Australian Open. The position of the player showed a similar distribution when playing winners, but more errors were hit from the baseline at the Australian Open. The data presented here support the ideas suggested in the literature, based on subjective judgements and experience. Providing objective support for these theories creates a sound base from which to build a framework of coaching and training in order to allow performers to reach their full potential.

Research into the effect of surface on play could be expanded to include more surfaces, such as the other surfaces on which Grand Slam events are played, and the effect of surface on matches between two specific players. Using this system, or similar systems, it would be possible to compare variables other than surface, for example, gender differences, varying match stages, and different standards of performer. By collecting data on individual players, databases could be set up on different players; from these it should be possible to identify any strengths or weaknesses, which would provide useful quantitative information for opponents.

5 References

Croucher, J.S. (1986) The conditional probability of winning games of tennis. **Res. Quart. Exerc. Sport,** 57, 23-26.

Franks, I.M., Goodman, D. and Miller, G. (1983) Analysis of performance: qualitative or quantitative? **Science Periodical on Research and Technology in Sport.** Ottowa: Coaching Association of Canada, March.

Hughes, M. (1985) A comparison of the patterns of play of squash. **International Ergonomics**. (eds. I.D.Brown, R.Goldsmith, K.Coombes and M.A.Sinclair, Taylor and Francis, London, pp. 139-141.

King, H.A. and Baker, J.A.W. (1979) Statistical analysis of service and match play strategies in tennis. **Can. J. Sport Sci.**, 4, 298-301.

Ladany, S.P. and Machol, R.E. (1977) **Optimal Strategies in Sports.** North Holland, Amsterdam.

Index